Shatter Me with Dawn

Sally Russell

Sally Russell

SHATTER ME WITH DAWN

A CELEBRATION OF COUNTRY LIFE

Illustrations by Katie Ridley

THE UNIVERSITY OF GEORGIA PRESS
Athens and London

Published by the University of Georgia Press
Athens, Georgia 30602
© 2001 by Sally Russell
"No. 323" reprinted by permission of the publishers and the Trustees of
Amherst College from *The Poems of Emily Dickinson,* Thomas H. Johnson, ed.,
Cambridge, Mass.: The Belknap Press of Harvard University Press, Copyright
© 1951, 1955, 1979 by the President and Fellows of Harvard College.
"A Gift of Horses" originally appeared in *Horse and Horseman* (August 1994).
Illustrations © Katie Ridley
Designed by Sandra Strother Hudson
Set in Minion
Printed and bound by Maple-Vail
The paper in this book meets the guidelines for permanence and
durability of the Committee on Production Guidelines for
Book Longevity of the Council on Library Resources.

Printed in the United States of America
01 02 03 04 05 C 5 4 3 2 1

Library of Congress Cataloging-in-Publication Data

Russell, Sally, 1942–
Shatter me with dawn : a celebration of country life / Sally Russell.
p. cm.
Includes bibliographical references.
ISBN 0-8203-2298-9 (alk. paper)
1. Russell, Sally, 1942–   2. Country life—Georgia—Barrow County.
3. Barrow County (Ga.)—Social life and customs.
4. Barrow County (Ga.)—Biography. I. Title.
F292.B27 R87 2001
975.8'195043'092—dc21
[B] 00-068273

British Library Cataloging-in-Publication Data available

As if I asked a common Alms,
And in my wondering hand
A Stranger pressed a Kingdom,
And I, bewildered, stand—
As if I asked the Orient
Had it for me a Morn—
And it should lift its purple Dikes,
And shatter me with Dawn!

EMILY DICKINSON

No. 323

FOR

FIELDING

SARAH JEAN

JULIA KAY

MARY GEORGIA

AND

OTHERS

OF THEIR KIND

CONTENTS

PREFACE

THE ESSAYS in this book came about because, like the poet, I am joyfully bewildered by the fact life gives much more than we ask. Although speaking thanks is often an inadequate endeavor, I have believed in trying. Gratitude may be what we came for.

These essays are also what I would call a salute to Old Blood. I have known for a long time that my soul was cast before the Industrial Revolution and that Old Blood flows in my heart. Not for a minute do I believe I am the only one in that condition, nor do I believe we are a minority. On the contrary, it is likely all of us have Old Blood in our veins. The Age of Supertechnology has routed ink pens, wagon wheels, candles, and wood stoves—as well as typewriters, record players, and electric mixers—but blood is harder to get rid of. What flows in our veins goes back into the night of Time and is not easily swept away, in spite of a world flooded with mobile phones, microwave ovens, laptops, digital TV, compact discs and players, mouse pads, and food processors. Old Blood will stir from time to time, insist we remember we are not, in fact, born to shop. Or at least remember we are not born only to shop.

In the frenzied getting and spending of the Consumer (Consumed?) Generation, we grow restless, dissatisfied. We complain when the mockingbird sings all night in the rosebush under the bedroom window; we forget to pause for the rustle of the river in its bed at twilight; we ignore the sacred whistle of wind in a wood duck's wings as it rises from the pond. Neglected Old Blood would remind us to hearken to the quiet rhythms of our own hearts.

For some reason I am at a loss to explain, I am good at checking the pulse of Old Blood. I know when it is in need of nurturing, and if the pulse feels especially weak, I do what I think I should to revive it. This is a gift. Through this book I hope to share the gift.

I grew up with three brothers and two sisters in rural Barrow County, outside the small town of Winder, in northeast Georgia, free to roam pine woods, explore red hills and cotton fields, wade creeks and "branches," build wash holes in them, wander down long miles of country roads afoot or on horseback. I remember with the sole of my foot how a red-clay country road gets smooth as tile in places in the summer, how delicious that silken spot feels in the shade to bare feet. I hear today with my mind's ear the musical beat of a horse's trot on the same spot.

I left Barrow County in 1965, after graduating from the University of Georgia, and spent most of the next ten years in apartments or subdivision houses. When I returned to the county in 1974 to take possession of a farm my father gave me, most of the dirt roads had vanished. Although hills, woods, and fields remained, many of these were doomed to the fate of the dirt roads: death by asphalt. Located forty-five miles from Atlanta, crossed by Interstate 85, Barrow County lies in an area that state economic forecasters liked to call the "emerging Northeast Georgia corridor" between Atlanta and Greenville, South Carolina. Economists did not take into account that some of us felt it was not emerging. To us it was disappearing.

Contented to live in the country again, daily amazed at the intricate and beautiful puzzle of Nature's kaleidoscope, I kept journals to record my farm's stories. I did this for my own pleasure, like the great French essayist Montaigne, and to help myself understand how, as the story was unfolding, my life fit into the puzzle. I wrote, too, from a deep belief that there is nothing more sacred than the Word, that the Word improves our chances with the sacred.

I was helped in this attitude by being born into a family that values the spiritual dimension of life, particularly as embodied in the Christian myth. We were not opposed to the good sense in other myths, but the Christian one was our birthright and we took it for the long run. I use the word *myth* in the highest sense of the word: that is, a vehicle by which humankind strives to explain something important about existence while understanding that it is essentially inexplicable. That may not be the highest sense of the word, but it sounds fairly elevated.

Like Herman Melville, I was "bred and born in the bosom of the infallible Presbyterian Church," where at an early age I learned to ask a solemn question: "What is the chief end of Man?"

Presbyterian children understood that Man referred to men, women, and children, because we children, usually taught by women, were required to learn the answer from the Shorter Catechism, which was this: "To glorify God and enjoy Him forever." I thought and still think that a satisfying answer.

The catechism definition of God, which we were also required to learn, was thrilling: "God is a Spirit, infinite, eternal, and unchangeable, in His being, wisdom, power, holiness, justice, goodness, and truth." Today it seems to me that "love" ought to be in there, but we were regularly drilled on a simpler version—God is love—so I suppose the omission is pardonable.

Although in adulthood I worked out my own salvation with notice-able departures from Presbyterian doctrine, I am grateful for a childhood that nurtured respect for spiritual forces in the world and awareness of power for good and evil outside myself yet within me and all other people as well. That these forces were inexplicable but not incomprehensible was another important facet of my early religious teaching. Without this training, I might have missed some of the lessons of my farm. I might not have glimpsed the Holy Spirit. Glimpses are the best we can hope for of the Holy Spirit, but they occur with generosity. We ought to keep on the lookout.

I need to say, too, that I am not trying to explain anything. I offer, rather, the tradition of observation followed by reflection. Or, as noted above, by awe. We can explain some things but I think (I hope) we do not explain much. This is an old-fashioned idea in an age when we are explaining (we think) everything from the weather to DNA. I find this compulsion to explain everything tiresome. Readers can expect not explanations but restful pauses, unruffled contemplation.

This book has been gleaned from journals kept over many years— a parchment-papered one with pages adorned by Hobbit-like creatures, gift of my sister Susan; another covered in red velveteen with a cat sketched in it in gold, gift of my daughter Nan; several college-ruled notebooks; one French school notebook, the kind lined with tiny squares whose purpose eludes me. Printed pages from the word processor found their way into a couple of folders, primary green and yellow. In creating the essays from this varied material, I wanted each composition to stand on its own so that readers could open to anyplace and find a subject to engage, puzzle, uplift, dazzle, beguile, amuse, gladden. That's close to what every day brought on the farm, and every day, though connected to others, ought to stand first on its own. The categories are perhaps arbitrary, but I find them fitting. After the introduction to the farm, readers may start with any category. I think of these as spokes of a wheel or pieces of a pie. Some readers may prefer to read from front to back, to get another story, one not told in any individual essay or within the separate categories. That story tells about how a woman not too different from other women of her region and time, whose soul was cast before the Industrial Revolution and whose family values were deeply biblical, adjusted these sails to live and love into the twenty-first century.

Given these conditions, I advise readers not to be too concerned with chronology. All essays are based on actual journal entries, but I often chose to coalesce to maintain theme. I reckon chronology is the least of the worries of the cosmos, if there are any worries in the cosmos. The best approach is that natural one that comes when getting to know a new friend. We listen to tales as we meet from time to time, and after a while, the chronology falls into place without much fuss.

Finally, I admit that sometimes I had to fall back on unwritten memory. Because places and characters were familiar to me, I did not always describe them in my journal, yet in bringing them to other readers I have wished to give identifying details. May I be forgiven if I fail to get the color of Mrs. Chastain's Cadillac or the style of her hair exactly as it was the day we moved the house. I beg pardon for recalling a star instead of a planet in M. LaMarche's swamp lake. I do not mean to be inaccurate. When memory balks at detail, which memory will do, we rely on primal impressions. I have reached deep for these, and I am satisfied that I give back what lives in primal memory, which deletes details but stores the essential.

ACKNOWLEDGMENTS

THROUGH THE LONG PROCESS of creating a book, the fortunate writer builds up a team that ensures the project goes to completion. I am a writer whose good fortune is spelled out in skilled and loyal teammates.

Lifelong friend Lynn Smith Roberts has been unfailing in her interest, her willingness to read, her desire to encourage. She is an extraordinary cheerleader. Everyone, whatever his or her work, could use a supporter of Lynn's abilities and dedication. Her kind of faith is empowering.

My sister Susan, close traveling companion, has shared experiences of farm life as we've shared so much else all our lives. Susan is much more of a farm woman than I am. She has raised and is yet raising cows and chickens in epic numbers. Her work puts food on many tables. Her home is a haven par excellence, sheltering and nurturing family and friends. Since I moved to England, her door has opened for me more times than I like to admit, lovingly and helpfully, however disruptive my arrival and sojourn might be. She makes as good a biscuit as I do. Maybe better. When I asked Susan if she has seen the blue of the heron's wings, she said quietly, "Yes, and I think I know where he lives."

Along with Susan, I thank her husband, Raymond Reynolds, for his constant support and outstanding example in farming activities. Without his expertise, tractors, hay balers, and cattle trailers, I might never have written this book.

I acknowledge with a mother's grateful heart the loving, patient support of my daughters, Nancy Jackson O'Neill and Jessica Jackson Keeley, through all these writing years. A great reward of my life is to know that both are adult women who appreciate what it means to live with the land.

To brother John I give loving thanks for keeping Somechoes house in the family.

A writer must have good editors, and I have been blessed with these. From the beginning of my writing endeavors thirty years ago, I have been encouraged and published by editors and publishers at the *Winder News,* recently rechristened the *Barrow County News:* Harry O. Smith, Ken Hudgins, Bob Poe, Myles Godfrey, Johnny Solesbee, Marsha Lane, LeAnne Turner, and Debbie Burgamy. I am grateful for their long-term support. In recent years Karen Orchard at the University of Georgia Press has generously offered skilled criticism and wise guidance. I owe Karen a debt of gratitude indeed bewildering.

Friends who read the essays as they were written and offered kindly suggestions from their considerable skill with language deserve a hearty thank-you. I offer my appreciation to my writing group here in England—Nancy Allison, Barbara Jagger, Ann Jones, and Pauline Prior-Pitt—as well as to stateside friends Buford Norman and Elizabeth Joiner.

Because I do my own typing/word processing in manuscript prep-aration, I have accumulated a notable debt to my husband, Les Warrington, a computer expert who keeps a well-trained and obedient machine. He shares his talents for computer management generously, cheerfully, and patiently, is ever gentle with my born-before-the-Industrial-Revolution soul. Although I would like to think I could, I never can thank Les enough for his help, which includes his constant insistence that I call myself a writer. He is the captain of this team.

Shatter Me with Dawn

SOMECHOES FARM

Queequeg was a native of Kokovoco,
an island far away
to the West and South.
It is not down in any map;
true places never are.

HERMAN MELVILLE

In 1975, through my father's generosity, I became the owner of a farm in North Georgia, ninety-five acres lying along the Mulberry River boundary between Jackson and Barrow Counties, on the Barrow County side of the river.

The Mulberry isn't much of a frontier, just a meandering, ol' shallow river, peaceful most of the year, no good for transportation unless it's spring and you're in a canoe, and then you'd better be also in an adventurous mood. Anybody I ever knew who traveled down a spring-swollen Mulberry has tales to tell. Its waters are coppery green in peaceful times and red clay orange in the spring floods. Basically. At any given time the color of the river is up for grabs. If you think you've got it, it changes. Proteus, that crafty shape-shifter, may have gotten his inspiration from the river.

The Mulberry is a good river for turtles (which some call terrapins), muskrats, wood ducks, beaver, kingfishers. Not much for bass, bream, trout. Though I've heard it has a few catfish and a few more carp, I hardly ever saw anyone besides the kingfishers fishing the Mulberry. It's a good river to walk along in contemplation, a place for soothing reflection or, in summer, soothing barefoot wading. I've exercised horses in it to build up their legs and gotten along all right unless the horse got imaginative enough to think lying down would be fun. At least two I had were that imaginative. I've taken to the river a few times on foot in autumn or winter, when something on the other side looked too good to miss, and though it was cold, it was bearable. An all-round friendly river.

The river frontage of my farm ran for a scant half mile, and westward my father owned several hundred acres of farmland, what we called the Horseshoe Bend Farm, after the shape of a bend in the river. Between us, we had about two miles of wooded river bank. Poplar and mulberry trees liked the sandy, wet bottom soil, and American beeches as well as a few birch trees could be counted on to prosper close to the water. Oak and hickory claimed the slightly higher land above the bottoms, and uphill in old cotton fields, the pines thrived.

Eastward from my farm lay Mr. Wingo's place, a farm of 129 acres, about 30 or 40 of which were swampland and pond. The river wouldn't stay in its banks near Wingo's. It liked to spread out in the lowland there. Two creeks also fed Wingo's pond, and it was a haven for waterfowl: mallards, mergansers, wood ducks, Canada geese, sandhill cranes, great blue and little green herons. A redtail hawk used to like to sit on the eastern bank, in one of the old beech trees, watching. She had a taste for something at Wingo's, but I never knew what.

Mr. Wingo was in a nursing home by the time I moved next door, and his small prefab white house sheltered among the oaks on the pond's edge was usually empty, though occasionally someone rented it for short periods. Old Clem, who must have been seventy, although it was hard to tell because he'd been rode hard and put up wet more than once, rented Wingo's. Clem arrived with all his worldly goods in a battered station wagon and about half a dozen head of horses delivered by the kindness of a friend who had a large cattle trailer and, I surmise, the same kind of heart. Clem didn't pay his rent and pulled a pistol on Mr. Wingo's sister, Mrs. Means, when she tried to collect it. I got along okay with Clem, though, because we both loved horses and I didn't have anything to do with his rent.

Thus, I generally had the run of the Wingo farm because nobody cared if I wanted to watch the ducks down there. The Harbins, who bought the farm after Mr. Wingo died, lived in town and only grew their summer garden out there. I'll never forget the night Mrs. Harbin called me in tears because my daddy's cows had gotten into her garden and how I went down there in the dark to drive them out—too late, of course.

The tomato plants were trampled, the bean vines mangled. Still, the Harbins never held my daddy's errant cows against me.

North across the river from these farms was a vast plantation owned at one time by a longtime friend of my father's, Mr. Dan Williamson. The Williamsons owned almost three thousand acres near Hoschton, and my daddy could tell you exactly how long they'd owned it, who had married whom, when they'd married, and maybe why. He'd doctored them all since 1936, when he returned to Barrow County to begin his medical practice. The Williamson place hadn't been farmed in years. It was 75 percent pine woods, 15 percent hardwoods, the rest broom sedge fields decorated with the usual hawthorn bushes and persimmon trees. The whole formed a haven of wild beauty and serenity.

A couple of years before I came to my farm, the Williamson place had sold to a contractor in Atlanta, and about three years after I moved to the farm, financial troubles forced him to sell. By the grace of God, he sold to Michel LaMarche, a wealthy Belgian businessman who didn't speak English. When M. LaMarche came to inspect his farm, the tenant farmer, a student of mine, called on me to interpret.

In spite of a crushed ankle resulting from falling suddenly sideways with a nine-hundred-pound quarter horse between my legs, I spent two days with M. LaMarche and Harold Carter, our state Fish and Wildlife man, exploring that bewitching farm. We covered old logging roads in Harold's truck, but we walked through woods inaccessible by vehicle. We must have made a puzzling sight threading those deep woods, open under February sun: a slim, thirty-seven-year-old woman in jeans and blue-plaid flannel shirt with a grubby walking cast on one leg and a worn hiking boot on the other; a portly, balding gentleman in his late forties wearing a smart gray business suit and shiny black shoes; and a much taller, Gary Cooper–type lawman in his campaign hat and forest-green uniform. Perhaps the sounds of Harold's country Georgia drawl, M. LaMarche's impeccable, slower than Parisian (i.e., Belgian) French, and my American-accented French switching into southern-accented English were equally incongruous.

I made a southern supper for M. LaMarche and his wife before they went home to Belgium. In her forties, Mme. LaMarche was small and dark, had sweet, expressive brown eyes. I served southern-fried chicken, black-eyed peas, turnip greens, sweet potato soufflé, cornbread, and biscuits. I had cream gravy or sorghum syrup to adorn the biscuits, pecan pie for dessert.

After he'd eaten a couple of pieces of fried chicken and taken a good dose of pot liquor from the turnip greens to his cornbread, M. LaMarche told me I could ride my horses on his farm all I wanted and treat it as my own. Perhaps I would be so kind as to report any signs of unauthorized hunting to Mr. Carter? I, however, would have the right to shoot one deer a season, no more.

I assured M. LaMarche I would shoot no deer, and I thanked him a thousand times, which wasn't nearly enough. I felt I'd been handed that farm on a platter of fried chicken. It was mine in a tangible way, and I didn't have to pay taxes on it. Like Thoreau, I could enjoy others' farms and withdraw when I'd enjoyed them enough.

The truth be known, I never did get enough of enjoying the LaMarche farm, and eventually it had to be taken away from me. The LaMarches owned it for about seven years, then sold to Scott Hudgins, the great Gwinnett County mall guru. Mr. Hudgins was uneasy about his neighbors crossing the river onto his place. It was a sad day when red "No Trespassing" signs went up at our main horse crossing on the river.

To the south of my farm, across County Line-Mulberry Road, my father owned the land, what he called the Captain Williams Place, about two hundred acres, bordered by Rocky Creek, a bright, strong, light-on-dark, dancing-over-rocks creek that also liked to swamp up in places before emptying into Whiddon's pond, not far from Wingo's. The Whiddons owned the farm across from Rocky Creek, and although their pond wasn't as wide or deep as Wingo's, it also attracted flocks of waterfowl. The Whiddons raised a few cattle on their three hundred acres but lived in town. My daddy hated it that Mr. Whiddon bought that farm before my daddy knew it was for sale.

My uncle Dick, Daddy's oldest brother (there were seven brothers), used to call my daddy the "baron of Barrow" because he bought up so much land. Uncle Dick said it with a twinge of envy. He was bad about buying land himself, but his youngest brother had gotten too far ahead of him and won the title in spite of birth order.

For nearly twenty years I lived within the boundaries of these old farms with freedom to roam and to love them every one. Cattle were the chief crop, but we raised horses on ours and a few cows. For me,. however, the most valuable crops were those that grew where people did not encroach. The Great Spirit was husbanding exciting crops, as the Spirit is wont to do: deer, fox, the waterfowl already mentioned, and numerous other birds—owls, whippoorwills, and chuck wills, hawks, indigo buntings, bluebirds, swallows, mockingbirds, quail, meadowlarks, doves, crows, red-wing blackbirds, to begin the list. Wild plant crops included the well-lauded blackberries and muscadines, complemented by the unsung fruit of crabapple and persimmon trees.

I was not farming in the sense that I was making my living off horses and cows, though I spent many hours in true farm work—feeding and tending stock (with the help of Dr. Jim Powers, I got to be a pretty good vet), hauling hay, mending fences, mucking out stalls, spreading manure. I joked that the only prosperous farmers in the county were the lawyers and doctors because they could afford their farm losses. A teacher, I struggled, taking in horse boarders, teaching riding, and occasionally taking in human boarders to make a little cash for taxes and horse feed. I tried to sell some timber once, but after the loggers had cut a few trees, I told them to go home, I couldn't stand the carnage. I felt like Judas. The most important crop of my farm I consider my two daughters. Growing up there strengthened their spiritual and physical bones.

As a teacher I had it over the lawyer- and doctor-farmers in the county in one important aspect. I spent a lot more time on my farm than they did on theirs. I taught French language and English composition and literature at Gainesville College, a twenty-five-minute drive from the farm. We were on the quarter system then, and my schedule changed every eleven weeks. Sometimes I taught between 8:00 A.M. and 2:00 P.M., and sometimes I taught only one day class, usually an afternoon one, and two night classes, which met for two hours each, two nights a week.

That left many hours at home, scheduling that another kind of job would not have allowed. I rarely taught in summer. My time was worth more to me than the state's money, and I enjoyed long summer days in the country, sometimes never leaving home for anything at all for a week or more. I loved company to come to see me, but I felt little need to go to town. I had too much to do in the country. Following Thoreau's example, I kept broad margins to my life.

My farm was part of the original Captain Williams Place, where there had been a fine, single-story antebellum farmhouse, four generous rooms, two each off a spacious hall, with wide, golden-brown heart-pine floors, walls, and ceilings. My daddy liked to show how the heavy front door still hung balanced on its hinges—he would push it closed with his little finger—after 125 years. He rented this house, and after the renters lived there for five years without paying any rent—Dr. Russell wasn't good at collecting rent—he finally told them they'd have to move. They moved, and the next night the Captain Williams house burned to the ground in one of the saddest fits of dog-in-a-manger on record. Old Clem's pulling a gun—I don't think it was loaded—on Mrs. Means was, after all, not so bad.

Dr. Russell moved another old farmhouse to the site, one without the age or character of the Captain Williams house, and fixed it up for renters. They turned out to be the Johnson family, a husband and wife and three young children. They didn't pay any rent either, but my daddy never asked them to move. He did ask them to help keep the cows out of the road, and they were faithful to do that. They borrowed a phone call now and again, and Jackie liked to send me a mess of butterbeans from her garden when they came in. Although the Johnsons were simple in various senses of the word, I am thankful they were my neighbors in this isolation because in addition to being rustic, they were honest.

Although I'd long wanted a heart-pine farmhouse, after the Captain Williams place burned, it looked as though I'd have to build a new house on my land. Then one day a friend called to say the Dee Kennedy house was for sale, to be moved. She thought I might be interested.

I drove out to the house, which was on Dee Kennedy Road, eight miles through the country from my farm. The house was all heart pine, one of the oldest in the county, built about 1870. It had four good-looking columns on the front porch for ostentation (in spite of a prodigious woodpecker's hole near the top of one of them) and a cut-out string of Victorian gingerbread railing along the second story balcony. It was basically a working farmhouse, two rooms up, two down, off pleasant hallways, with two shed rooms and a kitchen off the back on the ground floor. The first family to live there were the Maynards. They raised nine children in that house.

Dee Kennedy had been the most recent owner. When I went out with my daddy to look at the house, an old woman living nearby came over. She'd heard about the idea of moving the house and felt obligated to tell me how they found Mr. Kennedy dead on the back porch.

"Hanged hisself," she said. "Ain't that right, Dr. Russell?"

"He knew he was dying of cancer," my father answered.

I fell in love with the house and agreed with the new owners of Dee Kennedy's farm, who had built a ranch-style brick home behind the old house, to take it off their hands for five hundred dollars. Everyone in the county, with the exception of my father and possibly my husband, Dwain Jackson, thought I was crazy. Fortunately, being crazy in Barrow County is not an unknown phenomenon.

Dwain did think the idea of moving a house a little insane, but to his credit, he saw how deeply in love with this house I was, and he had enough confidence in me to let me handle the affair.

Clarence Chastain from Toccoa moved the house. I interviewed three house movers before deciding on Clarence, a tall, straight-standing, straight-talking man of fifty or so. He was the kind of man who can wear a red baseball cap, which he did, with dignity. During the interviews, I learned that house movers are a special breed. Ego they do not lack. Most of them will tell you they can move Stone Mountain if they can just jack it up. Clarence assured me he could move the house, but not until he had thoroughly inspected it, rafters to underpinning, crawling over, under, and through in his dark green coveralls. He said if he didn't make it, I wouldn't owe him anything, but I'd have to clean up the mess on the side of the road. If he did make it, I'd owe him three thousand dollars. I shook hands on that deal.

Clarence came to move the house on a bright April morning. His house-moving trucks, two of them, looked like rejects from *The Grapes of Wrath*. Okay, maybe not that old, but pretty old. I didn't say anything. Not in the presence of that ego.

After our carpenter, Lloyd Roberts, had taken off the roof and columns, the moving crew jacked the house up, so that moving day all we had to do was hitch up and get going. Clarence had brought a burly young man who didn't look more than eighteen or nineteen to drive the moving truck. Two other men were in the second, smaller truck, which would be needed when we had to leave the road and take to pasture.

My brother John asked Clarence later why he chose such a young driver.

Clarence said, "Because he don't think he knows anything. He does what I tell him." Clarence sat up in the cab of the big truck with his driver or got out and directed him, sometimes from the front, sometimes the rear.

Mrs. Chastain came too, an attractively plump woman in her forties. She chose blond hair well-coiffed and a stylish polyester pantsuit for the occasion. Her outfit almost matched the rose-beige of her shiny Cadillac, which she drove to lead the procession. No flag flew from the Cadillac. With Mrs. Chastain driving, there was no need for a flag.

It all happened easy as sweet potato pie until we reached the wooden bridge.

We had asked the county road crew whether they thought the bridge would hold a house, and they said it was on steel girders. It ought to. School buses went across it.

Later they reported they'd taken the heaviest piece of highway equipment they had across the bridge and lived to tell it, but there was no way to be sure that a caterpillar and the truck to haul it weighed as much as my house. So I waited with prayerful heart at the bridge with my friend, Bud Draper, who was serving as volunteer architect for the house renovations. Dwain was busy elsewhere, cutting overhanging tree limbs along the road with his chainsaw to make way for the house. He'd said all along if the house fell in the creek, he didn't want to see it.

Bud, my father's contemporary and friend, was a man of imposing intellect, stern character, and aristocratic demeanor. When two well-weathered men in khaki work clothes showed up, coming to stand near us, Bud engaged them in casual conversation. Although one stuttered badly, it was soon revealed they worked for the county road department. I had a sinking feeling I might be cleaning up the mess of my house from Little Mulberry Creek.

Across the creek John pulled up in his blue pickup truck and got out to stand with a few other people who had stopped to watch. At twenty-nine he looked like a younger version of my daddy (except he still had plenty of hair): slight of build and short, full of energy and quiet charisma. John was in the Georgia General Assembly, so it was natural to see him shake hands with the folk standing around and speak to them before he waved and smiled big at me and Bud.

It took almost thirty minutes for the house to cross that fifteen-foot span, not because the bridge threatened to give—it never did cause great concern for bearing the weight—but because it was barely wide enough for the trailer wheels. When this circumstance became apparent, Clarence had his driver back the truck off the bridge and line up again. When he shouted "Roll it!" the truck brought that trailer along inch by inch, with part of each outside wheel over the bridge edge.

As we watched the house roll onto the pavement from the bridge, the little crowd applauded furiously, including Bud and me. Turning to us, the stuttering road crewman smiled broadly and said, "P-p-p-p-p-p-pretty good bridge!"

At Countyline School an important telephone cable had to be disconnected before we could pass. The company manager was there to see that his crews did the job properly. Losing that cable would put sixteen thousand people out of their phones, he said.

The teachers let the children—about a hundred of them—come out and stand near the roadside to see the moving house. Mrs. Chastain waved to them.

Three miles past the school, as we were preparing to turn off the road into the pasture and negotiate terraces to the hilltop, it started to rain. Clarence's crew had filled the ditch with railroad ties as a makeshift bridge, and the rain had made them slick. The truck rolled across all right, but house and trailer slid sideways into the ditch. Rainwater had collected in a sagging plastic covering we had put over the house, and as the house tilted, this water rushed over the side with all the terror of Niagara. Although the house righted itself immediately, it did so to the ominous sounds of floor joists cracking and windowpanes shattering.

By the time my heart had returned to reasonably normal beating, Clarence had surveyed the damage, declared it reparable, and said he'd be back to finish the job when things dried up some. This being April, he couldn't say when that might be.

House and trailer sat in the ditch, a corner of the house jutting onto the road, for a week. The house looked like something a flood had left. Its unexpected roadside presence was especially eerie at night, when its few unbroken windowpanes caught the beams of my car's headlights.

These difficulties did not permanently trouble the house, however, and once Clarence had deposited it on the chosen hilltop, with Lloyd Roberts as carpenter, we faithfully restored it to a dwelling to shelter us with competence and a certain style. Lloyd, a black man, was a craftsman unafraid of old houses, which he approached with respect and skill. With him and Bud Draper on my team, I couldn't have failed to turn Somechoes house into a thing of beauty and usefulness.

By the time Lloyd had finished polishing her up, everyone in the county wished they had my house—or so I supposed, because of the many visitors who drove up in the yard wanting to "see the house." A good number of these pilgrims said they used to live in it. I sort of doubted that at first, but they had authentic stories to tell. When a house is more than a hundred years old, it can easily have sheltered a half-dozen families for a long while. Given the larger families of yesteryear, it develops a well-populated history.

I framed for the living room a photo Mr. Paul Maynard gave me. He was ninety when he visited the house where he was born. The photo shows him and his eight brothers and sisters with their parents. The big children are all standing on the upstairs balcony. Paul is a two-year-old in a long white gown, holding his mother's hand on the front steps.

I called the house Somechoes, pronounced Some-Echoes, because calling from its porches, back and front, produced ringing echoes in the surrounding woods and because I felt the house itself was an echo of the past, with its heart-pine walls, ceilings, and floors. No one could pronounce the word right when they saw it on the sign by the front door. They usually said SomeChoes. To avoid embarrassing a mispronouncer who wanted to know how we came by the name, my sister Susan answered that SomeChoes was the name of a Cherokee Indian maiden who died on the Trail of Tears and was buried out there in the oak grove beside the house.

But really, we called our place Somechoes (Some Echoes) Farm.

Herman Melville wrote that Queequeq's tropical island home of Kokovoko was not down in any map because true places never are. Although this seems to be impossible, Melville is quite right. The reason true places are never down in any map is that they are not about place. They are about time. A true place exists in time, not space. By a true place I understand a place where people live long enough to appreciate what it contributes to their daily life, to their particular history of joy and sorrow, love and hate, plenty and want. It's a place that harbors the most personal memories: cutting and hauling stove wood with your brothers, creeping downstairs on a long string of Christmas mornings, learning to conquer your fear of the crickets in the basement, getting ready for the prom, accepting an engagement ring in the front porch swing, bringing the babies home from the hospital or, if you're among the luckiest, birthing the babies. It's where your grandfather hanged himself on the back porch so your grandmother, not a hopeless siege with cancer, would get his life savings.

Life happens to people in something we call time, and once our time has passed, the place where we spent our time is gone, too. That's why many of the visitors to my house who claimed they or their grandparents lived there were disappointed.

"There was a fish," several of them said. "I seem to remember it was carved over the front door. We knew the carpenter was a Christian and left this sign on all the houses he built."

We never found that fish, though we looked. It had passed away with some of the early occupants. Nevertheless, the fact that it lived in memory to comfort and make proud their descendants is evidence that the house is a true place.

For memory is where true places *are* down. They reside in the memories of those who have been fortunate enough to live in them. By memory I understand deep heart-memory, where even Time may cease for a true place as it lives on in stories told by children, grandchildren, great-grandchildren.

When I review my life on Somechoes Farm, I feel somewhat embarrassed to admit it, but like Thoreau on Walden Pond, it appears I am more favored by the gods than others, richly endowed with this true place. Having been taught that those who are highly privileged have a corresponding responsibility to share with those less fortunate, I am happily obliged now to open the gate at Somechoes Farm for others, even those who never lived there, and to invite them warmly to have a stroll around, to remember their own true places, and to relearn that, as Thoreau reminds us, time is but the stream we go a-fishing in. We drink at it, but while we drink we ought to see the sandy bottom and detect how shallow it is, how "its thin current slides away, but eternity remains."

I doubt there's an adequate definition of eternity in any dictionary. I'm willing to bet, however, that what we learn of its definition, what we learn about timelessness, comes by paying attention to life in true places. To that end, I offer Somechoes Farm.

Part One

KITH (AND KIN)

KITH, a collective noun, is an Old English word, meaning one's friends, acquaintances, neighbors; also country and kinfolk. I extend this definition to include animals. Geneticists claim humans share 60 percent of our DNA with fruit flies, a higher percentage with birds, horses, dolphins. This should not astonish. Ancient myths of many cultures illustrate our blood kinship with the rest of creation. They mourn and celebrate our aptitude for metamorphosis. It is likely unwise to pretend that such creatures as mermaids and centaurs do not exist.

AN EPISODE OF
SANDHILL CRANES

In November 1979 the first sandhill cranes came to Somechoes. Separated from my husband of eighteen years, I was grieving the death of our marriage. Although I resisted the idea of divorce, it seemed more and more evident that we had long ago separated at some unrecognized crossroads and that our lives were no longer going in the same direction. That they ever would do so again seemed doubtful. I wanted to accept this change without bitterness or recrimination, but our circumstance had turned Dwain so frustrated, angry, and violent that I had to ask him to leave the house. My heart ached for the children, who were eleven and eight that year. I had been through divorce with my own parents. It's a pain you don't forget, yet I seemed unable to stop what was happening.

This was also the year we became impassioned with horses, and in this we were blessed because we were able to spend most afternoons on horseback. Nan's first pony was an almost fourteen-hand bay gelding named Mr. Peabody. His saucy personality made us think he ought to have been called Mr. Somebody. Jessica claimed a twelve-hand chestnut and white mare, Yo-yo, who simply could not have been more serene and cooperative. Scout, a good-natured four-year-old quarter horse, was my mount. We also boarded Jennifer Lowry's white pony, Hobbit, who was part unicorn. Mellow autumn afternoons in the woods and fields, finding new trails along the river, getting to know and love our horses, being together in exciting new circumstances, all this was healing for us.

After a long, happy trail ride into the blue of a perfect autumn evening, I had hung around the barn longer while the children had gone to the house to do homework before we were due at my mother's for supper. I was turning Scout out to pasture, and he was eager to rejoin his buddies down near the front pasture lily pond. A gleaming chestnut paint, he had his head up and his ears forward as I pulled his halter off. He cantered off toward the pond, and I stood listening, as I loved to do, to the sweet music of his hooves, when I heard a more insistent sound in the sky.

I had never heard such music. It was a vibrant, all-pervasive trill, deep and, yes, I think, happy: *karoo-oo, karoo-oo, karoo-oo* filled the sky and rang in my head and in my veins. Looking up, I gasped to see a flock of giant birds sailing toward me, not too high, singing and swirling, no longer in formation, though I could see they had been. Their ragged lines spoke of former direction. Their swirling spoke of excitement about something.

The air rang with their cries—*karoo-oo, karoo-oo, karoo-oo, karoo-oo.* Somechoes Farm's talent for echoes made the clarion calls that much more thrilling. I stood spellbound as the birds passed over. There must have been at least forty of them. Wingo's pond is only about a quarter of a mile from the house, and over the woods between my pasture and the pond, I could see the birds dropping, disappearing behind the trees, landing on Wingo's.

Captivated by their siren song, I had draped Scout's halter and lead line on the gatepost and turned toward Wingo's when I heard Nan call, "Mama! Mama!"

She was running across the paddock toward me, her little face glowing. "What was that sound?" she asked. "I heard it in my room!"

She, too, had come under the spell.

"Some kind of wonderful birds," I said. "They went in down at Wingo's. Let's go see!"

It was deep twilight now, and we crossed the back pasture with quick steps to reach the band of dark woods separating our pastures from the natural lake. As soon as we entered the woods, we could hear the birds trilling softly and cooing, delighted about their evening's accommodations. I couldn't blame them. Wingo's is lovely at any time of the day, but at twilight it's five-star—and more stars to come.

We crept quietly forward for a few steps, but listening to the contented sounds, I took Nan's hand and said, "Let's wait. If we disturb them now, they may not find a good place to spend the night."

So we turned back and walked hand in hand across the pasture, not speaking, but Nan sang the bird notes softly with accuracy and delicacy.

At Mother's we found my brother Alex, visiting from Alaska. He is an outdoorsman of great skill, a doctor but also a hunting guide and bush pilot with many years' experience. I asked him what kind of birds he thought our visitors might be. Nan made the sound and he made it back to her. They were singing bird language.

"They're probably sandhill cranes," Alex said, "though the whistling swan has a clarion call as well. I'm glad you didn't disturb them. They make a long journey—Alaska to the Gulf of Mexico. They're a little far east, but the drought in the Midwest has driven them this way, I guess. Tohawah, the Indians call the whistler," he said.

When we returned home, I looked up whistling swans in the encyclopedia and confirmed what Alex had told us. I also learned that in some Indian lore the whistling swan and her young are believed to be the souls of a young wife and her children, forced to flee a jealous and cruel husband.

I decided I would get up before dawn and go down to Wingo's to see what kind of birds those were. If the girls wanted to come, I said, I would wake them up. A heavy frost was forecast. They would have to wear lots of clothes and keep quiet and still. They both voted yes, but I was sure that when I woke them in the dark, they would vote no.

At 5:30 I was threading my way across the back pasture under a cold, star-studded sky with two little girls gloved, capped, and scarved to the eyes, coming along behind, not saying a word. The sky brimmed with stars. At least one tumbled out. A quarter moon waning to crescent gave enough light for us not to need a flashlight. The air was biting, filling our lungs with winter prophecy.

The pond lies almost due east of the house. By the time we reached the western shore, the eastern horizon was beginning to show a flush of royal blue that spread to the dome, painting out stars behind it. We could hear the birds talking, but they had settled in on the northeastern side in the shallow waters where the river's spring flooding forms a bountiful swamp of reeds and lilies between the deeper part of the lake bed and the river bed. Over the open, deeper water a white mist swirled almost imperceptibly.

We paused a moment to appreciate the mist. Suddenly, close to shore, a beaver, shiny-wet brown, fat and curious, popped his head out of the water for a cautious inspection. He swam importantly back and forth, drawing black, disappearing lines on the dark, smooth surface of the water. At intervals he smacked the water with his tail and dived. Surfacing farther out, he paddled back, daring us to be dangerous. When he finally satisfied himself that we were not, he sailed away in disdainful silence.

It was still too dark to see well far out on the lake, even with our binoculars, and it was clear we needed to go to the eastern shore for a truly good look. We skirted the southern edge of the pond to reach a promontory that juts into the lake very near where the birds were feeding. I whispered to the girls that we would have to go slowly and be absolutely quiet.

The eastern horizon went pale blue, and the mist began to flow toward us. Stars winked out in the dome. We crept forward a few feet at a time, stopping to watch and listen.

Soon, with binoculars, I could see that the birds were tall and gray with red-patched faces. Most were feeding, but three were clearly sentinels, watching the peripheries. The birds seemed almost to float on the shimmering dark water rather than to stand in it, and their long graceful necks gave them an attitude of swans. Nevertheless, although I had never seen a sandhill crane, I was pretty sure we were looking at a good-sized flock of them on Wingo's pond.

We lay in the leaves beneath a sycamore, propping our elbows on an old log to steady the binoculars. We passed them back and forth without speaking. The birds chatted and fed.

I don't know how long we remained there, sharing dawn with these magic birds. Long enough for Nan to dare to sing to them, sailing the high, laughing, flutelike trill across the morning, a sound as free as the creatures she sang to. The birds did not answer, but they did not take flight.

When Jessica whispered that she was going to move forward, I thought Nan's song might mean a child would not be alarming to the birds. I nodded.

But we had reached the safety line. No sooner had Jessica slipped across the fallen tree than the alarm cry went up and the flock took to the sky, heading north toward the river, their great wings swinging slowly as they gathered air, their cries throaty and strong, rising, ringing.

Over the river they banked and came back toward the lake, low, in faultless V-formation, their slim necks stretched reed-thin and long, long. The sun, reaching the ridge top, turned the lake silver-blue. On its surface the flight of the cranes was perfectly reflected. As they passed over the lake, three more birds got up—the faithful guards, I think—and joined the flock now headed south, singing, blessing the sky, the water, the wooded hillside, and us with their passing.

The rapt look on the faces of my children as the birds flew over matched the rapture I felt in my heart. We were free in that moment from all sorrow and fear.

When the wooded hillside no longer echoed the birds' cries, we crossed to the back pasture again, headed home. The sun had risen over the trees, and in the field every twig on the thornbushes, every blade of grass and sedge, every needle on the pine seedlings, even the barbed wire fence, wore a crystal garment that sparkled with prismatic light, matching in beauty the song and flight of the sandhill cranes.

STEALTH BOMBER OF THE
NATURAL WORLD

ONE AFTERNOON last week I was in the hayloft throwing down hay for the ponies—it was a warm but windy almost-spring afternoon—and I heard an owl hoot, close, then an answering call, farther into the woods toward the lily pond. Again the nearer owl called. I strained my vision into the bare branches, hoping to see, for the sound was close. It made my blood dance, so deep and throaty and clear it was. *Hoo, hoo-hoo, hoo-o-o.* Again the answer. *Hoooo, hoo-hoo.* I felt as if I were a bird, up there in the loft, listening for a mate, half crazy to find him, half afraid to find him. The sound was almost tangible to my skin, not only to my ears. The afternoon sun was low, the horses were crunching their grain, and the owls were singing. I felt unspeakably privileged. I have often enjoyed night owl songs, but this daytime crooning—ah, spring!

A day or so later, I was riding Took across the big pasture up at Horseshoe Bend, and I let him gallop to the top of the hill. This sudden introduction must have enabled us to surprise two large owls at the edge of the woods, on the ground, intent on each other. In broad daylight.

With spring in the air, I knew what was going on. And why not? People court at night, when they're usually not working. Owls are wise to court in the daytime, when they're not working. Of course my horse startled the lovers, and they silently took to the air. I thought there was a note of regret in their flight, and I felt sorry we had disturbed them.

The next day Took and I were trotting down Tortoise Shell Trail, headed for the Unicorn Trail, both of us happy in these deep woods we love so well, where the trees are old and strong and the river glints through them in the afternoon. I can tell when Took is happy because his trot is light and springy, a trot that makes me happy.

The trail winds through the trees and isn't easily negotiated at the trot, so I was concentrating on giving accurate leg signals to protect my knees when I again spotted the owls. Facing each other intently, they were perched on the trunk of a hickory tree that years ago died in a storm. I slowed Took to a walk, then halted, but it was too late. The owls took the air as I called out, "I'm so sorry," hoping I hadn't deterred the owl population growth on our place with my blundering.

Riding on, in my mind's eye I replayed their intensity and their silent flight as they separated in the high trees, and I knew I'd witnessed something powerful and eternal, as if I'd *seen* the life force of spring or at least a corner of that mystery we humans limit by calling it sex.

Back at home I looked up barn owls in my birder's handbook and learned that although owls, like other bird species, possess a remarkable breeding signal that helps them produce the number of eggs they will most likely be able to raise—more eggs in time of plenty, fewer when food sources are scarce—rapid urban sprawl has encroached on much owl habitat; nevertheless, the barn owl is such a talented and successful hunter that it is arguably the most widespread bird species on earth.

Reading that, I breathed less guiltily and read on to try to understand about owls' hearing, their unique weapon in the battle for survival. Because the owl hunts at night and thus gave up the use of his eyes, which are excellent (I'll use the masculine pronoun here because the book says the males feed the females during incubation, though both incubate the eggs and feed the young after hatching), he must have worked hard at some juncture, evolutionarily speaking, to develop extraordinary hearing. It couldn't have been an easy decision, giving up daylight to hawks and eagles. Owls know about leaving comfort zones.

Over eons, barn owls developed asymmetrical ears and learned to locate their prey by the time it takes the sound to reach each ear. For example, if the prey is straight ahead, the sound will reach both ears simultaneously. If the prey is slightly above, the intensity with which sound strikes each ear will differ, and the time difference at which sounds reach each ear, from left or right, will accurately locate the target. Combined with a clever (and attractive) facial ruff, a concave surface of stiff, dark-tipped feathers that functions as a reflector, channeling sounds into the ears, these asymmetrical ears enable the owl to accurately pinpoint a sound within 1.5 degrees in both horizontal and vertical planes.

In addition, it is believed the owl has special brain cells that are activated only by sounds from certain directions, giving him a sort of aural map of space. I never thought of space as having or in fact needing a sound map. Owls did think of this and became the undisputed masters of the night shift.

In spite of his superior technology in nocturnal hunting, the owl, says my handbook, leaves nothing to chance. He establishes his territory and *learns* his territory. It seems to be especially important that he know the heights of perches and of hills. A good thing to remember for any species: nothing substitutes for knowing the territory.

Supper at Susan's to celebrate my birthday, March 10. The sweetheart called to say just come, we'll celebrate with what we've got, which was pot roast and vegetables. Her scrumptious biscuits and sorghum syrup were the cake. Delicious. There's nothing as dear on earth as a beloved sister. I know this from loving and being loved.

Present: Susan, Raymond (cleaning chicken houses but came in later), Mother, John, and seven-year-old Alexi. So wonderful to have my mother out of the nursing home for a meal. She told me again how there were three inches of snow on the ground the night I was born. I thanked her again for my birthday.

We got to talking owls. John is spending a lot of time in the woods these days, finding solace in them as I do when other fronts are besieged, and he said he found a great horned owl down near the road at Rocky Creek, killed by a car.

He made the *hoooo, hoo-hoo* sound that I heard in the barn. "That's a great horned," he said.

John makes accurate birdcalls. He's especially talented with crows and ducks. I like to think of him stalking the woods, listening, learning. A man ought to have woods skills.

He said an owl is a killing machine—the stealth bomber of the natural world. He described how most birds make a fluttering sound, a whir, when they fly. But not the owl. He said when he inspected the wing feathers of the dead horned, they were lighter, downier, not smooth.

Although I was glad John had taken this opportunity to observe owl feathers, I hoped the killed owl was not one of those I heard singing. The car is the unnatural enemy of all creatures on earth, including humans.

John said he found where an owl had killed a hawk and eaten everything except the wings, even the feet. Imagine eating hawk feet. The owl would likely have caught the hawk roosting; thus, we could say the hawk paid the price for daytime hunting privileges. Do owls, knowing well their territory, check out droppings that indicate roosting places?

John told of reading that an owl was put in a totally dark place with mice, and the next morning all the mice were gone. Also a bald eagle was put in the same dark place with the owl. Next morning the eagle was dead.

I was surprised to learn that the owls I saw and heard were great horned owls instead of the common barn owl, which does not hoot but instead makes a variety of harsher sounds. John says the great horneds are among the earliest to mate in spring. His words gave me chills and thrills.

Which culture is it that believes hearing the owl call your name is a sign of impending death? One of the American Indian tribes, perhaps the Eskimos.

The next night, walking to Wingo's at twilight (owls will hunt crepuscularly, says my handbook, and early twilight hunting surely encouraged the development of their asymmetrical ears), I skirted the back lily pond and came out into the pine thicket that is taking over what used to be the back pasture. As I was about to step onto the open path where the broom sedge is ahead—but barely—of pine seedlings, he was there in the sky in front of me, his wings cupped in the classic dive posture. It was a huge owl, low over my head, and whether a warning or a benediction, I didn't know. My sudden emergence from the wood disturbed his dive, and he deftly shifted his aerial attitude and sailed off into the pines. Not a sound from his wings, though he had to twist and turn with agility to fly toward and through the trees. I know about trotting through woods on horseback. Think of flying through them with great silent wings. The path skirts the edge of the thicket, but before I left it behind, I peered in, sure he was there, watching. I could see nothing but dark and the black shapes of tree trunks, shadowy brush. I was glad not to be a rabbit, a mouse, or even a hawk.

In the broom sedge there was still glow of sun, and as I walked through the golden fronds, I wondered how we began to define the Intelligence that creates the owl with powerful automated skill in finding food, inexorable in its links with death, and creates, too, another creature to understand the owl and explain it, in spoken stories and written word, one capable of inventing more lethal and less useful methods of destruction.

Blake called it a fearful symmetry. Frost called it a design of darkness to appall. But I'm not sure it's either fearful or appalling. Perhaps we simply do not understand. We see through a glass darkly, or not at all. In our struggle to define, to understand our Creator, we have assigned to humankind certain responsibilities—at least some of us have—for what we perceive as wrong with the world. The pain of death makes us think it is wrong, and we ask why should we be the only ones on the planet (which may be an arrogant supposition) to suffer for death. Donne said it best:

> If poisonous minerals, and if that tree
> Whose fruit threw death on else immortal us
> If lecherous goats, if serpents envious
> Cannot be damned, alas, why should I be?
> Why should intent, or reason, born in me
> Make sins, else equal, in me more heinous?

It's a tough question, unanswerable by any lights we have at present, yet in the twilight, as I threaded the shining broom sedge and entered another dark wood, I was not afraid or discouraged. Watching for that first glint of lake shine from Wingo's—the pond holds light long after the sun has set—I felt peaceful, certain the order of the planet is trustworthy.

WHERE SHE BELONGED

I HAD NEVER HEARD MUCH that enhanced the reputation of Irish setters. On the contrary, I had heard that in spite of their beauty, they were crazy or, at best, dim-witted.

When my brother John gave five-year-old Nan an Irish setter pup named—what else?—Kelly, I was ready to kill him. Not because I had that much against setters, but because I had also two-year-old Jessica, and we were about to embark on a two-hundred-mile trip, returning to our home in South Carolina after a week's visit with my mother in Georgia.

Of course when a child's beloved, handsome young uncle has given her a squirming, sleek, copper-glow puppy, her mother, unless she is willing to star as the Wicked Witch of the West, will not refuse.

We had the station wagon packed, and the girls were off for one last trip to the bathroom. John brought the puppy from the pen in the backyard. He was also carrying an old bath towel. I recall it well: it was Pepto-Bismol pink.

"You might need this," he said, handing me the towel as I sat the puppy in the back seat. "She gets carsick."

Dwain Jackson planted himself behind the wheel so firmly and swiftly that I knew there was only one person who was going to get to hold a carsick dog in her lap for two hundred miles.

The journey burned itself into my memory so indelibly that I have been ever after able to recall it in vivid detail of stench, soggy, slippery towel, and sad-eyed pup, especially when my daughter dares to accuse me of insufficient motherly devotion.

After this inauspicious beginning, life with Kelly did not improve. She put to shame the imbecility of legendary setters. If dogs in general had been half as dumb as Kelly, we would never have bothered to domesticate the species.

For starters, she could not be housebroken. She wet the floor without the slightest provocation. Merely speaking to her had a good chance of evoking this watery response. Shouting at her in frustration or crooning sweetly guaranteed it. She never learned to go outside and tend to business with any degree of regularity that would inspire confidence.

In addition to puddling indiscriminately about the house, she also bumped into furniture with surprising strength for her size, sending lamps, curios, magazines, cups of coffee, crashing.

She refused to obey the simplest commands, "stay" and "come." Either she did not understand, or she did as she pleased.

Trips to the vet for shots or for boarding remained messy. At first Dwain and I would toss a coin to see who had to hold the dog for the drive, but after losing the toss a couple of times, I figured the wisest way was for one of us to hold her going in and the other coming back. It was a matter I preferred not to leave to chance.

The most irritating thing about Kelly, however, was that she did not know how to take love. If we gave her the slightest bit of petting, she would beg for more, and she could not accept no. She would climb in our laps, paw our legs, knock us down with leaps, even after we had given her long minutes of cuddling and caressing.

The only time we could safely pet her a little was at mealtimes, when we could rub her head while she was preoccupied, for she ate like a garbage disposal on the rampage.

Having enjoyed house dogs for years, I persevered, but after nearly a year of mopping up urine, buying new lamps, and doctoring scratches on the furniture, me, and the children, I was disheartened. I had never believed in keeping dogs on a chain or in a pen. A dog should be part of the family, coming in the house after playing in the yard or romping in the park. Naturally, we wanted to take our dog on picnics to the lake and on overnight camping trips.

Kelly was also disheartened. She crept around the house, her head hanging in fear that she would do something wrong. I shouted at her much too often.

About this time we moved back to Georgia. There was never the slightest chance that Kelly would ride in the station wagon again. Instead, she had to share the back of a pickup truck with two ponies. All three arrived no worse for wear, and as we moved into our Somechoes house, I decided that Kelly would have to become a yard dog.

Living in far country, and as a result of refusing to adapt to people's demands, Kelly had the chance to live a life closer to that of her ancestors, a true dog's life, but without the stress of being solely responsible for her daily ration. She roamed at will through fields and woods, hanging out at the house only at night and for daytime naps and meals. In this environment she proved intelligent, catching rabbits, squirrels, moles, and mice. She ate what she killed. There wasn't much traffic on our road, but she learned to avoid what there was.

Looking out the living room window on a breezy winter morning, I would smile to see her trotting confidently across the big front pasture, a rich auburn splash in the dun and brown of winter weeds and grass. She'd be headed for the bright glint of Wingo's pond to chase beaver (she had sense enough not to catch one) and to watch the wood ducks and mallards come to feed. She liked the deep woods along the river, where the squirrel population was heavy.

Kelly loved going on the long trail rides I took almost every day as I conditioned horses for long-distance competitions. At last our two worlds had come together, and Kelly and I spent many hours as happy traveling companions. I enjoyed the flash of her rusty coat emerging from the woods or broom sedge. My horses learned from her not to spook at unexpected appearances, an important skill in a trail horse.

At the barn I could pet Kelly because she would rarely insist on more, once I turned to groom, feed, or tack up a horse. We would sit together for a moment on the steps of the tack room while I rubbed her head, which she would lay quietly in my lap. She liked sleeping in the tack room.

Lean and tough as a lighter knot, she grew older. Her muzzle went gray, and her teeth wore down to nubs. Still, she never missed a trail ride unless she was off hunting, and thus she covered forty or fifty miles a week with me at good speeds over rough terrain. I was surprised one day to realize she was past thirteen years old.

The inevitable day came when I noticed that she didn't always go with me. She would lie in the tack room, or she would go part of the way and turn back before we crossed the river. I'd find her sleeping or lying with her head resting on her paws when I returned. She stopped hunting. She spent most of her time under the back steps or in the tack room. It was autumn, the time when I loved to ride best, and I missed her companionship.

Then I came home one day from work, and no Kelly greeted me in the driveway. No Kelly under the back steps. No Kelly at the barn.

I knew, but I kept watching for her, whistling into the twilight as I put her feed out. Days passed, but Kelly did not come back.

I never searched for her. I like to think of her off for that last trot through the November woods, her path thick with rustling bright leaves. With the wild thing's instinct, she knew her old heart was giving out. I'll bet she found a safe, snug spot, maybe at the base of a grandfather black gum tree deep in the swamp between Wingo's pond and the river, where she curled up and drifted off to sleep, dreaming of squirrels.

NESTING

As a woman I have had one overriding ambition: that my home be a place of refuge. Whatever else I am doing, I want the place I call home to offer comforting shelter to those I love and to others who might pass my way in need of a haven.

I came by this ambition honestly. My grandmother Russell raised thirteen children and managed to make her houses, which were always simple and sometimes quite small, feel like the warmest, most desirable places in the world to all of her offspring, their spouses, and their children. In addition, she offered a home to two of her sisters, her widowed brother and his three young children, and her husband's brother. A rather distant cousin lived with her for more than three years. Although she found his staying power a bit much, she did not abandon her ideal of loving hospitality.

My mother had also the gift of making a house a home, a nest, a longed-for shelter. Bedlam Ridge, in spite of its zany name, was a large, gracious house to look at, but what made it a home was the way my mother felt about it. It was her crowning glory, a symbol of her achievement that remained when my father left her for another woman. My mother knew the house represented her as the First Wife, the one who bore the children and the hard times. It was rumored that her rival had bragged in a drunken moment that she would have the husband and the house, and so my mother, no matter how small her finances shrunk, would not give up her home. When it sank toward serious dilapidation, when selling it would have given her much-needed income, she hung onto it.

But not just as a symbol. In all its seasons, the door to Bedlam Ridge was open: to her children, their friends, myriad nieces and nephews, her family, Daddy's war buddies. After we were grown, every one of her six children came home, though thankfully one at a time, with their families to live for a few months or a year or two. When Dwain Jackson and I split up, he went to live with my mother until we could decide what to do. Bedlam Ridge was a haven.

Standing on the balcony of my house at Somechoes Farm on a cloudy morning in early spring, I watch the world go lighter. The clouds are low and thick, no triumphant sun at the horizon. Just a quiet revelation of fields and trees, peaceful, comfortable. The air is warm, and I smell rain while standing alone on the balcony, which Mrs. Philips, who lived in the house before I bought it, called a widow's walk. I was determined not to call it a widow's walk, though I am now in my house alone, having survived the departures of one husband and one lover.

Although these departures were not without heartache, I have not given up the ambition that my home be a haven. I like having a partner, but a woman can make a home without a man. Several of my women friends have lived here for months at a time, one for over a year, while they sorted their lives out after divorce, job loss, illness. My daughters and their friends come for weeks of vacation or months of study. I am satisfied that Somechoes has earned its haven badge.

From this second story of my house this morning I easily spot old wasps' nests hanging from the high porch ceiling. Four swallows' nests, a bit crumbly after winter, sit cozily near the ceiling at the top of porch columns and in the corners where the house and porch are joined. Cobwebs festoon the gingerbread molding around the door and drape the light fixtures, too. These are old homes, old places of safety, that will be repaired or replaced as the seasons swing. We are living here together, the swallows, the wasps, the spiders, and I.

Yesterday afternoon Jessica came home from her paralegal class in Atlanta and climbed into bed with me where I was reading and having tea. She had a cup of tea, too, and we were good friends, talking and laughing. Then we snuggled together for a warm nap. A bed is a nest within the house, a good place to welcome your closest friends, to share the solace of its covers and its peace.

It pleases me to recognize nests within my nest on a spring morning with the rain gathering in the gray clouds. I'm glad my home is a place of multiple homes, like the earth itself, a haven. I go in with this vision of my house like a Russian doll, hiding others of its kind but not exactly like it, yet each reflecting something of the character of the larger nest.

We have had swallows' nests for almost as many years as we have had the house. When the first barn swallows built on the front porch, at the top of one of the columns, I rejoiced. Nolan Willard, who was building the carport and storage building out to the side of the house at the time, told me I'd be sorry if I didn't tear that nest down right away because the birds would come in greater and greater numbers as the years went on. He painted a dire picture: the entire front of the white house covered with red-clay swallows' nests.

"Now wouldn't that be a topic," was all I said.

If I'd thought he would understand, I'd have told Nolan that there are worse things than swallows' nests to have on your front porch, like a washing machine, an old refrigerator, or a freezer locker, but I didn't think he'd understand. Besides, he might have had cousins with such as that on their front porches.

I'll take swallows' nests over satellite dishes, which are recently appearing on porches. The nests provide much more entertainment, and if you don't count the cost of hospitality, which I don't, it's free. Besides, the swallows over the years have repaid our hospitality a thousandfold in tender of joy, surprise, delight, and home education courses. If anything, we owe them.

Watching these clever and industrious architects build or repair the nests each year, daubing the wet mud into a sturdy cup, is a privilege. Only once did I disagree with their house site. That was the year a pair started a nest in the gingerbread molding at the top of the front door. This molding serves as a brace for the balcony. At the first sign of red mud architecture, I got a chair and stood on it to wipe away the mud. It was rock hard and had to be chipped away with a screwdriver. I persevered, thinking how inconvenient going in and out the front door would be for us and for the swallows.

Next day while I was at school, the birds put back what I had taken down and added several new layers. I chipped away again, but they were undiscourageable. After they rebuilt the third time, I gave in. "Okay," I said, "we'll use only the back door while you are nesting."

The way a pair of swallows work together has given me comfort when my own relationships were painful. The males are as handsome and as hardworking as you'd want a partner to be. Debonair in their rich blue coats and burnished orange vests, they bring globs of mud in tireless trips, while the females chirp and twitter about where to plaster. When the nests are done and the females are brooding, the males line up on the porch in the sun, standing guard. Sometimes four swallow gentlemen sit on the telephone wire running to the house, apparently awaiting orders.

The satisfied look on a female swallow's face, in her entire demeanor in fact, when she pokes her head over the edge of the nest and finds her partner faithful nearby stirs my heart with joy and longing. Her pleasure when her brood hatches and she perches on the nest edge to survey them reminds me of something I've known in my own being many times, watching my babies and my grown daughters as well. Nesting brings a deep satisfaction.

As the years have passed, I enjoy thinking that more and more swallows are out there with Somechoes in their blood. The most nests we had during a single season was six. I figure we put more than three dozen birds into the world that year because several of the pairs hatched two broods of four or five chicks. The usual number of nests is four, and double broods are not guaranteed, but they are common.

Every so often I go out on the porch in spring, when the swallows first come back and begin their repairs, and I remind them that there is a perfectly good barn behind the house and that they are, after all, barn swallows. They pay no attention, go on with their brick making.

In summer, watching them teach the young to fly, I learned not to take the flight of birds for granted, to recognize a yearly miracle, this laying of eggs, hatching, feeding, flight training. I knew greater satisfaction in my own work of child care and training from observing the swallows. The flight lessons once helped me make a difficult decision.

Nan was seventeen years old and wanted to go to Six Flags over Georgia for a day out. I didn't mind her going. What took my appetite, kept me awake nights, and turned my hair grayer was that the plan she presented was that she drive there herself with three girlfriends, one of whom was her fourteen-year-old sister.

She couldn't be ready for the perimeter traffic, I told myself. Besides, it was to be on July 3, when vacation traffic made highways more apt to be lethal. I simply could not say yes to this plan.

But I believe in adventures. I said I'd think about it.

One afternoon, sitting on the edge of my bed, wondering what to do, I heard a wild twittering from the swallows' nest in the east corner of the porch, which I can see clearly from my window. Looking out, I saw that the nest was empty except for the mother bird, who was giving desperate instructions to a fluff ball perched on the balcony railing.

That bundle of froth looked as if it would never fly. It would lift one foot, tremble violently, then cling like chewing gum to the railing.

Mother kept after him in a voice so shrill I thought she must be begging him to come back to the nest and safety. She must be sure he was not ready.

About this time, a thunderstorm stomped in, the wind got up, and rain poured. Shivering on his precarious perch, that bird looked stuck for good.

But his mother kept talking, and pretty soon Papa Bird showed up to give short demonstrative flights from the boy's side to the top of the nearest column.

Next a brother came skidding in, landing most ungracefully but unhurt, living proof that virgin flights succeed. After preening his slick feathers, he was off again in the rain.

Papa called from his perch on the nearby column. Mother urged from the nest, and the baby finally took off, fluttering like a heart falling in love. And he was in about as much trouble.

Although Papa's perch was very near, the youngster could not reach it for all his fluttering and twittering. Mother had, I expect, turned her face to hide her eyes. The baby tried to land on the rail again but missed.

Then he spotted the light fixture hanging from the ceiling and grabbed hold of that lifeline, breathing hard. Sitting sideways, he couldn't last there for long.

Swooping down beside him, Papa must have caught him in his draft because before you could say Charles Lindbergh, the youngster was soaring, out in the open, *flying!*

Mother took off right behind him, not too close. Papa veered away then, and the little one was on his own. Within a few minutes he was back at the nest, where his brother and sister had also returned. All three were chirping wildly about the joys of flight. No one looked fluffy anymore.

I knew that within a day or two the nest would not hold the flyers. A nest is a fine thing, but it isn't for everything. I let Nan drive to Six Flags.

In early autumn the swallows gather for flight, and one inevitable morning I miss their twitters, an alarm clock I value, and I miss their graceful swoops over the lawn at evening, writing an invisible but indelible lesson in the balance of nature. I scrub the bird droppings off the front porch, knowing there will be no more until spring. The porch feels lonely.

In the dark before sleep, I imagine the swallows on their southward trek. They are as uplifting as prayer, these swallows in my mind, winging their way across the earth. I smile at the thought of Somechoes Farm riding in the blood of such airy creatures, Somechoes Farm alive in the beating hearts of many swallows, Somechoes Farm patient, waiting for the nod of the globe to activate its power, waiting for the right moment to call them back to their nests, to call them home.

COONS AND COON HUNTERS

THE MEN come to the door at twilight, hat in hand if they have a hat—likely a baseball cap—and ask if they can hunt the river or the creek bottoms tonight near the house, north and south.

I say yes because I've found that as a breed coon hunters are reliable. They close gates, they put out their fires, they don't leave beer cans and sandwich wrappers. Most of the time they don't fire guns.

Also to their credit are those rangy, sleek-coated hounds, baying all night long down the river with voices God must have formed from night along the river, their noses quivering, their hearts beating, for coons. Their singing makes my heart pound to a different rhythm, understand something about the delirium of hunting.

Sometimes a coon hound gets lost from the pack, and they have to leave him and he ends up in my yard the next day. These dogs usually have tags, and I call for the owner to come get his dog, but in the meantime, I have a good-looking blue tick hound on my front porch. A southern front porch always looks good with a hound on it.

My brother John says I never want to see a pack of hounds catch a coon. I'm sure he's right. I don't like the idea, but there are plenty of coons, and adversity never hurt any of us. If the world were completely safe, we'd be so lazy and bored, we'd die of lethargy.

Our coons are so cautious I hardly ever see one, which is a good indication that they are up on survival skills. Coon signs abound in the woods: scat, little handprints in the river sand and in sandy spots along the creek. Once I saw three kits climbing a sapling near the riverbank, and I got a good look at them. Nature makes coon babies mighty cute.

I had no urge to touch them. I knew the mother was close by. One of the worst things about seeing a pack of coon dogs catch a coon is what the coon does to the dogs before they finish him. I did not want to risk a mama coon's taking my admiration for her babies the wrong way. I kept my hands behind my back while I looked. I walked away soon.

One thing coons do that is not a good survival technique is to eat too much. When they've been greedy, they go to sleep on the spot, like the coon in the persimmon tree essay in part 5. I have also seen a coon curled up in the middle of the horse trail after feeding on too many yellow jacket larvae. I stirred up the yellow jackets one day by rattling a log on the trail while riding—a memorable ride.

I approached the spot with great caution the next day and was surprised to find the log turned over, the yellow jacket nest exposed and emptied of all the larvae. A little farther on a coon was curled up tight, fast asleep in the middle of the trail. He woke up hissing and spooked my horse almost as bad as the yellow jackets did, but I was grateful to him for eating the yellow jackets, and I forgave him. I've waked up hissing from a few naps myself.

I don't know how or why coon hunting got started. Coons are not much good as meat, and I doubt they were ever much of a menace. Today's coon hunters are not hunting for food or to rid us of vermin. They want to wander dark woods with their dogs, to squat by a fire, talk with buddies, escape the hectic, impersonal pace of daily life. Most of them are older men who have been coon hunting for more than forty years, but some are in their thirties and forties. I think we should keep men around who care about nights along the river, hunting coons.

They leave little notes, written on the backs of envelopes or scraps of tablet paper, stuck in the back door screen: "Mrs. Russell, we are across the road hunting the creek tonight. Thank you." Or "My name is Tony Smith from up at Blairsville and you said over the phone I could hunt coon, so I am down on the river tonite."

The notes make me feel my part is appreciated or at least acknowledged with respect.

I ask that the hunters let me know when they are on the place. I don't worry about much out here on the farm, but truck lights in the pasture might mean cattle thieves instead of coon hunters.

Once I had to call the sheriff on a bunch of coon hunters who came unannounced and were running a big pack of dogs down on Rocky Creek. They got to shooting and shouting, and the cows and the horses were racing up and down in the pasture, terrorized. I wasn't frightened: I was mad.

The sheriff came straightaway, and it turned out these hunters, from over in Gwinnett County, were drunk and hadn't asked permission. But that's the only case in sixteen years of a disrespectful coon hunter on this farm.

The worst problem I have had with coon hunters is that the coon hounds sometimes get mixed up or frustrated or mischievous, and they tree one of my cats instead of a coon. Since I have only two cats, and since they have a distinct job around the barn and the house where mice are concerned, and they are good at their job, I don't want to see them lost to a confused pack of coon hounds.

The first time this happened—about a hundred yards from the back door—I knew instantly what the problem was. The air was booming with hounds baying and barking, and because Scarborough was a new cat, raised in a city apartment, I figured she had gotten herself in trouble. It was a black night, and since I did not know how many dogs were in the pack, I got in the car to drive to the edge of the woods from which the ruckus emanated as if there were a loudspeaker down there.

The coon hunters themselves, some local boys, arrived before I got there and were calling the dogs. We had a good laugh. I could see the cat's green eyes glowing in the tree, and once she figured out she had an exit, she hightailed it for the house.

Another night about 10:00 I hear a similar ruckus a bit farther down in the woods. The cats have been out since dusk. Uh-oh.

It's a rainy, dreary night after a cold, dripping April day. I am ill-disposed to venture out to rescue a cat, having already put on sweatpants and shirt, my sleepwear. I am also working at the computer, trying to finish an article.

Migno throws in her beagle notes, high and frantic, and there is nothing to do but go out there and investigate.

Hoping for the best, I don't put on shoes but my terry cloth mules. I try to skip over the wettest spots going out to the car.

I drive to the edge of the woods, but the pack is deep in the woods, nowhere within headlight range. Their barking and baying echoes across the hills like the finale of a football band contest.

Migno stands beside the car, barking frantically. I sit there, contemplating my philosophy of death. If that cat can't take care of herself, is it my job to do so? Maybe this is her time?

It sounds like a big pack of hounds, and I figure the cat up the tree is probably Scarborough, Jessica's little town cat, whose woods skills need work. I decide to find the hunters to come and call the dogs.

I drive slowly over the pastures, but I see no truck or car. When I finally turn back towards home, I see in the rainy headlight beams that Migno has followed me. She is panting, so I let her in to ride beside me, muddy feet and all, in the front seat.

The dogs are still singing to praise Jesus in the woods. I will have to go in the house, put on shoes and socks, find a decent flashlight, get a shovel or a hoe or something to beat off dogs if necessary, and tramp God-knows-how-far into the woods.

I consider again: If they've been barking this long, the cat must be pretty far up a good-sized tree. Judging from where the barking originates, I know the oaks and hickories are strong, their trunks thick. There aren't any little trees in that part of the woods to speak of. Fog is dripping off the trees. The broom sedge is sopping.

"Shoot," I say aloud to Migno, "that cat won't be fool enough to try to come down into the teeth of a dozen coon hounds. I'm going to bed."

When I get to the back door, both Pandora and Scarborough are sitting there waiting for me to let them in.

"Well, ladies," I say, "do you have any idea of the confidence I was about to exhibit in your survival skills?"

They don't look back, flow unconcerned into the house.

I wonder what the dogs have treed. Then it comes to me: a coon. Which is what they are supposed to tree. I am confident a wily ol' Somechoes coon isn't going to come down out of his big hickory tonight.

I go to sleep listening, guilt free, to coon-dog music, faint now, drifting across the foggy fields.

HOUSE OWL

I DON'T RECALL being afraid of things that go bump in the night. My father was a country doctor, and he had a small farm on the side because he preferred farming to doctoring. He couldn't make enough money farming to raise his three sons and three daughters, so he doctored and tried to assuage his farming passion with a milk cow, a mule to plow the garden, two ponies for the children, and five thousand laying hens.

Nighttime could be busy at our house with the phone ringing for the doctor, children walking/talking in their sleep—Mother caught John going out the back door more than once when he was little, sound asleep—and critters getting out of the barn or in the henhouses. One night a big king snake got into the basement, where we usually had about three thousand eggs to clean, grade, and box for the hatchery. The snake knocked something resounding off the freezer locker, prompting an investigation that resulted in our mother's saying, matter-of-factly, as she eyed a hoe-handle-thick and plenty long snake lying on her basement floor, that we might as well go to bed and let the snake have a few eggs. He deserved something for keeping the poisonous snakes away.

I inherited my father's passion for farming and, I hope, my mother's good sense about bumps in the night.

Consequently, when I was awakened at 3:00 A.M. by a resounding thud somewhere in the house, I lay quietly under my down comforter, not eager to get up in February cold to investigate a nonemergency. Although I had become aware of the sound in my sleep, once awake I was relatively certain the bump was internal, not a horse loose eating grass and cozying up to the house as it snatched the green and tender fescue next to the foundation.

I drifted back toward sleep. There came another bump and a clink. Probably the cat has a mouse on the run, I murmured in my brain. She'll get it in a minute.

Silence. There was a full moon, and the world outside lay in silver and shadow. So did my bedroom. Snuggling deeper under the down, I reaffirmed my opinion that night is a lovely time and that it's a shame we don't enjoy it more.

The next bump came louder, the clink tottered at the verge of crash.

I was at last wide awake. What in the world? Pandora may be old, but she can dispatch several mice in half that much time. Besides, she wouldn't be chasing a mouse over tables and other things downstairs. She is a much more subtle huntress.

I directed my attention to the attic, hoping the source of the thumping was there. Squirrels, I said, though in fifteen years we have never had a squirrel in the attic—at least not one indiscreet enough to make himself known, day or night.

Another thump. A definite crash. I was going to have to sally forth.

Although I was not considering a burglar, I crept down the stairs with caution. About halfway down, I heard the thump again. It came from the living room. Crouching, I peered over the stair rail into the living room. Sofa, chairs, the usual.

I took another step, reached the bottom one, then turned toward the living room. That's when the owl tried again to get out the window, flying across my line of vision, crashing into the window, falling against an end table, and setting a lamp tottering and clinking, before thudding to the floor.

My heart didn't know whether to stop or race.

In the shadows under the end table he looked as large as an eagle. Struggling to rise, he could not get lift. There was no sky to fly in.

I figured the best thing to do was to close the living room door.

"Oh, Great Spirit," I breathed, pulling the door to, "I've heard of barn owls, but house owls are not within my realm of knowledge. Help."

Safe from terrified owl talons, I tried to think what to do. The owl was jumping about, trying to fly. Peering in again, I watched his sweep of wing brushing the walls. He was, quite literally, climbing the walls. At the top, he would fall to the floor, thud.

Since he returned to one of four windows with each attempt at flight, he often landed in a corner with a lamp, a table, and a chair. The lampshade was nearly demolished, the lamp clearly doomed. Each time he fell, he fell under a table, where he would rest a few minutes before coming out to try takeoff again.

He looked, breathing hard under the table, about two feet tall. Tall. With long, prominent talons showing.

Time for reinforcements.

I crept back upstairs to wake my daughter Jessica, who is as good as an entire army. She has lived for weeks in the wilds of Montana to dig dinosaur bones. She worked on a French farm for a summer when she was only fifteen. She is a can-do person. The Great Spirit led me in her direction.

"Jessica," I said, putting my hand gently on her shoulder and waiting for her to wake up. When she mumbled, "What is it?" I said, "There's an owl in the living room."

She got out of bed without a word and went downstairs, putting on her glasses as she went. She peered into the room, then quietly closed the door and confirmed: "Yep, it's an owl all right."

"What shall we do?" I tried to speak matter-of-factly, like my mother and the king snake. "If we wait for morning to call the Fish and Wildlife people, he may kill himself or destroy the living room, both occurrences that I would like to avoid."

"While you were away last weekend, a young hawk got on the screened porch. Steve was here visiting Monique, and he caught it with a towel and set it free," Jess said. "We could throw a blanket over the owl and carry him outside."

We stood silent, considering this proposition.

"Are *you* volunteering to bell this owl?" I asked.

Long moment of silence.

Although she is nineteen, I am her mother, and here my maternal instincts took over. I could not take a chance on her being clawed by a desperate owl.

"Of course you aren't," I said. "I am."

"Well, you've got to get ready," she said. "Put on gloves and your down jacket and a hat."

I did all those things. There I stood, looking as if I could compete in the Iditarod except for my floppy flannel pajama legs and tatty blue terry-cloth scuffs.

"We'll turn on the light," Jess said. "Maybe that will quiet him, like daylight."

We turned on the light. He was under the table, and he swiveled his head to look at us with bright, dark eyes. His face was a creamy white heart, gracefully concave. His feathers were grayish brown, lighter underneath. His legs were long. I gazed and he gazed. How bizarre I must have looked to him in tweed hat, puffy blue down coat, and scuffs, things with no meaning to him.

He appeared beautiful to me, gazing calmly, in spite of the panic he must have been feeling. When had he ever been in a house—a place that for him was a complete *huit clos,* a no-exit, where light came through but when he flew for it, there was no sky. Although his talons were fit to strike terror, in that moment I did not fear them. Something of the grace of his construction, the body shaped for flight, the face for gathering sounds, even the sharp claws, entered my perception of the wholeness we all share, every animal, on earth. I knew myself part owl, he part human.

I lacked, however, confidence that he was human enough to understand if I offered him my arm and explained I would escort him to the freedom he longed for.

"I am your friend," I said aloud. "I know you are frightened. So am I. But we will think of a way."

He struggled again to fly. I jumped back, and his wide, confused wings carried him into the cramped air and across the room. He fell behind the television set in the corner.

My heart racing, I thought perhaps we could throw a blanket over him there.

Jess was standing at the door, ready for flight herself. I threw a sheep-skin from the back of the recliner. Then I threw a camp blanket. The owl poked his head out of the space between the wall and the TV stand, uncovered.

Within seconds, he was out and had flown back to fall again under the table by the recliner.

I edged over to the TV and retrieved the blanket.

Again I studied him as he studied me. After a moment, he hung his head and shook it sorrowfully from side to side.

"I know," I said. "I feel the same way. Quoth the raven, 'Nevermore.'"

I felt deeply sorry for him. My sympathy flooded the room. I was sure he must feel it. I wanted to call someone more adept than I to come and set him free. Someone with a net for such an express pur-pose. Someone who would not throw sheepskins and plaid blankets at him.

But it was 4:30 A.M. and the thought of waiting until daybreak at 7:00 while he tried to crash out the window and hung his head full of sorrow at his failures was too painful.

"Let's move the chair," I said. "Maybe we can cover him if it's out of the way."

We inched the chair out. He sat still. We inched some more.

He took off, if so it can be called, for the TV corner again. We scrambled for the door, which was closed. We huddled against the door. He fell behind the TV. My tweed hat fell off.

We could not help laughing, but the intense desire to rescue had become need in my blood, which nevertheless ran fearful at the thought of touching him, of not being able to match his power and his fear. After all, an owl is a bird, not that different from a chicken, and from experience with chickens, I knew birds can be stupid animals, incapable of the least rudiments of thought. Riding quietly over a knoll in the pasture, I saw a hawk once on the ground. It looked just like a chicken and, because we were downwind, was not afraid of us. My horse was Easter, famous for spookiness, and so I stopped, not wanting a hawk takeoff to send Easter into takeoff. The hawk kept scratching around after something in the grass, for all the world like a little red hen. I half expected it to say, "Buck-buck-buck-buck-buck."

Chickens know about only one thing—food. Eating and a little squawking and flapping, that's it for chickens. This owl could not be much different, except that what he knows as food is different, and his equipment for getting his food is more honed, more dangerous.

When it appeared that momentarily, at least, he was not going to soar from behind the TV, Jessica and I decided we would both try to put the blanket over him. That way we could spread it out fully and drop it more softly. That plan, of course, precluded anyone from standing at the door to open it in the event the owl attacked, which was why we had not considered this idea earlier. Oh, well.

Jessica took one end of the plaid blanket, I took the other. We inched toward the television set. Lifting the cover and spreading it at the same time, we nodded to signal the moment to drop it lightly onto what we hoped was the owl. At this point we could not see him.

Then we jumped back. There wasn't a flutter. Nothing moved, especially not us. A long pause. Still nothing.

"I think we've got him," Jessica said. "Let's pull the TV out a little."

I swallowed my fear or at least the evidence of it, and we tugged on the TV stand. The blanket slid all the way down and sure enough, the owl was under it. He did not struggle.

I wanted to get him out from under that heavy cloth as quickly as possible. It could suffocate him. But remembering those talons, I thought the old camp blanket looked kinda thin.

"Let's put an army blanket over this one," I suggested. "Then I won't be in the least afraid or likely to drop him."

Jessica went for the army blanket, and I pulled the TV stand all the way out of the way. We spread the army blanket over the plaid one and I started to gather the two up toward the lump that was the owl. Slowly, gently I worked, and soon I had a glob of blanket under the owl and was headed toward the door.

I was holding a wild owl in my arms! The sense of kinship I had felt earlier came back, and I was relaxed, confident. The owl did not move. Jessica opened all the doors to let us pass.

On the front porch, I said, "What now?"

Jessica, still the cool head (but she was not holding an armful of owl), said, "Go down in the yard, put the blankets on the ground, then pull them back. Be sure to stand to the back so he won't fly into your face."

Good point.

A February full-moon night is mercurial, silver, a fine distillation of cold, light, shadow, stars. I place the blankets gingerly on the ground and find a corner I can safely fold back. I lift the blanket carefully, carefully. Suddenly the owl is revealed.

More than suddenly he takes flight, his wide wings strong, stroking air. He vanishes. We do not see his gray form disappear into the deep blue light and shadow in the pasture. He vanishes.

We stand peering into the silvery light we mistakenly call darkness, amazed that such a presence can be so swiftly gone.

It is cold. I pick up the blankets and we go back in the house, turn out the living room lights, congratulate each other on a job well done and go back to bed.

It's nearly 5:00 A.M. The moonlight streams across my bed and I lie awake, wondering where the owl is. Is he flying, hungry, driven to hunt even after such a harrowing experience?

He must have come down the chimney. But owls are famous for knowing their territory. How could an owl not tell a house from a hollow tree? Did he simply land on the chimney, feel curious, take a peek? He knows he can get out of a hollow tree. Why not out of a chimney?

Even an owl can get into a jam where his fabulous survival skills are of scant use to him. But things came out all right. There is empathy in the world.

In the evening when I come home from school, it is dusk, almost dark. I stop at the bottom of the long driveway to get the mail. As I am getting out of my car, the owl—I know it is he—flies low over the pasture and crosses the road almost over my head. If I were courageous enough, I could reach up and touch him.

DEER HUNTER

I WALKED to Wingo's this afternoon, slipping sideways down the steep bank at my land line to get into the river swamp. From there, I had good walking out onto the flats, where water, sky, and swampy ground blur their boundaries.

A big flock of woodies was riding the middle of the lake, splashing, raising their wings to shake rainbow water from gleaming feathers, the males arching their necks to flash the iridescent brilliance of their green-blue-purple crested heads. I like the dusty blue of the female's wings, less often glimpsed but surprising with warm beauty when it is. The wind was in my favor, coming over the water toward me. I moved slowly, slowly, and the party went on uninterrupted. I reached the sapling oak on the patch of dry ground nearest the water and sat down, clasping my knees, resting my chin on them. Soon the lake eased into my whole mind and body. I relaxed into the poetry of wetland.

Traveling in Wales with Les last summer, I learned that Welsh has a word, *dôl,* that means "water meadow." *Dôl* originally meant "bend in the river" and then came to mean the land enclosed within that loop— water meadow. When Les told me that, Wingo's rose in my mind. I could see it lying gracefully between two creeks and the river, a water meadow.

I lay back on the grass under the moving sky. A deep happiness coursed in my blood. I thought about Les's coming visit and wondered if we would come down here to lie under the stars, listen to the frogs singing, and make love. It seems a good idea, to participate in this great life pulse by making love.

Coming home across the back pasture, I jumped a whitetail doe— TALL tail, small deer. Although flying her flag high, she was not too frightened, glided off a ways, tail quivering, and stopped, looking back. I stopped, too, looked sideways at her. If I really want to see a deer that sees me, I do not look at her directly. I call on peripheral vision. The space between us was about twenty yards. I let it be. She dropped her tail, shot it up again. Then she increased the distance between us little by little until she was lost in the brier patches. I walked on, glad we parted friends.

Because the ninety-five acres I call Somechoes Farm is surrounded by more than four thousand uninhabited-by-humans acres (I consider it highly presumptuous the way we humans designate land "uninhabited" if humans don't live on it), I enjoy plenty of deer neighbors. They leave their scent in the woods and fields, a sign different from that of cows or horses. Riding late in the evenings, coming home by twilight or moonlight, I smell deer in the dog fennel patches behind the Johnsons' house. I imagine several deer, and in my mind's eye I see them lift their heads to test the air, hold their grassy ground, decide this horse-human smell is not alarming.

Their odor also perfumes thickets along the riverbank, where they like to curl up during the day. I feel a little like Goldilocks, seeing the flattened brush and grass, the slight depression in the sand where they lie. Unlike Goldilocks, I try not to take advantage of this unexpected intimacy. I leave everything as it is.

I know the places the bucks scratch their antlers against the scrub oaks in my back pasture, behind the lily pond and at the top of the steep rise overlooking Wingo's, when they're in rut. The signs of their pawing and stomping, showing off their sexual readiness, thrill the core of my being. I have never seen them at this activity, though the evidence of it is considerable. The voyeuse in me would like to see them snorting and prancing, shaking their crowned heads, itching for a fight.

In the autumn the deer come to eat persimmons in the pasture with the horses, and the deer harvest the crabapples, too. It is not unusual to see the deer enjoying these treats at daybreak alongside a couple of equines. Deer come to the salt lick I provide for the horses, especially in winter, up by the front yard pasture gate.

When deer season opens in late autumn, I am deprived of riding early in the mornings because then the woods are liable to be (over)populated by deer hunters. Most will be family members, well aware of riders, but some will be poachers, hunting our land without permission, sneak thieves for whom I have no sympathy. Whatever time of day I ride during deer season, I put jingle bells on my horse's bridle and saddle. I wear a bright orange vest. I whistle and sing. I want everyone to know we are coming.

Although I am on the side of the hunted, wishing for every deer to escape the hunter, I respect responsible hunting, acknowledging that deer are here for hunters and hunters for deer. Theirs is an ancient and wise partnership, like that of the hawk and the mouse, the fox and the rabbit. The oldest message throbbing in all our blood may be that life is created from the shedding of blood, the source of life. Most of us must hunt. Those who crusade against hunting have probably never been truly hungry. When venison has been harvested fairly, I enjoy eating it. To provide nourishment is a universal reason for being.

The skill and courage of the hunter's blood flowing far back into the night of time brought us into the light of history. I bow before the power of the hunting urge. Hunting grounds are holy ground.

The trouble is this: there are those who have no respect for hallowed ground. We have had our share of that kind of deer hunter: dishonest, sneaky, wastrel. They come under cover of darkness, cast beheaded deer carcasses in their wake, often with numerous empty beer cans scattered around. Finding these beautiful creatures slaughtered in the woods for the sake of displaying their stolen heads as trophies provokes a nauseating awareness of man's inhumanity to nature. I wish no one had a share of that kind of hunter.

Yet their kind go back nearly as far as careful and caring hunters. Blood lust has infected humankind at every epoch, longer ago than Cain. Practicing patience (before big guns, patience is advisable), I prefer to focus on the fact that the deer survive and thrive because responsible hunters are in the majority and have established short deer-hunting seasons.

My season for hunting deer on horseback is long—all the year except for a few weeks of the legal season. I never ride out intending to hunt, but I often find deer because neither horses' scent nor the sound of their hooves alarms the deer. I am rewarded with exciting close-ups of the shy creatures, especially if I see them in time to slow down and approach at a walk, stop a few yards off. From horseback I have enjoyed watching deer nuzzling leaves for hickory nuts in the deepest woods on Horseshoe Bend Farm. I gazed my heart full of their graceful forms.

My mare Dalal and I once came upon a pair of deer splashing in a deep swamp pool on a hot May afternoon, having more fun than a barrel of beavers. In places the deer became nearly submerged, and they swam with vigor and joy. We watched for a long time, until Dalal decided she wanted to join them. I hated to turn down the suggestion but had to.

"They might not mind your presence, lady," I said, "but they would certainly mind mine. Let's not spoil the fun."

By far the most exciting deer hunting I have experienced on horseback involved a chase, none the less thrilling for being unintended.

Jessica and I went out on Took and Dalal on a December afternoon, Jess riding Took, who started out as her horse, surrendered to me only when she lost interest in riding during her midteen years. They share a special affinity, and he seems to know that he has more freedom to run when she is aboard than when I am there.

Took loves to run, revels in his Arab speed, shows joy in flight. In the barn and paddock, he is far down in the pecking order, waits humbly for others to precede him, but in the pasture, when the herd goes to running, he's out front, tail flying high, showing 'em how it's done.

The day of the deer chase, we started off briskly in the cold air. Dalal has a long, smooth trot, and we took the lead at this pace. To keep up, Took sometimes had to canter, but he never minds cantering. Both bays with black manes and tails, the matched horses made an agreeable picture, and may I be pardoned for appreciating the sight of my pretty, blond twenty-year-old daughter, trim in her black riding pants, boots, and hat. A forest-green jacket set off her riding attire perfectly. After riding an hour, we were all—horses and women—pretty high.

We paused for a moment near the river, where the old bridge is bent, to watch the muddy waters swirl and foam around the twisted girders that once spanned them. The bridge was part of old Highway 53 and the roadbed, never paved, carries on up the hill to Daddy's barn.

"Shall we take the road and go home by the barn," I asked, "or go through the woods and out into the pasture?"

"I vote for the pasture," Jessica said, "and I'll lead."

She turned her mount into the woods where a narrow path twists among the trees, letting him trot fast. Dalal had no trouble keeping up. These woods are mature oaks, hickories, a few poplars. They blend into a patch of young pines planted at the edge of the pasture, through which we years ago cut a wide trail for the horses. I figured Jessica had in mind a long canter through the pines and across the big pasture. The horses sensed the run coming, tugged against the reins.

As we entered the pines, a doe got up from the undergrowth, leaping onto the path beside Took. Within two bounds she had taken the lead, but Took did not give up easily. Jessica, a brave and adventurous rider, leaned forward to help him answer the challenge. The three of them— deer, horse and girl—kept pace through the pines until the deer lengthened the distance between them in the open pasture. Faster than a horse and unburdened with a rider, she soon left her challengers behind. Took galloped gamely on until the deer bounded out of sight into the woods on the far side of the field. When Jessica asked him to heed her tightening rein, he graciously slowed.

Dalal, not known for speed, was happy to canter, allowing me to watch the show. That view of girl, horse, and deer in flight composes a memorable picture I call *A Few Strides of Glory.* As mother, equestrian, and deer hunter, I am glad I didn't miss the shot.

A NEIGHBORLY TALE

It was the autumn after I came back from a superb eight-day horseback ride through the Loire Valley in France, followed by four weeks there with my friend, Maryvonne Demeneix, that I told Ben I could no longer consider living apart, he on a marsh island off the Georgia coast and I at the farm. We had started the dream of building a house on the island together, but Ben became increasingly possessive of both house and dream, pushing me farther away each time I went to the island. Hurt and puzzled, I finally arrived at the day when it seemed wisest to make a clean break. Living on a Georgia marsh island with Ben was a dream hard to let go, but the summer in France gave me courage. Complete separation from life here, from language to landscape, provided calm release from the emotional pain I'd suffered for more than a year. I was emboldened to think of selling the farm to move to France to open a bed and breakfast and write.

If pain doesn't make us consider alternatives, it's fairly useless.

At a Sunday dinner, my brothers and sisters and their spouses, as well as Mother, Daddy, and his wife, Kate, were gathering at Bedlam Ridge to celebrate a visit from brother Alex and his wife, Judy, from Alaska. I thought I might want to know my family's opinion of my idea. I expected them to be surprised that I would consider leaving Somechoes. Perhaps they would try to talk me out of it or make a joke of it. My throat tightened while we were seated and eating around Mother's big dining table, and I could hardly enjoy Nancy's good lasagna casserole or Susan's broccoli cornbread. I decided to get it over with.

"Johnny Fleeman's coming out this week to give me an estimate on my house and five acres. I think I might sell and buy a bed and breakfast place in France," I said.

Alex picked up on the important part of this statement right away: "Johnny Fleeman's selling real estate now? Too bad he had to give up the abattoir after Goodman died, but I guess it was inevitable. Finding good help's got to be hard, probably impossible."

Daddy was next. He'd been the Fleeman family doctor for about forty years: "Not many folks'll work like the Fleemans. Lord, they could work like horses."

Smiling dreamily, Susan remembered that Johnny Fleeman made our preteen hearts beat faster when he drove by on his tractor. He was three years ahead of us in school and was the fastest man on the football and track teams in three counties. Legendary speed. He had a shy, appealing smile.

Then I remembered the time I was happiest to see him driving that tractor. I figured we wouldn't get spanked for telling about it now.

"It was when you had that old Ford Jubilee tractor, Daddy," I said, "and I was learning to drive on it."

"It wasn't old then," Daddy said.

"I was only thirteen," I said, "but Alex showed me how to change gears, and I got to driving the tractor pretty good around the pasture, having a heck of a time."

"I rode with her," Susan said, "standing on the sidestep, hanging onto the fender for dear life."

Everyone was listening attentively now.

"It didn't take long for the pasture to get boring," I continued, "so I suggested we go on the dirt road, by way of the back gate, where we couldn't be seen from the house."

"Yeah," Susan said, "if Mother hadn't officially disapproved of an adventure, we could always plead ignorance of the law."

Everyone laughed, remembering what a tyrant we thought our mother was. She blushed, quiet in her wheelchair but still at the head of the table.

"So off we went," I said. "We'd been bumping along for about a mile when I decided I'd better get back home, not knowing anything about the gas supply. Susan, with a little sister's unshakable faith, wanted to go all the way to Johnny Fleeman's house. How could I disappoint her?

"When we got near to the Fleemans', I realized I was going to have to turn around because I couldn't go breezing into the Fleemans' yard for no reason. This meant going into reverse in the middle of the road. I hadn't had much practice with reverse.

"I managed to get the tractor sideways in the road and figured if I could back it a little we could turn around. But I wasn't smooth enough with my shifting. The tractor jerked backwards like a crawdad in the creek, and there we were in the ditch. I forgot to keep the clutch in. The motor died with a shudder.

"Susan looked a little pale, but she started laughing, and so did I. We always laughed when we got into trouble. Nerves, probably.

"I didn't have a clue what to do, but the Good Lord was looking after us. We heard the sound of a tractor motor, coming down the road. In a minute there was Johnny Fleeman driving a tractor with a plow.

"'Afternoon,' Johnny said, stopping his machine. 'Looks like you've got a little problem.'

"'Yes, *Sir*,' we said, figuring respect was owed to anybody who could drive a tractor and use it too.

"'Why don't you get down and let me see if I can drive it out?' Johnny said.

"We scrambled down, and before we could say *Jubilee*, Johnny had the tractor out of the ditch and headed toward home.

"We remounted our respective steeds, motors rumbling. 'Uh, Johnny,' I said, 'I hope you don't need to mention this to anybody.'

"He smiled his shy smile and tipped his baseball cap. 'My lips are sealed,' he said."

John said he had a better rescue story than that on Johnny Fleeman.

"You remember the time we were going to canoe down Marburg Creek at the flood, don't you, Alex?" he asked.

"Boy, do I remember *that*," Bruce, our baby brother (he's now thirty-eight), said. "Let's see, I must have been about seven years old."

"John was thirteen," Alex said. "I don't know what got into my head that day to take my little brothers into those wild waters in a canoe. No life jackets. I was twenty-one and should've known better."

"I can already tell I'm glad I didn't know about this until now," Mother said.

"We carried the canoe down to the bridge near Bethlehem below Johnny's house. It'd been raining for a week, and the water was almost over the bridge, moving like Time itself." Alex likes Faulknerian elements in his tales.

"We thought we could ease into the backwater below the bridge," John said, "and have a good ride once we got into swift water. We usually didn't think canoeing that lazy old creek was worth the trouble."

"As we were getting into the canoe," Alex went on, "I looked up on the bridge, and there was an old blue Chevrolet pickup stopped. It was Johnny Fleeman's. He got out to watch the show. I shoved off the canoe like I knew what I was doing."

"We didn't get far," John said, "before the current caught us, and in less than thirty seconds we had spun sideways. There was no way we weren't going over."

"We came up at the same time, don't you remember?" Alex looked at John. "We were shouting, 'Where's Bruce?' About then he popped up like a fishing cork, and I grabbed him. I knew you could swim. 'Get to the shallow water!' I shouted. The current was sweeping you away from us."

"Yeah," John said, "I couldn't believe how strong it was. You were making progress toward the bank, but I was swept downstream, struggling to stay afloat. After a few minutes I noticed someone running in the backwater. It was Johnny Fleeman, high-steppin' it to the rescue. He reached out to me in that curve near the wash hole and hauled me in. I was so tired I could hardly move."

"I lost my glasses that day," Alex said, "and we didn't find the canoe until the next week, when the creek went down."

"I don't know how I raised a single one of you," Mother said.

When the laughter died down, Nancy said she had a Johnny Fleeman story about the night the WAG house burned.

The WAG house was a shack that Daddy had Will Thomas build from old barn lumber for me and Susan and six friends. We called ourselves the Winder Adventure Girls. It was a tiny one-room place, housing only a rickety old table and seats of boards nailed to the walls. If all eight WAGS were present at once, we could hardly get us all inside, but this clubhouse was the pride of our lives. I was in college by the time Nancy was taking her friends down there for hot dog roasts. The night in question, she and cousin Sally Nelson were having an adventure.

"A problem flared up," Nancy said, "because we built our hot dog fire too close to the clubhouse. The wind got up, blew our fire against the house, and those old boards blazed up like kindlin'.

"When we realized the house was on fire, Sally jerked off her shirt to try to beat out the flames. Sally was twelve, a year older than I, and had her first training bra. The fire made short work of her shirt, and two terrified girls were trying to beat the flames out with a shovel when Johnny Fleeman came driving by. He must have been working his way through the university by then.

"Johnny pulled us away from the fire, put his vest on Sally, and sent me home to call the fire department. As I dashed away, he broke a pine sapling and attacked the flames.

"When the fire department arrived," Nancy finished, "he got in his truck and drove off, with never a word to anybody. By that time the WAG house was nothing but a heap of ashes, but the fire department saved the dry autumn woods."

"I saw to it he got his vest back," Mother said.

Nobody said anything else for a few seconds, remembering that secure, neighborly feeling you had for people like the Fleemans. They lived three miles from us, but at the time there were only three other houses between our farm and theirs. Today there are three subdivisions.

"Johnny's girl, Faith, is a super cross-country runner on the high school track team," brother-in-law Raymond said. "Isn't she a good friend of Jessica's?"

"Yes," I said, "and Jess's first crush was on Faith's older brother, Sean. He is a good-looking thing."

Again no one wanted to speak.

"Leaving these roots would be a violent move," I said into the silence. "On the other hand, if I need to do it, having Johnny Fleeman help me out is a reliable tradition."

They all knew some of the heartache I'd suffered, but no one looked inclined to comment.

Then Daddy said, in his easy, nonjudgmental way, "Might be a good time to sell."

Part Two

ARTHROPODAL

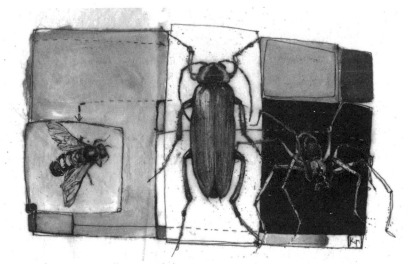

ARTHROPODAL. Of or pertaining to the phylum *Arthropoda*, in this instance encompassing insects and spiders, creatures having segmented bodies and jointed legs/limbs, numbering six (insects) or eight (spiders). These creatures progress through life using a series of metamorphoses in one of two types, gradual or complete. From the Greek *arthron* (joint) and *–pod* (foot).

WASPISH

THERE'S A WASP flying around the dining room in the warm winter sunlight coming through the tall windows that face south. Heat from the wood stove and the sun has fooled her into thinking it's spring.

She drones over my head where I am sitting at the dining table, which is festooned with a poinsettia-printed Christmas cloth and green candles in two well-used silver candlesticks. Alone in the house, I am trying to enjoy my lunch. But a wasp droning over my head is not given to lighthearted Christmas anticipation or to peaceful dining at any other season. I duck awkwardly between bites if the flight trajectory seems to warrant ducking, and I soon grow tense, start to sweat a little. Fear keeps me from swatting at the thing lest I anger her into unreasonable attack.

I learned when I moved into this old house that I would have to cohabit with more wasps than is the wont of most moderns. The board walls, floors, and ceilings harbor wasps, and they creep through the cracks into my space. Which would not be so bad if wasps were a little better natured. It's tough trying to get on the good side of wasps. They don't care much for intimacy of any kind.

My cousin Harry Eaton on my mother's side is the only person I've ever known who could be in the least intimate with a wasp without regret. While I was repairing this house, Harry came up to check out the famous mobile home he'd been hearing about. My mother's contemporary, he was an antique collector and dealer and thought it reasonable to move a hundred-year-old heart-pine house eight miles through the country in order to save its life. He was proud to have a relative who was up to such a stunt.

We stood in this room and talked about the renovations, and Harry noticed a few wasps flying against the windowpanes.

"Well, you'll have to get used to wasps," he said. "They've been wintering in these walls for a hundred years. They aren't likely to stop because you've put in plumbing."

"That's good news I hadn't expected," I said.

"Oh, they don't bother you if you don't bother them," he said.

"Ha!" I said. "I've never wished a wasp malice aforethought and I've been stung plenty of times."

"You know, I never have been stung, not in sixty-five years," he said. "I can actually hold a wasp and it won't sting me."

Harry was a big talker and tall-tale teller, and I raised my eyebrows at this statement. Without a word, he walked over to the window and put his hand in front of one of the big red wasps crawling on the pane. She crawled onto the back of his hand, and then he transferred her gently to the palm of his other hand. She crawled out of there and started leisurely up his arm.

He was a big man, like most of the Eaton men, and the wasp crawled a long way up that brawny arm while he stood there cool as rocks on the creek bottom. The Eatons had a lot of cool, most of them.

"Don't know why, they just aren't afraid of me," he said, as he put his finger out for the wasp to crawl onto. Then he put her back on the windowsill.

Remembering that wasp on Harry's arm makes my heart race, as does the sight again of the current wasp floating past me, near, her long legs primly held at the wasp-dangle angle—the one they say means she is not being aggressive. Nevertheless, I find this angle most unattractive. For all her poise, she crashes into the windowpane on the west side of the room and gets caught in a cobweb there.

Living in an old house like this means a plentiful supply of cobwebs, which I take advantage of to catch wasps. I figure this is fair warfare because wasps eat spiders, paralyzing them and then poking them, still alive, into nests for a newborn wasp snack. If spiders have their day, who can blame them?

The wasp struggles against the web, but she cannot get out. She buzzes, groans, and strains, remains caught fast. Now I have a moral dilemma. Do I go ahead and kill her, smack her with the newspaper rolled up by the fire (no longer afraid that she will fire back at me if I miss), or do I let her die an agonizing, struggling death?

I read somewhere the opinion of an insect expert that wasps are more nervous than mean. I am fully willing to concede that such may be the case, but I am nervous about having a nervous critter armed with a sharp-pointed, poison-laced weapon skittering about the house. If wasps are going to be nervous anyway, I figure I'll give them something to be nervous about.

I get the rolled paper from the fireside and smack her. She comes apart, and her stinger portion falls to the floor—it's the heaviest part of her and the ugliest, attached or detached, the part whose ugliness inspires movies like *Alien*. Weighted with fertilized eggs at this time of year—one name for part of the wasp abdomen is ovipositor—it carries that wicked stinger noticeably protruding. I don't look at stingers any more than I have to.

Nevertheless, there's half a body moving around on the window sill, which isn't a pleasant sight, so I start to squash her under my finger on the paper. Although I know the stinger is gone, I hesitate. This second half of her falls behind the deacon's bench. I go back to my tuna salad.

When I go upstairs to take a nap, I find another wasp hanging on the curtain beside my bed. How can I enjoy a nap with a sword of Damocles wasp hanging over my bed? But how to dispose of this bugger? She's cuddled down within the folds of the blousy, unbleached muslin. I find the fly swatter and bat a couple of times, which action serves to send her deeper into the folds, wherein to wait malevolently for me to fall asleep before taking her revenge. So I take the metal end of the fly swatter and pin her against the window, once more separating abdomen from thorax. The pieces drop behind the blanket chest window seat where there are lots of cobwebs. A brief buzz, then silence.

As I snuggle under the comforter, I chide myself for being intolerant of wasps. I know I ought to think of their talents. They are builders—those compartmented nests of paper they make with rotted wood and their own juices are clever—and they don't capture the spiders they feed their young without a fight. I once watched a wasp carrying a spider across the back lily pond, a spider almost too big to be flown with. But the wasp managed it some way, her efforts nothing short of heroic.

Another thing to admire about wasps is the way they protect their nests.

Now right here I have to admit that something I said back there to Harry Eaton was not exactly the truth. Because in fact, I *have* wished wasps malice aforethought. When we were children on the farm out at Russell, one of our summer amusements was to bombard wasp nests. Whenever we spotted a likely one on the wagon shed or the barn, we would go off and collect weapons—rocks, magnolia seed cones, maypops, chunks of stove wood—and then we would blast away at the nests, but only if they were in a place that allowed us space to run like hell after each assault because the wasps, naturally, dashed out, dive-bombing all over the place.

One day I spotted an enormous wasp nest—it was at least as large as a basketball—in my grandmother's rosebushes, along the path between her house and ours. I could not believe how big that nest was. I ran to tell my brothers and sisters and several visiting cousins about this exciting target. Off we all went, like Pharaoh's army, my mother said, to fight the wasps.

We numbered about ten youngsters, boys and girls, ages four to twelve, so the first assault was a good one. But from a nest so large the defense team was bound to be impressive. When that black cloud of wasps rose up, we all ran like jackrabbits, scattering far and wide, squealing in terror and delight. When we had regrouped, breathless, at the mule lot fully two hundred yards away, my big brother Alex said we need not have been so scared. If you stood perfectly still, the wasps wouldn't bother you. Alex, being the oldest, spoke with authority, but most of us were old enough to recall that we had never seen Alex stand anywhere near perfectly still during a wasp fight. Unfortunately, our brother John, then four, thought his big brother knew what he was talking about.

We marched again, approaching cautiously to be sure the wasps had settled down. Then we let fly another volley and screamed off again. All but John. Out of the corner of my eye, headed toward Grandmother's front porch, I saw the little fellow crouch down, still as still could be, only a few feet from that huge nest.

I also saw four big red wasps land on the back of his neck. Two of them stuck there. His screaming had no delight in it.

I knew my sisterly duty, and I did it, and I was not the only one who went back for him. Cousin Mary Ina got to him before I did. We raced with him around the house straight to the kitchen, where Modine Thomas, the cook, met us on the back porch, her black face stormy. "What y'all doin' to that baby?" she asked.

"Nothin', Modine, honest. He's been wasp stung."

Modine knew what to do for wasp stings, and that day her quick action may have saved John's life. She slapped wet tobacco right on the spot where he'd been wounded. Tobacco juice will draw wasp poison out with a strong, quick pull. I don't recall whether Modine got the tobacco straight out of her mouth—she usually kept a pad of snuff tucked between her lower lip and gum—or whether she made up a little paste fresh. She probably used what was ready.

Modine ordered us to leave that nest alone, a totally unnecessary command. We knew the wasps had won that fight. They, however, were taking no chances. A couple of days later we noticed an amazing thing: they had moved the nest. At first we thought we must have knocked it down, but no, there was no nest anywhere in the rosebushes. We finally spied it in the boxwoods close to the house, in a spot we would never dare throw at.

There are few things I regret in my life, but one of them is not seeing those wasps moving that nest.

In the spring I remind myself of the advantages of wasps to humans, especially those humans who live on farms. I recall well the year the army moths ate the pastures down to nothing because the winter had been so cold that almost no wasps had made it through—I think it was the winter of 1975–76. Wasp diet includes army moth larvae, which feed on grass like our pasture fescue. No wasps meant that the army moths were routing the fescue roots, and the sad results were we had hardly any new spring grass and bare pastures the entire summer. It was a bleak time.

Thinking about wasps and moths and green pastures inspires me to try to let outside all the wasps that, having overwintered in my walls, mistakenly come inside the house as they awaken in spring. After all, who wouldn't be a bit groggy after sleeping for three or four months? In spring I suspend for these moth-eaters my general rule that critters who wander into my house do so at their own peril.

The kind of wasp we have at Somechoes is the paper wasp, recognizable because they rest with wings folded beside the body rather than over the back. I have inspected a few living wasps in the house but confess I do not like to get too close to them. I base my identification on the fact that we have numerous papery wasp nests under the eaves of the front and back porch, in the garage storeroom, and in lots of corners of the barn and on the fact that the wasps are large, reddish-brown, and mean looking.

Paper wasp reproduction techniques are curious. Throughout the spring and summer there is never a wasp without a stinger, and only females have stingers. So where are the boys? Shouldn't there be as many of them as there are of the girls? What could these boys be doing with their time and talent while the girls are building nests, catching spiders, battling army moths, and in general making themselves useful?

Hard as it is to believe, there are actually no male wasps at this time. Only fertilized female wasps live over the winter. These pregnant females, called queens, emerge in the spring and go to work making small homes in which to lay eggs that will eventually become female worker wasps. As soon as the young queens have their workers, they settle down to doing nothing but laying eggs, which all hatch into worker wasps— female but sterile. This is a relatively peaceful time. The wasps are working hard, going to bed early, getting up early. The nest grows bigger day by day, and everyone seems satisfied.

Then in late summer, when the nests are bulging with eggs, alas, sex must come into the picture. Certain eggs develop into fertile females and fertile males, and when they hatch, guess what happens?

All you-know-what breaks loose, which is what you would expect to happen in a social order that has been going along ignorant of sex and then has a big dose of it splashed all around. The sterile females stop working, the queen stops laying, and the newly hatched fertile females go sashaying around where the males are hanging out—usually the warm side of a tall building, a dead tree, or a power pole. The high white sides of Somechoes house, east and west sides, are favorite wasp courting spots. The males sort of perch up there, bodies raised high, wings held out at the ready, watching. They ignore bees, flies, grasshoppers, mosquitoes, gnats, other male wasps, and sterile female wasps.

When he spots a fertile female, the male darts toward her with great energy, knocking her to the ground, where he mates with her. Which proves my earlier point that it's hard to be intimate with a wasp. Some experts say the females are not necessarily sexually drawn to the males but are instead looking for a place to spend the winter (like in the walls of Somechoes) and so are innocent and unsuspecting. I really couldn't say.

This mating dive is pretty exhausting for the males, and they don't last long. As autumn wanes we have only pregnant females hanging around the eaves of the house, trying to find a crack to ease through to overwinter safely on the dark side of my warm rooms. The males have taken to the woods to curl up and die.

I suppose a system like this does simplify the question of sex. Keep one of the halves out of things until reproduction is absolutely necessary, and then it's no holds barred for the previously barred sex. This might also explain why the males don't need stingers: no one has time to get nervous.

BUMBLING CARPENTER BEES

IT IS A BALMY MARCH DAY, and the bumblebees are out in droves at the barn when I go down to get the horses up because Gus is coming to ride. Actually these have to be carpenter bees. I said *bumblebees* out of habit because the two species are alike, and when I was a child we always said *bumblebees*. I don't know how carpenters differ from bumblers except that the carpenter bee is less hirsute, has a shiny, show-off abdomen, and builds her nest as part of a barn or house. Bumblebees build their nests in secret woodsy places that are pretty hard to spot.

I walk through the swarms of bees as they hang in the warm air in the sunny barn aisle, sniffing out house sites. I come and go from the feed room, putting feed in the horses' troughs and closing the stall doors with a clang, and the bees are not bothered.

When I ring the farm bell hanging in the loft from rafters that the bees are seriously inspecting for houseworthiness, the insects do not become alarmed. Hearing the bell, nine horses come running, and after I have let them into their stalls, I sit on the grassy bank in the sun beside the barn to watch the bees.

The gentle way they navigate the air this warm morning is appealing. I feel happy watching them. Gus says I shouldn't let them nest in the rafters, door frames, or anywhere else because they will destroy the barn, boring so many holes that they eventually weaken it to tumbling.

Gus teaches computer science at Georgia Tech and is a serious brain. I am sure he knows a lot about some things, but I doubt he knows much about carpenter bees. Yes, there is a good bit of sawdust at the mouth of their holes, but I suspect the bees have a kind of sixth sense that tells them how many bee apartments such a barn will safely support. A good carpenter needs to know things like that. They will stop short of this number, sending other bees to other barns. Their version of zoning. They need the barn, have no interest in destroying it. Those ancient, crumbling barns we see over the countryside—it isn't the bees that bring them down. It's wind, rain, sun, bees, frost, tired nails, storms, neglect.

Gus sometimes strikes at the bee swarms with the shovel, bringing a few bee citizens down around his bald head. I find the dead littering the barn aisle. I tell him I'd rather he didn't do that, that I will keep the barn standing, not to worry, but Gus doesn't listen to me. I teach what he calls fuzzy studies (humanities) at Gainesville College. What could I know?

The experts, people who teach at places like Georgia Tech, I suppose, say that physically the bumble- and carpenter bee should not be able to fly. The experts say this with amazement, which I find amazing. They are amazed that the bee can fly, and I am amazed by the presumption that we think we understand everything about flight. There are all kinds of laws we have not begun to understand and perhaps never will. Physical and moral laws. We are ready to accept that a natural—that is, physical—law is immutable, yet there is the bumblebee right before our eyes, disproving the law. But what is proof? The morning is too delicious to think about proof.

I walk through the bees again to let out the horses who are not going to be ridden. I am grateful that the bees are not fearful. I would be terrified to enter a swarm of wasps like that. Wasps study the situation, keep a brigade ready to defend, another ready to attack, but I waltz through the bees without a blink, without a fluttering pulse. They slide away in the air without agitation. They hang, they hum.

I walk through swarms of honeybees the same way, those feasting on the plum bushes in full white glorious bloom along the drive. I have faith that the bees are too busy or too contented to bother much with a human walking along with no ambition toward plum blossoms.

I know, however, that it doesn't do to have too much faith in bees' forbearance. When I was five years old I learned to catch the white-nosed bumblebee. My older brother, Alex, who was nine, told me the white-nosed ones would not sting, and he was right. I think they are the males.

I liked to catch the bees and hold them gently, listen to them buzz with my careful fist held close to my ear. I would let them crawl across my palm before taking flight.

Then that rascal brother told me the honeybees in the flowering bush by the front door wouldn't sting. With all the faith and naïveté of five, I reached up to take hold of a honeybee. I can still feel the burning pain, see the stinger that stuck in my palm, right at the base of my thumb. I never liked holding any kind of bee after that, but I am willing to trust them in flight.

I wonder if the reason bees are less aggressive than wasps is that they feed on nectar instead of on spiders and larvae as wasps do. Getting started in life from spider meat cannot make for the kindest character. Bees, however, wake to life in a golden, sweet honeycomb and move on to plum blossoms. I would expect the natures of creatures so nourished to be different.

Gus drives to work from Lawrenceville, fighting downtown Atlanta traffic every day. Sometimes he goes in to school at 6:00 A.M. and stays until 10:00 P.M., to avoid the traffic. I spend almost sixteen of every twenty-four hours here on this quiet hill, and my drive through the country to Gainesville College is not stressful at all until the last mile. I guess it isn't surprising that Gus wants to knock down bees while I admire the grace and agility of their flight patterns.

I doubt humankind ever got anywhere much going to battle against bees with a shovel, but anyway, while Gus is here, I'll take mine up to the house and stand it behind the kitchen door.

HORNETS AT HOME

THE FIRST HORNETS at Somechoes Farm built their nest high up against the west chimney, under the eaves. It was a magnificent nest, bigger than a human head, and because it was so high, it posed no danger to us. All summer long the hornets came and went, doing whatever they do in the nest, and we came and went, parking the car, tending flower beds, watering and feeding the dogs beneath the nest, and not a cross word between us. Hornets are not bothered by people unless the people get in the way of their path to the nest door.

Obstructing a hornets' nest door guarantees big trouble. Hornets are ferocious fighters at their doors, and they have wicked weapons that they use without the slightest hesitation. You do not get a chance to say, "Excuse me, I didn't mean anything. I was just walking by." If you knock into a hornets' nest in the fields or woods by accident—and it is always an accident; no one knocks over a hornets' nest on purpose—for example, when you are bush-hogging or clearing trail for a bridle path, the hornets come out in well-aimed swarms. A man, a tractor, and a bush-hog are a formidable team, mowing down everything in its path. But when the man suddenly abandons his tractor and bush-hog and hightails it across the pasture, arms waving about his head, you know he is battling hornets—and losing.

This attitude of refusing to listen to reason when they think the nest is threatened has served hornets well through the ages. They are not an endangered species.

I know a little about what hornets do in the nest because once they built on Daddy and Kate's kitchen window, boldly stuck the nest to the windowpane. Standing at the kitchen sink, anyone could see inside the nest with perfect clarity and safety. To Kate's credit, she let the nest grow. It was high off the ground at the back of their house, and people could easily avoid the yard below the nest. The window, which had a storm window component, remained closed all summer.

When the nest was only hand-sized, the inhabitants were a few smallish females and an obscenely large queen—three or four times larger than the others. There did not seem to be much advantage to being queen. The handmaidens spent long days gathering papery bits from dead tree limbs in the nearby woods, the floor of the gazebo in the side yard, arms and backs of rockers on the front porch, old lumber stacked in the backyard. The females brought these bits to the nest for making papery sheaves for the walls and for stiffer-sided little chambers inside the nest. The queen kept busy laying eggs in the resulting chambers. It didn't look as if anyone had an easy job. The nest grew apace, and the queen soon was lost somewhere in the center, surrounded by her children. They rolled, crawled, and buzzed when they were not flying out to get paper material. I have to say hornet society seems satisfied and peaceful with good work for everyone.

The second year at Somechoes the hornets chose the back end of the garage, high and dry under the eaves at the peak of the roof. The only time we had to go near was to cut the grass back there, and then Ben simply gave that spot a wide berth. The horses grazed there with impunity, however, and kept the grass down. The hornets did not seem to mind when a horse bumped against the garage.

Having discovered equine company to be pleasant, the hornets built the next three years at the back of the barn, again under the eaves at the highest point of the roof. We lived in peace with them there, too, because this nest rode high above the gate into the barn. The horses came and went every day on the ground below, and by keeping the back doors to the hayloft closed above, we never threatened the hornets' home.

We enjoyed watching the hornets collect their papermaking material from the barn walls. Their industry and single-mindedness is admirable. Although I know their sting to be vicious, I cohabited with them long enough to prove that hornets are not prone to attack. I have sat in a rocker on the front porch while several came to comb paper makings off the arm of the chair. I have sat on the steps of the tack room while hornets swept needed materials from the door frame beside my head. I found that this practice gave me valuable exercise in relaxing under tense circumstances. I gained practice in remaining nonthreatening but alert. I learned to trust my own nerve and the nature of hornets.

I confess to pride at being tolerant of the hornets and for sharing my space with them in spite of the danger. I felt a peculiar sense of achievement from living in peace with such historically warlike creatures.

The thinness of the line between war and peace with hornets was revealed to us one December afternoon when Jessica and I were riding one of our most-used trails. With summer foliage gone from the hawthorns, we spotted a hornets' nest in a bush beside the trail, a spot we must have passed hundreds of time in the spring and summer. It was a large nest, so big that we marveled we had not previously seen it. Jess and I had cleared this stretch of trail in preparation for a Georgia Endurance Riders fund-raising event to which almost one hundred riders had come. Every one of them had ridden past that nest on a single day, and no one had been attacked. It was above head height for riders of average-sized horses, but those on tall horses would have easily risen to the nest's height. The reason we riders had escaped hornet bombardment was simple: the door of the nest was turned away from the trail. Hidden in the thorny and leafy limbs of the hawthorn, their pathway to home unmolested, the hornets had not been bothered.

Then the spring day came when we discovered hornets were building their nest in the boxwood beside the front doorsteps. Ben was cutting the grass, and I was planting petunias and impatiens beside the steps on the side opposite the boxwood. As Ben swept by me on the riding mower, I looked up and saw him duck his head, then swing an arm out. Stopping the mower, he jumped off and headed back across the lawn and down the driveway, swinging his arms about his head and shoulders and swatting at his thick blond beard and long blond hair.

I knew he had hit a bees' nest, but whether it was hornets or yellow jackets, I didn't know. If it was yellow jackets, the nest would be in the ground. Hornets would be in the shrubbery.

I was afraid to move for fear of moving the wrong way into the line of fire. My eyes swept the ground between me and the mower. I could not see any yellow jackets swarming. Raising my gaze to the shrubs, I saw the hornets that had attacked Ben returning to the boxwood. I backed away hastily.

Poor Ben was coming back up the driveway by this time, his feelings seriously injured. He had been one to speak up for cohabitation with hornets, and he did not appreciate their ingratitude. Shirtless for this hot job, he had two red welts from the stings, one on his shoulder, another on his back. We went into the house, and I put ice and a little baking soda on the marks.

When everyone had had time to calm down, we went back to the porch to get a better look at the boxwood, where we were sure the nest must be. Sure enough, there it was, about the size of a softball, hanging near the ground, close to the steps. We watched the hornets come and go for a long minute. Their flight path clearly would be interrupted from several directions by anyone who was in the yard or going up the steps. It was early May. The nest was bound to grow much bigger and become a danger to visitors and to us. It would have to go.

The way to get rid of a hornets' nest is to burn it. At night, when the insects are quiescent. You do not ask yourself moral questions. You move quickly. Smarting from his afternoon wounds, Ben was prepared to do the dark deed.

Of course we felt guilty about destroying this home, but the fact remains, every creature in nature must take its chances with nest-building. Sometimes we pick the wrong spot. These hornets had picked the wrong spot.

As soon as it was good and dark, Ben doused the nest with gasoline, threw a match at it, and jumped back. Standing on the porch, I saw the nest and the bush take fire. The hornets tried to get out of this inferno, but almost none of them escaped through the narrow door. They were doomed. The nest went up like a wad of newspaper, gone before it had time to get hot enough to ignite the green boxwood to any serious degree.

Where the nest had hung, the boxwood lived scarred that season with a few scorched leaves and twigs. Neither Ben nor I liked to go near it for a long time, though not from fear of hornets. I don't know why exactly. Perhaps we were mourning, as humans are wont to do, our involvement in the inevitable. Consciousness makes us so mourn. Consciousness gives us the idea of the inevitable, then confuses us with the suspicion that nothing is absolutely inevitable. We might be better off if we were like the hornets, asking no questions when anything appears to threaten the path to home.

WRITING SPIDERS

It is September 21, and for the past two days, the air has been an autumn elixir of sun and bracing air that puts the glory of spring and summer to shame; though autumn days grow shorter hereafter, their fleeting character intensifies their sweetness. It is also possible that autumn days are sweeter because they are about harvest. They make tangible the results of the swing of the sun more than do spring or summer days. Autumn and winter, about harvest and death, are hard to ignore. Of course, resurrection is pretty hard to ignore, too.

I went early to the barn and tacked up KJ, a young Arab mare I am training in hopes she will be suitable for my niece, Betsy. The mare shows good sense but hasn't much experience. Gracefully compact in her dappled gray coat, she has the classic Arab dished face, and liquid, enchanting dark eyes. As we were setting out, Gus drove up, so I said I'd go the back trail and meet him again at the barn in a few minutes. A couple of miles with good old solid Bandit, Gus's Appaloosa gelding, would be good for KJ.

KJ took my suggestion of trail with good will, and we went down by the river and back up to the lily pond among the pines, where we saw the great blue heron. He was breakfasting late—it was Sunday, after all—on the frogs in the pond. I smiled as he lumbered into the air, awking at us.

When we joined Gus and Bandit at the barn, I asked KJ to lead. She did pretty well, all things considered. She is certainly cooperative and responsive. I had to keep only the barest contact on the reins. I like her. She has that "maybe-I-won't-believe-you-and-I'll-panic-anyway" streak that most young horses have, but I believe experience will allay that. She's 100 percent better now than she was six months ago.

The air felt so good that in spite of other duties, I stayed out longer with Gus than I intended. I finally turned home, leaving him to take the last part of the river trail alone. KJ likes Bandit but did not object to leaving him, another good sign of her cooperative spirit.

When barn chores were done and all the horses put out, I stopped by the grapevines on my way to the house. The muscadines clustered thick and richly purple. I gathered a good bowlful in my shirttail within two minutes. I felt like the richest woman on earth gathering in jewels. I did not neglect to taste a few of these beauties as I picked. In the kitchen I washed the smooth amethyst orbs in the sink, treasuring my treasure in my hands, admiring the dusky, sun-flecked skins.

Suddenly I noticed a spider on the sleeve of my purple sweatshirt. A big yellowish spider with prominent black legs.

My heart started to pound and, like KJ, I thought about not panicking, but unlike KJ, I did, sweeping the creature off my upper arm in total fright. This resulted in the spider's lurking somewhere in the kitchen without my knowing where. I felt like screaming, but to my credit, I did not scream.

I scream where wasps are concerned, for I have the feeling that they react to the sound waves, are reassured by my terrified sounds that they have me on the run and therefore there is no reason to keep dive-bombing at me. Spiders, however, are quieter, less openly aggressive, so screaming does not seem an appropriate response to their presence.

As I peered about the room, realizing that the yellow spider was not going to show well against my yellow kitchen floor, I took several deep breaths to calm my pounding heart and wondered about our antipathy toward arachnids.

What does a spider represent? A female predator, fangs, poison, webs, entrapments. Okay. But why can she not represent beauty of design, disciplined craft, successful provision, patience? Of course she can represent all those things.

I do not rout all spiders in my house as I do the wasps, for spiders have much more to recommend them. Their webs are works of art that I enjoy, and they sometimes catch wasps for me, too. The spider herself is quiet, unobtrusive.

Thinking of Ariadne's plight, the first spider-woman, I feel sympathy for her. She risked everything for Theseus, and then he betrayed her. Why should that make her abhorrent? It ought to make *him* rather undesirable. Are women instinctively afraid of spiders because of a fear of ending up like Ariadne? Probably more than half of us have trusted untrustworthy men.

After a few minutes, I went back to washing my grapes, and I did not see the spider again until I started to the phone to call Nan. The spider was making her way cautiously toward the back door. With our positions known, I was calmer and went over to study her.

She was worth studying. Shiny yellow-green, luminous, like tinsel, her body seemed wrapped in shiny paper. Not a color I would have chosen for myself, but it was attractive. I could not help admiring it. She had the odd appearance of seeming to go upside down. It was as if the tinsel should have been her belly, not her back.

I scooted a piece of paper under her and lifted her closer. I wished I had chosen a larger piece of paper as she continued to crawl toward my hand. I noticed her hairy legs and again the shimmering raiment.

Although wild critters (birds excepted) that come into my house generally do so at their peril, I figured I had brought the spider in on my sleeve from the grapevine through no fault of hers, and therefore smashing her did not seem fair. I advanced cautiously toward the back screen door, holding my spidery paper at full arm's length.

She came closer and closer to my arm. I lost my nerve and turned the paper over, intending to dump her (this was better than my earlier all-out panic), but she let out her lifeline and floated in the space between paper and floor.

This I had to admire. Seeing her yellow-and-black-striped belly, with her legs starkly black next to this alternate color design, I again had the impression that she was upside down, but her legs were working in their normal way, a strange motion akin somehow to a person doing a back bend and "walking" on all fours in that attitude.

I let her down gently to the floor and scooped her back up with the paper. This time I made it to the back doorstep, where I put her down on the railing. She crawled away, and I watched her shiny side glow. Her underside was quieter, a dark velvet.

What is the purpose in this design? Hanging in the web, she does not have a back and a front. Perhaps she has found the designs work well in tandem, camouflage and seduction, and her evolution pleases her. Who doesn't have two sides—at least?

We have numerous spiders of this kind at the barn and in the orchard this season. I have heard them called writing spiders after marks in their webs that some people think resemble writing. There is a folklore associated with those scribblings that says if the spider writes your name, you will get your wish. Or is it that you will die soon?

I have inspected these spiders' webs for years, and so far I have not seen anything that could properly be called writing, much less be my name. I doubt Zoroaster could read such scrawlings. But there must be a purpose in them, and it probably has to do with entrapment.

If that's the case, we could say these spiders make a living from their writing, no mean accomplishment in any species. I salute them.

FIREFLIES

THE FIREFLY is an insect that has never frightened me. When we were children, we caught fireflies in mason jars, making a game of it, a lively summer evening contest among my brother Alex, four years older, and my sister Susan, a year younger, and me. Sometimes our cousin Mary Ina, who was Alex's age, was in on this game. We learned to go quietly at the pulsing lights to catch the prize in our hands. I remember the pungent, not unpleasant odor of fireflies on my hands. In spite of the care I took catching the slight creatures, my palms would sometimes glow from holding fireflies before stashing them in the jar.

I cared little about winning the contest. It was too hard to try to count how many bugs were in a jar, and it was no good accusing anyone of dishonest counting. But to have a jar of light to hold against the night, to sit glowing beside me on the porch steps while the grown-ups talked and rocked on the porch—this was rare treasure and pleasure.

I was uneasy, nevertheless, knowing it could not be fun for fireflies or anybody else to be caught in a jar. Although we punched the tin lids with an ice pick to allow air in, I opened my jar often to let in lots of fresh air and never kept my fireflies for long. Before bed, I would release them back to the night with gratitude for the light and the feeling of treasure. I imagined they were grateful to me for freedom.

Alone in the house for supper—I hate eating alone—I was trying to forget painful things like how the break with Ben still throbbed, how Sharon had gone and it seemed right to both of us for her to find her own place (I am too much like her ex-husband, Harry, and she is too much like Ben), but she could not say thank you.

Why do I expect gratitude? Of course the long-ago fireflies were not grateful. How could they have been?

So I decided to take a walk before dark. I took along my clippers and cleared a little of the trail for the Poker Ride, scheduled for June 20, when there will be a hundred or more horses and riders here to enjoy our woodland trails and take a chance on winning a poker hand they will draw on the trail. They pay ten dollars for this game, and the money goes to the Georgia Endurance Riders Association.

I chose for the trail most of that which runs along the river and then crosses the county road at the Beckemeyer farm to meander beside Rocky Creek. The path is about eight miles and on a hot summer day will be a delight.

After the storm this afternoon, the trees dropped water on me, but the evening was warm, and the water felt good. I wore my Australian hat, old black sweat pants, and my bright blue "It's Hard to Be Humble When You've Finished the Old Dominion 100-Mile Endurance Ride" T-shirt, thin from much washing.

Clipping and clearing branches and vines from the trail, I stopped from time to time to watch the river run in the fading light. I let those muddy, reddish swirls and the soft swishing of the river's swollen burden headed for the Oconee, the Altamaha, the Atlantic, whisper sweet nothings to me and take my heartache along with them to the sea.

I ended up at the top of Road Trot Run pasture, where the grass was so tall I could hardly walk through it. I was soon soaked, but I was happy, feeling strong in my good bright body. I walked all the way to the big barn.

The fireflies came out as I crossed the pasture. The storm clouds were low, snuffing out twilight, and the glowing, flitting creatures, like sparks of hope and courage, lifted my spirits as had the music of the river. Fireflies are lovely, giving off their pulsing, pitiful brilliance against the dark. Tonight hills, trees, bushes bowed in deep shadows with their water burden, and fireflies sang songs of light. I felt almost as if I had stepped into another dimension of shape, sound, and light. A strange but appealing perception.

Tired of the wet grass, I took the road home, thinking of when Took and I rode the Old Dominion in 1986. Next to the gallant spirit of that half-Arab bay pony, it was the fireflies kept me going the last dark and lonely miles. The T-shirt says it's hard to be humble when you've finished the Old Dominion, but actually almost anyone who has finished this hundred-mile trail through the Shenandoah National Forest in Virginia—in twenty-four hours or less—has the good sense to be humble about it. So much could and often does go wrong.

Took cleared the ninety-six-mile vet check down in the creek bottom about 1:00 A.M. without a hitch. He was going well, had smelled home camp. It was the rider who was tired—the vet crew helpers had to boost me into the saddle—and when we had left the lights of the vet station behind, the dark road felt so bleak and black that although I kept telling myself that I should let Took do it, that he could see much better in the dark than I could, I grew more and more tense. We were on a good dirt road that we had covered that morning going out, so it was not strange territory. I knew it would cross the Blue Ridge Parkway in a couple of miles. Then it was just two miles through the woods to the finish line. Four miles is nothing when you've done ninety-six.

I said this out loud for me and Took, but the road was DARK. There was only the rind of a moon, and it made no headway at all against dense hardwood foliage. On our left at the road's edge I could feel an abyss that I reminded myself sternly had looked at dawn like a fairly gentle slope down the mountainside.

I dismounted, thinking we would be more secure with me walking and leading the way. It took about twenty yards for me to walk right off the left-hand side of the road and tumble a few feet down the slope, losing the reins. Took did not go anywhere. I could not see him, but I could feel him waiting up there on the road, in the patient way horses often have as they wait for us to get something figured out.

I scrambled up the bank, picked up the reins, and thanked Took for his good sense in not trotting off. I put my head against his mane, letting the warmth of his neck and the rich horse odor of him cheer me. I was worried about whether I could get back in the saddle.

When I lifted my head, I noticed the fireflies for the first time. There were thousands of them, and they were flashing, pulsing, flashing with such exquisite rhythm I did not know how I could have missed them earlier. If ever light makes a sound, fireflies will be the originators. They were playing light music, filling the dark with a powerful rhythm. I have since read that there are many species of fireflies and each has a specific time for its nocturnal activity. It is possible these fireflies had only just begun their serenade of light. For indeed firefly light does have to do with mating, though I am absolutely sure that their light is not simply about mating any more than our love songs are. There is the pleasure of the song itself.

Seeing these fireflies—*feeling* them, I should say, for in spite of the intensity of the tiny lights, it was their pulsation that lifted me—I walked on, reassured by firefly light. I did not try to remount until we had almost reached the top of the trail, and then I did so without a problem. The fireflies stayed with us until we left the woods to cross the finish line, trotting easily.

Remembering those Virginia fireflies on my solitary way lit by Georgia fireflies brought another memory.

John has brought his daughter, Alexi, to spend the afternoon with me. At seven, Alexi is a fairy child, petite, her golden hair in tangled curls, angel hair. She turns cartwheels on the lawn, leaves little piles of leaves and shells and stones all over the house and the back porch. I feel fairies on the place again, like I did when I heard my own little girls playing with their imaginary friends. Jessica's was Lucran; Nan's was Cathy.

I grieve for this family in turmoil, for sad circumstances that have brought Alexi today, but having a child in the house again is a gift. John comes back at supper, and we eat on the porch, by candles Alexi lights proudly. She burns mint leaves in the flame as night closes in, standing by her beloved daddy. Their faces look less strained in the candlelight. The night and the quiet country, the peace of Somechoes, have offered a respite.

Alexi asks me if I have fireflies, and I say yes, assuming she knows what fireflies are. I look across the lawn to the woods, but none are flashing, so I say, "You'll have to come back and see them another time."

But as Alexi and John are leaving, going down the back steps, she sees fireflies illuminating the dark woods and exclaims, "Oh, Daddy! What is that?"

"That's the fireflies, Alexi," he says in his quiet way.

Her face transforms to delight, exultation, exaltation. "Yes," her features are saying, "Yes! Fireflies!"

Tonight as I walked, I tried to catch a firefly. I did not try very hard, but I could not catch one. Perhaps it takes a child to catch a firefly.

Then I remembered a weary midnight on Lake Burton, at the home of my brother Bruce, and his wife, Debbie.

The house, which I call the Castle on the Rhine, rides the steep mountainside with grace. With sisters Susan and Nancy, Bruce, Debbie, and I are in a third-story room many feet above lake level, in the treetops. The lakeside house wall is mostly window.

We have been campaigning all day in Rabun County because Bruce is running for superior court judge, and the election is next day. Although exhausted, we sit for an hour telling campaign tales, laughing and groaning. At last we wind down enough to head for bed.

When we turn out the light, we see, to our astonishment, that there are fireflies in the room, inside the wide window, glowing, pulsing, glowing, pulsing. We all exclaim over this extraordinary occurrence. For a few moments we watch the display, quiet, unworried.

Curiosity gets the better of me and I switch the light back on. If fireflies are in the room, I want to know how they got through the closed windows.

They are not inside. They are outside the window, showing that fireflies might be called light ventriloquists, throwing their light for magical shows or, better, to give their light where it is more needed than in their own bodies.

As I flick the lights off again, Susan says, "Fireflies are a gentle insect."

Part Three

ELEMENTAL

ELEMENTAL. Of the powers of nature; suggestive of the great forces of nature; basic, primary.

ON DARK AND LIGHT

WHEN WE were putting Somechoes house back in order after hauling
her over from Dee Kennedy Road, one of the first things we had to do
was to have the power put in. The people from Jackson Electric asked
me didn't I want a farm light in the yard, one of those modern wonders
they were right proud of, you could tell, from the way they said it like
they knew I'd want a light that comes on automatically at evening when
the dark is at a certain shade, gives a permanent twilight to the farmyard until morning, then goes out automatically. As good as a streetlight
in town.

I told them no, thank you. I wasn't interested in a streetlight out here
in the country. I was moving to the country to get away from streetlights.

I am not afraid of the dark, and unlike most people I know, including those in the country, I don't see a great advantage in light perpetual.
I like for the dark to come in, settle down, have its turn, and I like wandering around in the dark, which isn't dark if you give your eyes time to
adjust to what light there is. In my experience, there's always light somewhere.

Like the time I went for a walk in the April rain, coming in late from
school with rain and dark falling fast. I needed to let go of some
worries, and so in spite of rain and night, I set off for Wingo's, knowing
I could get there on paths I knew well enough to travel blindfolded.

Pretty soon anxious thoughts and feelings quietened, as they will
during a woods walk. I was happy, walking under the warm spring rain
in my old blue rain jacket. I was cheered, thinking over the sweet way
Nan had agreed to put the spaghetti casserole in the oven and set the
supper table so that I could have my walk.

Because the rain clouds were passing, a delayed brightness came to
the evening. I decided to go through the swamp on the northwest side
of the pond, the part that dried up when they started pumping sand on
the other side of the river. Maybe I could catch a glimpse of the heron

before he caught a glimpse of me. I like to watch him fish but seldom get to see him waiting, watching, then flashing his beak into the water. He usually lumbers into the sky at my approach.

I didn't see the heron, but I startled some woodies that flew off down the river, scolding me with their shrill cries. I followed them a little way, idly wondering how long I could walk in this once-wetland. It made my heart hurt to think how many wild creatures had lost homes because we humans wanted more sand to pour more concrete in Gwinnett County. The sandhill cranes hadn't stopped over in several years, spring or fall, most likely proving that the swamp was no longer big enough to give them the food or the protection they need on their long journeys each spring and fall. How would we like to be obliged to travel each year from Alaska to Mexico and beyond to reproduce, while along the way all motels and hotels, all places of rest, were vanishing?

While I was grieving over this loss, the dark came down again unnoticed, and soon I was thrashing about in the thick swamp underbrush, lost. Not only had evening given way to night, but the rain clouds had also returned, and I was in dark about as thick as any I could recall. I couldn't see anything. I wasn't afraid of being lost for long. I didn't know that part of the swamp, but I knew the river was on one side and the pond on the other, and I was bound to come upon one or the other pretty soon.

I stood still, listening. I could hear bullfrogs, close, on my left, and nothing like their reverberating chorus on the right. That meant the river was on the right, the pond on the left. So I started upriver toward home, and though I got turned around a couple of times, I soon could see well enough to make out spots in the brush that were more suitable to passage than others. Once I stumbled into a narrow clearing and smelled deer. I am sure they bedded down there during the day. I couldn't say where the light was coming from, but I could *see* the deer room, feel its absent inhabitants. It was a cozy place, and I liked it, but I kept angling toward what I thought was the riverbank. I was sure there would be some light gathered in the river, and I was right. At the river's edge a thin, silvery light emanated from the rushing water, enough to make following the river back to known paths an easy walk. Soaked to the bone by the wet bushes, I nevertheless felt warm and happy, satisfied that there is always light somewhere.

Maybe the reason I am not afraid of the dark is that when we were little we slept outside in the summer on what we called the sundeck, under the wide and starry and beautiful sky, and we loved doing this.

The sundeck was an idea my daddy got from a house he had seen in Germany during the war. This was an open, tiled deck, about twenty feet by twenty feet, off the back of our house, on the second floor, forming the roof of the master bedroom and nursery, which was a wing off the back of the main house on the first floor. The deck had a black, wrought-iron railing around it, but my mother worried a little about her children out there. It was at least twenty-five feet down from one end of the sundeck because the two-car basement garage, having been dug out of the side of the hill, was under the master bedroom. Mother thought she knew us well enough to expect to look out there someday and find one or the other of us—probably our oldest brother, Alex— getting ready to rappel from that iron railing, while Susan and I argued over who would be second.

Still, when summer nights hung unbearably hot in our upstairs bedrooms, we begged Mother to let us drag our mattresses out there to sleep, and after painting a few dire pictures of what happens to children who are careless in high places, she usually agreed. Otherwise, we were not going to get much sleep, and we sure as heck were not going to get any use out of the sundeck. A sundeck might be an okay idea in Germany, where the weather is cold and people soak up every ray of sun they can in summer, but on Georgia summer days, it was so hot on the deck that you could hardly stand to be anywhere near it. One scorching July day Mother said that she bet you could fry an egg on those tiles.

As far as I know, she never tried this culinary feat, but we children tried it, without success. Getting the still-raw egg up meant a mess. We tried it more than once, depending on how high the temperature went, of course not bothering to mention our exploits to our mother. We got away with it because of the five thousand laying hens my daddy insisted on keeping, which made keeping an egg count for anybody but Harrison Hatchery one of the jobs our busy mother did not consider doing.

Anyway, we used to think we were in high cotton when we'd pull our mattresses out there with a sheet and a pillow and lie cool, looking up at that deep, thrilling sky where stars were steady and sheet lightning was flashing. We knew sheet lightning wasn't dangerous, being far away and not earthbound, and we were too high for mosquitoes to be much of a problem. We'd lie there talking, peaceful about sundeck cohabitation, not really caring who got to sleep closest to the house, where morning shade lay longest. I remember sleeping peacefully there with Alex, Susan, Nancy, and John as well as an assortment of cousins. It's hard to be fractious under the "huge and thoughtful night."

I would fall asleep without knowing it while hoping to see Pegasus among the constellations. I never saw stars that looked like a winged horse, but I have galloped along the Milky Way, delighted at such stardust. I would wake early to the sun coming over the pine trees out toward Grandmother's house. That was the only trouble with sleeping on the sundeck. We had to get up early.

I don't think our little brother, Bruce, ever got to sleep on the sundeck because a couple of years after he was born, its weight began to pull the master bedroom and nursery wing away from the rest of the house. When it rained, water poured through the crack into the downstairs hall. Architecturally, the solution was to roof the entire deck, shutting out the stars. But by that time my taste for the night was formed, and to this day I like to be out at night, stargazing or moonwatching. I enjoy getting up early, while it is still night, to see dark and dawn together.

I got up in the dark this morning to see the moon set. It was the morning of the full moon before Easter, a moon early American woodsmen called the Pink Moon. She *was* pink last evening as she rose, and she went down this morning silver and slow. Her white light lying over the dark pastures and woods was an exquisite liquid, especially where it glinted off mud puddles in the driveway and the paddock. The sun turns puddles to wanton coppers, cast over the earth, too insignificant to notice, but the full moon makes them a king's ransom, silver chargers glowing against dark velvet.

Looking into the dome as the sky lightened, I experienced a brief time when I could not tell the difference in sunrise light and moonset light. For a few heartbeats, the sun and the moon were equal in their endeavors to fill the sky with light. There is no good trying to say what color of blue that is. It is the blue-when-the-sun-and-the-full-moon-fill-the-morning-sky-with-equal-light. The sun soon won out, turning the sky daylight blue, but I'm glad I didn't miss that mystical light moment.

The quality of light is easy to miss. An earlier morning this month, writing at my desk, I noticed a sweetness in the first sunlight filling the house, and I stopped writing to watch the light. Early April light, it had not yet its full strength of spring but instead had a clear, bright goldenness, a lightness of double entendre that made the house at once seem light of weight and full of light, seem to float in the light, detached from earth, in thrilling flight.

I puzzle how that light could be so extraordinary when an hour later the house has reverted to ordinary—light enough, because of many windows, but not lifted by that inner light, that miraculous, visible penetration. I think it has something to do with the angle of light. In that early morning spring moment every thing is at the right angle, the correct angle, for flying. The earth is tilting toward the sun in its annual dance of spring, and the sun clearing the horizon sheds its light at a new angle. For a moment, my house floats.

Out walking later in the evening, along the river, which is flowing fast and full after several days of spring rain, I notice again the way the angle of light makes so much difference in the doors of perception. Earlier in the day the river would have run full of light, for the river drinks light, as we drink water, sustains its vitality from light. Light may be to the river what water is to us. Tonight as the sun is setting, great splashes of light careen off the surface of the river, making it impossible to look at the river without shading my eyes to shut out the sun, low on the horizon. Even then the great glints make it hard to look at the river, but I must look, and when I do, I feel my entire body, grounded at Somechoes Farm, take the measure of a cosmic angle of earthshadow and sunshine.

STELLAR DEBRIS

IF YOU STAND in the open on a clear, moonless night, away from artificial light, look up, breathe deeply, and reach for the stars with your mind, while asking them to enter your bloodstream, you know space. Your mind gathers time and distance to it with warp speed, the stars come to meet you faster than you can think, and although you will not get stars into your bloodstream because it is only your mind out there, you will experience the wonder of interstellar.

Although you will be tempted to close your eyes, it is important to look at the stars while feeling space, to stand open-eyed at the brink of the world. To know that our eyes can see 2 million light-years, can cross the eternity of space between us and Andromeda, is not something to miss. I recommend trying it at every opportunity. I recommend making opportunities, even if it means leaving city lights behind, which it does.

An astronomer perhaps and certainly a physicist will correct me: our vision does not cross the universe. We look up and the starlight, hurtling at 6 trillion miles per year, bounces off our retina.

Okay, I stand at the edge of the world corrected. I like the idea of looking all the way to the stars with my naked eye, but starlight coming to me is miracle enough.

Ancient peoples made up stories about the stars, which they saw as connected. I admired the word *constellation* the first time my father explained it to me, when I was about nine. He liked to explain words. Mother bought me a book on star pictures, too, but it didn't do me much good. There were lines from star to star, which of course were not there in the sky. Except for the Big Dipper, I had trouble seeing the same thing in the sky that my book said ancient Greeks or Egyptians saw.

I longed to see star-studded Orion. Orion was son of Poseidon, god of the sea, and my affection for Poseidon developed early because he is the god who gave humankind horses. Naturally, Poseidon's son was a mighty hunter and warrior, and thanks to his sea-god father, he also had uncanny swimming abilities. He could walk in the water as if he were walking on land, with his head just above the surface.

Artemis, the goddess of the hunt, a goddess usually indifferent to men, sometimes called the chaste goddess, fell in love with Orion, and her brother, Apollo, the powerful god of the sun as well as of poetry and music, did not approve. So he plotted to kill Orion and accomplished this goal in a cruel way. Jealousy is deadly in divine or human form.

Standing on a hillside looking down at the ocean, Apollo saw Orion walking in the water. Knowing that Artemis was proud of her archery skills, which were exceptional, Apollo bet her that she could not hit the object bobbing in the distant water. She, seeing the object farther out in the water than a human swimmer would ever be, did not suspect she was shooting at her beloved. She pulled an arrow from her quiver, took aim, fired, and killed Orion.

Grieving beyond consolation but unable to bring her lover back to life, Artemis placed him in the sky as a constellation of many brilliant stars. Orion has his club uplifted in one hand and a shield of a lion's skin in the other, as he wards off the attack of Taurus, the bull. Three bright stars mark Orion's belt, and a sword hangs from it. His dog follows behind.

It took thirty years of stargazing for me to see Orion's constellation. I read about it and studied it on a map of the sky, but only recently have I begun to see Orion's upheld shield and the sword at the ready in his belt. There are numerous stars in Orion. The trick seems to be to pick the right ones on which to focus, to "perceive" as sword, club, or belt.

"If the doors of perception were cleansed, every thing would appear as it is, infinite." Blake had probably been stargazing when he thought of that. Sometimes I take my quilt out in the backyard on a brisk, moonless autumn or winter night and lie a long time looking up, and it feels like the doors of perception go cleaner. I don't exactly see anything. I feel it, and it has the feel of infinity.

More scientific than the ancients, today we think we know much more about stars than our feelings or imaginations tell us. For example, consider that at a 1992 meeting of the American Astronomical Society it was reported that NASA's Hubble Space Telescope had detected "strong evidence" of a supermassive black hole 2.6 billion times the mass of the sun. Seriously reported.

Does anyone have a clear concept of the mass of the sun, much less 2.6 billion times it? I suspect we will arrive at such a concept only by looking at the stars a long time at night, letting the mind wrap around them, easy, without demanding too much data.

A black hole, so they say, is an extremely dense, energetic feature (handily imprecise word, *feature*) formed by the collapse of massive stars. The holes perpetuate themselves by swallowing other stars and stellar debris, and their gravity is so intense that even light cannot escape.

The black hole Hubble thinks to have detected—although the Hubble was not believed to be working quite right—is in a galaxy known as M87. M87? I prefer poetry in naming things in space, the music of *Andromeda,* the whimsy of the *Milky Way.*

They say M87 is about 52 million light-years away. Recalling that a light-year is approximately 6 trillion miles, even with a Hubble in top working order, what can we see that is 52 MILLION times 6 TRILLION miles away? At that distance, what good would it do us if we did see anything? I think scientists have got a new storytelling gimmick, and although it may be okay, it is not as tenderly humanistic as the Greek stories. We cannot learn anything about ourselves from considering black holes and radio signals and gravity that sucks in entire galaxies, has no respect for light. On the contrary, looking at the stars from this perspective puts us out of the picture entirely.

I would rather go outside and lie beneath the stars and agree with Thoreau that after sunset, the stars are like troupes of entertainers, coming out gradually from behind the hills and woods.

It was like that lying summer nights on the sundeck at Bedlam Ridge when I was a child. Cool after the scorching heat of the day, we would lie there, floating, the house a ship attached to the earth-ship. We would look deep into brilliant darkness. We watched for shooting stars and celebrated each one firing across the sky, disappearing into the darkness from whence it had emerged. We watched, trying to keep count, until sleep lifted us, for all we knew, into the stars.

Galileo, the astronomer who in the sixteenth century got into trouble with the Church for saying the earth moved about the sun instead of vice versa, was an early discoverer/user of the telescope and would, no doubt, be delighted with the Hubble. He thought we could see stars better with what he called "artificial powers of sight." His instrument increased tenfold the number of stars in the sky. Naturally, he was proud of his telescope, which ended, he thought, once and for all the wordy disputes about what the Milky Way was. With the aid of a telescope, he said, anyone may behold that the galaxy is nothing else but a mass of innumerable stars planted together in clusters.

Up against infinite galaxies I don't have much hope for "artificial powers of sight." But that shouldn't stop us from imagining, whether in scientific or mythic thought. It's probably best, however, not to get too serious about it.

I like to remember that the stars are always there—even during the day. It is simply a shift in the position of the earth that puts the sun on our side, that makes the stars "go away." They are twinkling on us around the clock. At night when they "come back," I'm glad they're back, and I remind myself how many are out there that I can't see. What a tableau for the eye and the mind.

When Dr. Joseph Ford from Georgia Tech gave his famous chaos lecture at Gainesville College, he said that trying to conceive stars is trying to conceive the inconceivable. Humans are a perverse race; once we figure that something can be inconceivable, we have to try to conceive it anyway. So we are trying to write the history of stars.

That humankind of all creatures should write the history of stars! Our span of life on this shard of what we suppose is a "dead" star—that concept ought to be enough to prevent our being afraid of death— is not registerable against the life of the most insignificant star. The history of our entire race does not come up as a dot against the life of a single star, Sirius, for example. The best brain we ever birthed cannot truly understand a star.

Yet we continue to pit our infinitesimal gray matter against the gargantuan mystery of stars.

Humankind does not live long enough to travel 6 trillion miles, much less two, three, fifty times that; nor, should we succeed in this travel, could we survive a close encounter with a star. Our closest star, the sun, will not allow us to look at her directly for long. In eclipse, she burns us to blindness for impertinent, naked-eye glances. Perhaps this is why humans have loved stargazing. Stars are easy on the eyes.

Thinking about stars has led us to believe we can figure out how to cross space, reach other galaxies, land on stranger planets, speak alien tongues. In our imaginations we can do and do all those things with relative ease. The stars fire the imagination.

I do not forget the first time my children saw the Big Dipper. We were about to move Somechoes house to the farm, and after an afternoon of cleanup of the house site, Dwain, the children and I had gone for a walk at twilight, enjoying the freedom of our own fields and woods. The blond, blue-eyed girls, who were four and seven, were ebullient.

It grew dark, a moonless, clear night. Happy to be out, we did not hurry back. There were cattle in Daddy's nearby pastures, and their throaty lowing gave peculiarly personal music to accompany us. The grass-milk-meat smell of cows in the dark is an embodiment of wealth. I do not wonder that early gods demanded cattle as sacrifice.

The girls danced along in front of us, chattering. Passing through a thick patch of pines, we suddenly topped a hill, and the star-spangled sky spread before us with the Big Dipper gleaming in the northeast, like an exquisite brooch on the breast of a goddess. I realized I had never bothered to show the children the constellation.

As they skipped ahead, I called, "Wait, I want to show you something." They came back to where I stood.

They knew well what a dipper was because their Grandmother Jackson kept an aluminum one hanging beside her kitchen sink. She believed in drinking copious amounts of water, and though the days of well buckets and water jugs had given over to the miraculous faucet, she liked to drink her water from a dipper. The children enjoyed the privilege of drinking from the dipper when visiting Little Mama.

"There's a big dipper in the sky," I said, "made of stars. If you'll look over that way you can see it. See? It's sort of hanging in the sky with the handle slightly bent over the trees."

They looked. At first they did not see what I meant.

"Think about how you would draw a dipper in a dot-to-dot drawing," I said. "And think big. It's a BIG dipper."

They looked. Adoring their star-lit faces, I was washed in the joy of flesh, blood, and bone a mother's children bring. Then they recognized the heavenly dipper. Amazement swept their features. They laughed. They clapped their hands. They danced, too, looking up as we walked on. Laughing, twirling under the stars, growing dizzy, all the way home through the dark fields they danced, stopping now and again to steady themselves by the lights of the Big Dipper.

RAIN

R AIN POURED for the third day in a row. The ground on campus
squished under the least weight, the weight of the last ginkgo leaves
lying under the black, bare, water-slick branches of their trees.
Pessimists expressed concern that the entire college might float out
to Lake Lanier. Students arrived shaking off water, left great puddles
in the halls. Everyone griped about the rotten weather.

I try not to complain about the weather and certainly not about rain.
Living on a farm should teach appreciation of rain as much as of
sunshine. I walk each evening into the dark, wet woods and know a
peculiar fascination, a strange peace. I agree with my father, who says,
"I'm glad I'm not in charge of the weather."

Home from school I decide, because it is raining, to have a cup of tea,
then take a nap. It's nearly dark, the rain is making kind music in the
drain and on the roof, but I can't sleep. My tea has revived me, so I
forsake the warmth of the comforter, put on a vest, my blue raincoat,
and Ben's old navy wool hat. I pocket a little flashlight and head for the
woods. With rain pouring, Migno is a bit reluctant, whines from the
porch. "So much for canine loyalty," I say to the dark world. Soon I hear
her padding along, catching up, but without her usual bounding-ahead
beagle attitude.

It isn't cold. Before long I wish I hadn't worn the vest. I stay in the
woods because the pastures are so wet and the grass high and because
trees shelter from the rain. I am happy and excited, planning meals for
Les's visit, planning a dinner party and a trip with the horses to Talladega
National Forest. I wonder if we will spend the night together in the
camper.

After a few minutes I reach the big pasture at the bush-hogged trail
and come to the place where my thirteen-year-old niece, Betsy, and I,
out riding on Sunday, had seen an oddity: a dead cat, a plastic custard

cup, and a plastic spoon, as if someone had dined on cat and custard. Because the horses were a little spooked by this sight, we did not stop to investigate. Tonight I take out my flashlight and inspect the cup— for Jello pudding. How did those four things get together here in the woods: a dead white cat, a white plastic custard cup, a white plastic spoon, and a leaf of cellophane? It will take imagination to figure that one out.

Switching off the flashlight, I walk on around the edge of the pasture and end up at the Teepee Place, where Ben lived in his teepee when he first came to the farm. Easter used to think that teepee housed timber wolves, but the other horses got used to it and would trot by unconcerned as Indian ponies. The girls and I were respectful of it. It was Ben's house, so we didn't go in uninvited. How long did he live in the teepee before he moved into the house? Odd that I can't remember. Not long, I think.

I stop to pee, chuckling to myself at the pun. The rain feels fresh and cool on my bare skin. Men like to pee on the ground, and I understand why they like it. Biology makes it easier for men than for women to have this little pleasure, but I don't deny myself the chance to pee on the ground. There's an earthiness about it, a communion with the earth, the comfort of a link reestablished.

As I start the last mile home, I recall my friend Chick Wallace's story of going to see her aunt, a North Carolina country woman, in a nursing home. "Are you happy here, Aunt?" Chick asked.

"Pretty happy, honey," she said, "but there's days I'd give anything to be able to pee on the ground just one more time."

It is exhilarating to be in the dark, the rain on my face fresh and fine, to remember poignant, earthy stories and good friends. I am a little tired, but my body is resilient, vibrant, a lovely, cherished instrument. I have a warm feeling of well-being and a grateful heart.

It rains all night, hard. At dawn it is still raining. Water stands in the pastures. I start to work at the computer. As the rain continues, I call my sister Nancy to tell her not to bring Betsy to ride. It's simply too wet.

About noon I call the horses up to feed. They are eager for dry stalls, grain, and hay. When they are all munching contentedly, I take to the woods, headed for Wingo's. Although I don't want to deal with wet tack and slippery trails, I don't mind getting wet. Migno trots along, proud and confident. What is prouder than a beagle in the woods, with a master/mistress to disobey?

As usual the woodies get up almost before I am in sight of the pond. They must have hearing sharp as God's. Their shrill cries pierce my heart, a wild sound I am privileged to know. There are about a dozen of them, and they fly fast across the lake and over the trees on the eastern border. A few times in my life I have come upon them close enough to hear the wind in their wings, a whistling sound of beauty and grace in the extreme.

There is nothing else on the lake. I look long across the water in the rain, and my blood pulses with the life that is here in these few acres, tries not to despair at human arrogance. What a blessing is a wetland like this, home for ducks, geese, beavers, frogs, fish, snakes, turtles, herons, to name only the largest creatures thriving in this shelter. Yet most of my species see it as a place to drain, so houses can be built here.

I make my way around the edge of the lake, holding to the steep bank about ten yards above the water. The rain is still coming down but in a fine mist.

I soon get out in the lake, in the part which used to be under water before sand pumping in the river lowered the bed. I jump a few streams, but in general, the marshy ground is good. When the sandhill cranes came the first time so many years ago, they feasted in this section. Without this place to rest and feed, they do not come.

I take zigzag paths through the swamp to reach the river and stand a long moment watching the brown water swirling, frothing, flowing. The graceful curves of its banks collect froth like lace. The riverbed is a place of life, where water is marshaled and given direction. It is a spirit place.

In the wet woods again, the rich odor of decay rises beneath my feet. In this soil being made, I smell death and life, and it is a good smell, the perfume of resurrection.

My wool cap and my boots and jeans are soaking wet. I pull the last steep hill to the barn steadily, thinking now about warm, dry clothes, hot tea, an hour under the blankets. It feels wonderful to peel off wet jeans, pull on my terry-cloth robe and woolen slippers. I make my tea, stand on the back porch to drink it, enjoy the warm mug in my hands, watch the rain. Then I crawl into bed.

Strangely, the security of a good roof and a warm bed reminds me that the world is not a safe place. I drift to sleep thinking that the moment we enter life, we are fair game for something. If not a timber wolf, then a leukemia virus, pneumonia bacteria, an automobile or another human roaring out of control.

But this is not reason to despair. Death is only one side of the balance. On the other side, there is this vibrancy of thought, this glowing body, the sound of rain on the roof, an easy sleep and waking to rain over, the long yellow light of late afternoon awash in the room.

PUDDLES

It rains for three days and nights. The river overflows twice, flooding water into the creek bed in Wingo's swamp, the bed that has been dry for almost five years, since they started pumping river sand over at Blankenship's. When the rains have gone, the coppery green water is still and clear. It reflects my form as I walk the beech log across the creek bed. I tremble at the acrobatic thought of myself upside down walking this log. I do not look down again.

In the night we have a dry, icy snow that cancels school. I am glad that in the South snow is more important than school. Up early to tune the radio to the good news that school is closed, I walk through my house, comfortable in my down robe, savoring the gift of a day off. The moon is nearly full, and at dawn amid thinning clouds, she rides away to the western horizon, clouds streaking her yellow face. On that side of the house, the oak grove and the hill pasture beyond are awash in white moon/snow light, but in the east, clouds obscure the sun's first brightness. Light seeps through the clouds, drains into the pastures. I admire each horizon in turn, glad again that living in such deep country means I don't have to put up curtains.

Ice coats bare tree branches in crystal, and plain pine needles wear snow crowns. The beauty of ice transformation is the rose with the thorn of cold weather. In Georgia, we are sure the rose is much more important than the thorn. The back porch thermometer reads twenty-nine degrees, and sun is forecast. The snow will not last long.

Because I need pictures of horses for an article on equine winterizing, I head early for the barn. Moment of panic when I cannot find my camera, then sweet relief as it surfaces in the flotsam in the bottom drawer of the downstairs file cabinet. Also surfacing are sweet thoughts of Les Warrington, who gave me the camera, of our happy Christmas here—the family caroling hayride, a Christmas tree hunt, a dinner party with friends from school when Barbara McMichael told fortunes by the fire as if saying poems of our lives.

The phone rings as I am going out the door. It's Ben, far away on the Georgia coast, wanting to talk. He talks about his work, and I feel his pride in it and that he wants me to share in that feeling. Part of me rejoices in that, but another part, which a few months ago would have given anything for this call, is floating free, enjoying Les, cautious about Ben, looking over her shoulder and asking, "Did you really like that song so much? Aren't you glad you learned to sing more than one love song?"

But I feel happy to listen to Ben's achievements. His voice always stirred me, stirs me yet. He rings off with, "I just wanted you to know I'm thinking of you and I love you." "I love you, too," I say, which is true.

The horses are standing up at the barn, wet, bedraggled, a sorry lot. I snap twenty pictures before you can say "winter storm," then feed the pitiful rascals. Their warm, furry smell is one of my preferred fragrances, and their winter pleasure in and gratitude for barn time makes my work easy. Gratitude makes much easy.

We have had an irritating epidemic of mailbox bashers, so I bring the mailbox in each night with the mail. The few times I have neglected to do this, the poor little aluminum box has taken a beating; it is now bent and scarred. Returning from taking it to its post this morning, I break a crystal-coated weed from the fence-line weeds, a tawny intricacy even without this winter coat of shimmering ice. Holding it up to the light, I sense a mysterious element, a basic of creation, undefined though visible. We are missing something.

Migno trots up as I consider this gift of the morning. She is compact and clean against the muddy, snow-patched driveway, a piston of energy and life, as contained and orderly—and as ephemeral—as the ice-coated weed.

"What a pretty puppy!" I croon, rubbing her head, which is silken and comforting under my hand, as is her shoulder and back. She is pleased with the caress, but with the beagle's cool, accepts it and trots off. She never fawns, never begs for love. An example to follow. The joy of her dignity is another gift of this morning.

As I straighten from petting Migno, I am conscious of the bare branches of oaks over my head, skeletal, harsh arms yet graceful, encompassing. With the crystallized weed, these giant black scripts may indeed be writing the underlying and ever-shifting order of the world.

Then I notice the branches reflected in the puddles in the driveway. The black trees are *in* the shining water as surely as they are in the red earth. They reach skyward in both places. I look down, I look up, and in both dimensions I have the powerful presence of the trees.

Consider these puddles, no more than whiffs of water yet reservoirs of huge oak trees, clouds, blue sky, a corner of my house. By circling the edge of the puddle, I change my view of the world. I watch it turn.

I, like the trees, am reflected in the water, caught but free, a magic creature kin to all others, dwelling between sky and water, dwelling on water, a crystal weed wand in my hand. Standing above myself in the puddle, I do not have a flattering view. To get a view less askew, I have to kneel beside the puddle and lean out over it, like Narcissus. I prefer not to worship in this manner. Instead, I imagine how the puddle sees me, not how I see myself in it. In this view, I am light and solid at once, part of the skeleton of the world, an immortal part, floating in a puddle.

In science class in grade school, Miss Esther Kinney told us there is life in a puddle. She was a passive woman, but she grew agitated, which may be why I recall her lesson, telling about bacteria and tadpole eggs in puddles. I went looking for tadpole eggs that day as soon as I got home from school. Today I prefer a different life in the puddle: tree branches, blue sky, gray clouds, Migno's face. I seldom pass a puddle without looking to see what it reflects.

In the village of Fontainebleau, in France, after nearly thirty years of long-distance friendship, two college friends and I managed to have what Aunt Georgia would have called a Lost Weekend, a time for women friends to go off and do what they want without having to explain anything to anyone. Because we had been French majors in graduate school together, the milieu had a heightened charm for us.

Each of us had lost mates to divorce or death, but at this juncture we were all happy with our families and each had worthwhile work to do that the others appreciated. We took long walks in the forest of Fontainebleau, reveled in the art and decor of the chateau in town, and dined on memorable French fare in quaint restaurants, talking all the while about work, home, family, literature, philosophy, religion.

Elizabeth wanted us to see Vaux-le-Viscomte nearby. "It's an exquisite chateau," she said, "and in the gardens there's a basin at least a hundred yards from the chateau in which the chateau is reflected. It's one of the most spectacular things I've ever seen. If the wind's blowing and ruffling the water, the view may be spoiled, but we can hope."

No further enticement needed for this puddle watcher. We set off from Fontainebleau, Suzanne driving. She did all the driving that weekend, from Paris and back again, brave woman. She said she'd always wanted to be a cab driver. She would have been a good one.

It was April and the sun was thin, breaking through clouds that the wind sailed across the sky like toy boats in the basins of the Jardin des Tuileries. Inside the mansion we heard about Fouquet, chancellor of the exchequer for King Louis XIV. Fouquet's passion for aesthetics led him to create this masterpiece, hiring Le Vau as building architect and Le Notre as landscape architect, the most famous artists of the day in their respective fields. The results were so spectacular that Fouquet's joy—and vanity—in his creation dictated an invitation to the king to come for a look. Louis accepted the invitation. When Louis saw Vaux-le-Viscomte for the first time, he was struck by its exquisite beauty—he was a man who knew and appreciated artistic beauty—but he was most impressed by the fact that he, although king, had nothing so beautiful.

Fouquet fell into complete disfavor, was accused of putting exchequer funds into his project—probably a just accusation—and ended up in prison. In the meantime, Louis, to show Fouquet who was in charge, went home and started the Palais de Versailles, taking Le Vau and Le Notre with him.

Elizabeth, Suzanne, and I spent a long time in the gardens of

Vaux-le-Viscomte that windy April day, walking down the long, tiered esplanade looking in wind-ruffled basins, disappointed not to see the chateau in any of them but pleased to be out together in the fine air. When it was time to go, we went back to the basin Liz thought was the one in question, but the wind was whipping the water into shivers. No hope of seeing a watery chateau there.

In front of the basin lay a ragged splash of a puddle, sheltered from the wind. Following my habit of inspecting puddles, I looked into it. The chateau, bordered by a cloudy, moving sky, had taken up residence there, as elegant in puddle water as in the prepared basin.

I would bet that Le Notre was a watcher of puddles. He knew about dimensions that matter, as true artists do. He did not waste time on formalities. He scandalized French society when he forgot to kiss the Pope's hand. Instead, he kissed both pontifical cheeks, asked the old man how he was getting on.

The day Louis came to view Vaux-le-Viscomte and its fabulous gardens, the fountains were playing, spotlighted like watery fireworks while fiery fireworks spangled the sky overhead. Louis would not have seen the reflection, but Le Notre knew that it was tough being head of state or church or being the treasurer of something as rich and poor as France. Maybe the fountain reflecting the chateau was his secret, a gift to be found in calm waters, in peace.

I'm sure there is a physical explanation for why a chateau reigning on the hill can be riding in a puddle two hundred yards down the hillside, but I doubt that Le Notre could have explained it. He simply saw the chateau in a puddle there one day and his genius lay in incorporating Nature's design.

I don't think he was able to repeat this miracle, however much Louis, who became known as the Sun King, might have wished it. His Palais de Versailles boasts a Galerie des Glaces—a chandeliered, glittering hall of mirrors—a stretch of man-made elegance that is world famous, but for my money, it isn't nearly as impressive as an entire chateau glimmering in a basin far down the esplanade of the garden, as if God himself had insisted on his own skyside view of this architectural jewel.

I think the reason a chateau can ride in a faraway puddle is that light charges the mind of the water with angles that allow the water to reflect much more than would at first seem likely. Water is greedy about such images, likes to reach for them. Once, riding Took late, I saw an evening star, low on the horizon, reflected in a natural lake across the river on LaMarche's land. The lake water was taking its blue from the night-coming-fast blue of the sky when we stopped in the dark woods beside the lake. With the single star shining in sky and water, the scene made all other reflection redundant. Then I realized the star was too low to be reflected in the ordinary, face-to-face way. That pocket of water in the swamp had snatched the star from the sky and pinned it to its breast, a badge to show what water can do with light.

The mind's eye operates from lights we do not understand. In a flash we experience suspected and unsuspected dimensions that change forever our view of the world.

How curious are the limits of sight, that we see through a glass darkly, that we are aware something is not meeting the eye, something we know is there yet are unable to grasp.

All day a frosty weed and oak branches black against the blue sky and black in silver-edged puddles at my feet shimmer in my mind. I shimmer, walking on the puddle, walking away from it.

I am assured by these presences. I am satisfied to know something without understanding it. I am certain that with age, my sight is improving.

HAUNTING GRAVEYARDS

I'VE BEEN BLESSED lifelong with romantic graveyards to haunt. The first and most important was our family cemetery, in the pine woods behind Grandmother Russell's home place that we called, after she died, the Big House, saying it fast, like one word, probably because Uncle Dick had bought the house from his brothers and sisters after their mother died, and he was a natural for his place to be called the Big House. Before that we called it Grandmother's house, but it would have been painful to go on calling it that after she was laid to rest beside Grandfather Russell and two of their babies who died in infancy.

Only a few years ago my father told me how he and his brother Rob walked the farm the morning of December 4, 1938, after their father's sudden death the evening before, and chose the spot for the family cemetery. They decided to put his grave on a little rise that could be seen from the kitchen window of the house, and the place was first called Papa's Hill. When the pecan trees in the backyard were in leaf, I doubt you could see the graveyard, right from the first, and by the time I was a little girl, pine trees had filled up the cotton fields between the house and the hill, so that the cemetery was a fine and private place for children to play.

For a long, long time there were only four graves: those of Grandfather Russell; the two babies, Lewis and Susan; and my sister Patience. My father also told me that the babies might not actually have been moved from their original grave site across the railroad tracks where they had been buried in 1905 and 1906. He thought the stones might have been put down as memorials when Grandfather's monument went in. This monument is a tall, rather phallic-looking stone, appropriate for a man who was the proud father of fifteen children. It took a big stone for all their names.

The graves are marked with modest headstones and long, flat stones about the length of whoever is under them. All the markers are of gray granite. Russell children have always played on the graves, leaping from one to the other. It was an easy leap from Grandfather's monument or from his stone to the babies'. You knew your legs were growing longer and stronger when you stayed airborne from Grandfather's to Patience's grave.

Having developed confidence in graveyards from this one, it was natural that we played in the graveyard on our home place, Bedlam Ridge, the house my mother and father built in 1949, about a quarter of a mile up the road from Grandmother's house. There a family cemetery belonged to people who had once owned the land, and my father said they could keep tending the graves, which they did. We played in the silky white sand piled on the four main graves, but we were careful not to leave them marred. Touching that cool sand under the oak trees in summer was almost like touching water.

We built playhouses near the oldest gravestones, the primitive, moss-covered ones. Some of these graves were sunken. Our Grandmother Eaton told us one of them was of a four-year-old boy who had died there while his family was on its way west in a covered wagon. Naturally we chose such a romantic, tragic spot for our pioneer cabins. Today I would doubt that story was true, except for the fact that Mama Eaton was not known for a rich imagination.

Someone in the family of those buried in the white sand graves is still tending that graveyard, though no one has been buried there in more than sixty years. I find that cemetery work a remarkable testimony to the respect the living may retain for the dead and to the power of love and habit over time.

Within walking or riding distance at Somechoes there are two old graveyards, and one is still haunted by living descendants. On my father's Horseshoe Bend Farm, which was owned by a family named Matthews back at the turn of the twentieth century, there is a graveyard at that bad bend in the road, the one many cars speeding down the empty road have failed to make and consequently have hit the oak tree minding its own business at the fence line. The oak so far has survived but wears warning scars.

The last grave to be put in the Matthews cemetery was in 1918, a boy seventeen years old, victim of the terrible flu epidemic. There are only half a dozen graves in all. The spot is surrounded by a low, granite wall with a crudely arched granite gateway for architectural adornment. Someone comes periodically and weeds the graves and puts down fresh gravel. Around the graveyard kudzu flourishes, and sometimes it climbs the graveyard wall, but it never gets too far inside before a phantom graveyard cleaner comes and cuts it back.

I saw the phantom at work there once and stopped to say hello. Ephraim Matthews, a fine-looking gentleman, white-haired, a little stooped in his khaki work clothes, but not too frail, said he was from Gainesville. His face red from his exertions, he leaned on his rake and said his family used to live in the old house that someone burned when my brother-in-law Raymond found a still in it. Ephraim Matthews sure hated to see the old place lost like that. It was he who told me the boy died of influenza.

Our other graveyard is across the river, in Jackson County, in the middle of Thad Pirkle's broad cow pasture on Highway 53, the one with the good cantering places. Dulcie and I discovered it the first day we found a safe fording place in the river behind our house, after Mr. Pirkle said I was welcome to ride on his place.

Whoever made the pasture left the graveyard and a few of its trees, a respectful and respectable thing to do. Noticing the little grove, I rode up to it and within the tall grass along the edge saw a rusty wrought-iron fence. In the shade of the fair-sized oaks, there was no grass and there were graves.

I dismounted and found a way to lead Dulcie in among the trees. She looked ghostly enough for the scene in her flea-bitten gray coat. The graves were old, some of them dating back to the early 1800s. I was surprised to learn that white people had settled that long ago in North Georgia.

Later I was trail riding with several little girls, six or seven of them, including my two daughters and Jennifer Lowry. Harry O. Smith, Jennifer's grandfather, was riding with us to help chaperone. Harry O. was in his seventies then, a short, robust, cheerful, and capable man. His love and knowledge of horses and his loyalty to me, born of a lifelong friendship between me and his daughter Lynn, were among my strongest assets in my early days alone at Somechoes Farm.

I told Harry O. about the graveyard, and he wanted to see it. Children like almost anything when on a horseback riding adventure, and this one meant crossing the river, so the little girls were all for it. They were still chattering about the "dangers" of the crossing when we dismounted and tied the ponies to the iron fencing to look at the mysterious graveyard. It did not look like anything most of these children had seen, being heirs to Forest Lawn places or at best the discreet sentinels of city cemeteries. I pointed out that the graves were very old and that if they'd read some of the inscriptions, which were remarkably clear considering their age, they'd learn how old.

An eager and bright nine-year-old, Elisa Krueger, went right to work reading inscriptions. "This one says 1829–1843." She took a few seconds to do the math in her head, then concluded, "Musta been killed in a car wreck."

Harry O. and I laughed long and loud in the cemetery that day.

The Russell Family Graveyard became the beloved project of my uncle Dick, a U.S. senator from Georgia for a long time. So long that when I was a little girl, everyone in Winder called him The Senator, with a casual disregard for the other ninety-nine. He was known as a fine legislator. He ought to be known for the way he transformed the spot where his mother and father were buried. As the years passed and the mortal remains of many of the family were brought to rest there, he turned a barren slash of red hilltop into a green and flowering park.

This cemetery is a spectacular gift to his family. We are rare who own our graveyards—and I feel a fine rarity because I have seen our graveyard fill up. I remember every funeral, except for Grandfather's. I do not find this a reason to grieve but rather a cause to rejoice. For those buried here whom I knew and loved are people who lived and died well. I find love and peace in our graveyard, and it is a portable feeling. This long association has given me the meaning of "hallowed ground" deep in my blood and bones.

Today I made a pilgrimage to the Big House, homing there because it's spring and pleasant childhood memories of spring rise from the rows and rows of daffodils my grandmother planted and from the heaped golden generosity of forsythia bushes in full blossom.

Front porch repairs were going on, and the front of the house looked beat up. Old boards, a sand pile, a stack of new lumber, and a battered pickup truck occupied the front yard, but no one was there. In the side yard, I noticed that the magnolias are aging, their limbs no longer young and supple and strong as when we used to climb in them. Yet the trees are less than eighty years old. Is eighty old for a magnolia tree?

The Japanese magnolia that used to bloom in the little space between the Big House and the Weaning Cottage is dead. Resplendent with pink blossoms, it was one of the first things to bloom in the spring. I thought Grandmother had put it there behind the other magnolias so that its special beauty would have to be sought. A secret magnolia garden.

I walked over to the Weaning Cottage, and the back door was open. How many times have I gone in and out of that back door? I lived there five years as a child and three as a young wife. The path between the two houses was well worn. Living with kin like that, private but close, was comfortable.

The house seemed small, especially the kitchen, which I once thought huge. The interior hasn't changed much. The sagging ceiling tiles still show leaks, notably in the dining room. When I invited my favorite French professor at the University of Georgia, Dr. John Downs, for supper, it rained all day, and water dripped steadily into a pan on the table. About dark Dwain crawled up in the loft and put down a pan to catch the water up there, and we made it through the supper dry, though I lived in fear of the pan tilting and pouring muddy water onto my meat loaf or worse, onto my professor.

The beaverboard walls are crushed here and there, all need paint. The fireplaces are as sooty as ever. Every year a family of chimney swifts lost babies in the living room fireplace. How I hated to hear them crying, knowing they were doomed, having fallen from the nest above. Dwain had to sweep them out.

I went out the back door, closing it carefully. I never remember locking that house the three years Dwain and I lived in it. We did not have a key to the front door. Nothing ever went missing.

It was late afternoon, and although the day had been warm, as the sun was setting the air grew chilly. I wandered in the yard and picked a pretty, tight bouquet of jonquils and what Mother calls dewdrops but I call white coral bells. I sang a childhood song about the coral bells as I walked in the yard. It felt good to be at home.

Then I did an odd thing for me. I got in the car and *drove* up to the cemetery. I don't know why. Usually I wouldn't miss walking that hill for anything. Today it was almost as if I hadn't intended to go there, but the car decided to go.

As I drove up, I thought the gray granite headstones looked like an alien convention, with the creatures attending sitting there, lumps. I smiled. Then I walked over the plot and read all the gravestones.

Reading them, one by one but in no particular order, I wept, though not from sadness. I wept, I think, for the spare beauty and truth of the words, for how much they encompassed, and for their witness to the human capacity for forgiveness.

Uncle Walter: His gift a love we never doubted.

Aunt Sybil: Her love knew no end to its endurance, no fading of its hope.

Fielding Jr.'s stone has three inscriptions. As Susan said, "They couldn't make up their minds. I'll bet they argued." In the end they were all inscribed and all are fitting. I like the Chaucer best, for a minister: "Cristes loore and his apostles twelve he taughte, but first he followed it hymselve."

The morning Fielding died, I woke up thinking I had never thanked him for his guitar, for the Sunday evenings while he was at Columbia Seminary, when he stopped with us on his way back to Atlanta after student preaching at Chestnut Mountain. We would sit on the front porch in good weather, in the library in bad, and while Fielding played the guitar, we sang folk songs: "On Top of Old Smokey," "Careless Love," "The Wreck of the Old 97," "Barbry Allen," "The Riddle Song," "Sweet Betsy from Pike," "She'll Be Comin' Round the Mountain," "That Good Ol' Mountain Dew."

Susan made up verses to "That Good Ol' Mountain Dew," for each of us. I remembered "My brother Alec, he is sort of a relic, not what you'd call real new. But he thanks he's bran' spankin' when he has been drankin', That Good Old Mountain Dew!" And this for me: "My sister Sally with a pen she would rally, wrote down a story or two. But she won the Nobel Prize when she wrote for everyone's eyes, the recipe for mountain dew." Fielding grinned when he heard these.

Lying quiet, dawn breaking, the tunes singing in my mind, I warmed to the memory of how good the singing together felt, and I sensed Fielding there in the room with me. I could almost see him. I thanked him for the joy and love he had been in my life.

I was dressing for school when the phone rang. It was Daddy, saying Fielding had died about 6:00 in the morning, over on Edisto Island in South Carolina.

There is no epitaph for Trip. The stone says "Reported missing off the coast of Macintosh County, Georgia, on August 29, 1981." As memories of Macintosh County rise, another pain edges in beside the old one. I know now the marina the three young men left in their boat that stormy August morning. I know the tidewater creeks, the marsh. I know the sea and the sky and what lured them, the openness, the wind, the wild beauty of the Georgia coast, for I loved being there with Ben on the marsh island where he said we would one day build a home.

My brother Bruce flew in the search mission for Trip. Bruce came home after a week, and we walked in the woods behind my house. He told how they hoped and gradually lost hope, forced to admit that their friends had perished in the dawn in rough seas.

"They were out there and their boat broke up and they drowned," he said, and his voice broke. He wept in my arms. I wept in his.

"He sought the good of his people and promoted the welfare of all their descendants."

That's the Scripture for Uncle Dick's stone. It's from the Book of Esther, and it's true. We are still benefiting from his life, his work. The entire nation.

The Senator's secular quotation makes me smile because I enjoy irony: "When the security of the United States was the issue, six American Presidents leaned upon this great patriot: He never failed them." Richard Nixon.

We had six presidents to choose from, and we picked Nixon. Like Modine Thomas said, though, about having her picture taken with Nixon the day of the Senator's funeral, "If I'd a knowed he was a crook, I wouldna done it."

Still, it's a good quote, and the picture of fierce Modine Thomas, her black face inscrutable, wearing a fur coat and a man's black silk top hat, standing in the Georgia Capitol with Richard Nixon and the Russell family—she was indeed part of the family—is priceless. I'm glad she didn't know.

"Then shall the dust return to the earth as it was and the spirit shall return unto God who gave it." Such peace in Richard Russell Sr.'s Scripture. Irony, too, for he was a man who moved dirt, usually in a wheelbarrow, all over his place for forty years.

"A lovely bit of heaven returned home to help brighten the kingdom." My sister Patience. An old pain, and a new feeling of loss as I enjoy my own maturity and that of my brothers and sisters. She was six when she returned home.

I thought of Grandmother Russell planting daffodils, which we called jonquils, rows and rows of them, new varieties each year. Her days must have been peaceful compared to ours. No radio or television to clutter her mind. She could be aware of the world at her doorstep, the world we should all want to know. She did not go gallivanting off in a car every morning. Home was a place to be, not a place to light. The flowers she left are her legacy. Uncle Dick planted those daffodil beauties on the path between house and hill. That too is part of her legacy. She left us the need and the will to plant flowers. And scuppernong vines. We are a rich family with this inheritance.

I went by the nursing home and spent some time with Mother. She was out in the hall in her wheelchair, visiting, when I got there. This is a good sign she is getting over the paralyzing grief of losing her leg. As much as one can get over it. There is no word to describe such loss. She is a woman who has had to learn much about loss. First Patience, then a beloved husband, not to death but to divorce, and now one of her own limbs. My heart swells with admiration for her toughness.

I came home in the dark, satisfied with the past and the present. Not satisfied exactly. More aware perhaps, more reverent. I felt purged, forgiven, and inspired. That's how I know my little sortie was a pilgrimage.

I had Bon Courage in the barn to rest a minor lameness and Dulcie to keep him company. Feeding the two, getting the riding ring ready for them to spend the night in it, carrying hay and water out there, I liked being under the wide and starry sky.

The verse from Ecclesiastes on my grandfather's grave turned quietly in my head. It is right that our dust return to the earth, and we ought not to be afraid to rejoice in that.

I released the horses into the riding ring, stood near them, breathing their perfume, the horse smell I love, and breathing too the sounds of crunching, blowing, and stamping they made over their hay.

Glad to be alive, I found myself saying aloud Stevenson's grace-filled "Requiem":

> Under the wide and starry sky
> Dig the grave and let me lie.
> Glad did I live and gladly die
> And I laid me down with a will.
> This be the verse you 'grave for me:
> "Here he lies where he longed to be,
> Home is the sailor home from the sea,
> And the hunter home from the hill."

Death should be felt as a homecoming, and earth is the home of our dust. Yet when I looked up as far as I could into the stars, absorbing the immense distance between earth and stars, I felt, too, that the soul, the mysterious, unnameable part, may indeed take to the sky, sail eternal paths in the darkly brilliant dome, and discover the soul's home place.

IT'S A BAWDY PLANET

IT IS NIGHT, and alone in my house, I am turning out lights before going to bed, my body dreamily recalling a long afternoon ride and how good it felt, galloping Took up the steep old power cut on LaMarche's place, how sure-footed the horse is trotting the rough downhill side of that cut and how easily I move with him then, liking our union, the joy of him between my legs, and how pleasure heightens in the sweet moment when we float into an easy canter over that mile of good logging road. We are both flushed and proud, crossing the rain-swollen river as if it's a garden path, and we swing home at the trot down the river trail, not tired after twelve miles.

An alarming howling in the backyard, a sound I have not heard in a long time, startles me into the present. Oh, no. Can it be that Migno has callers?

This thought makes me feel sick. No, it's not possible. She has had one litter of pups, but she was nearly three years old when they were conceived and had never showed a sign of fertility. We didn't know when or how she got pregnant.

Well, I guess we knew *how*. But not when, and certainly not who.

It has been a year since those puppies were born, four of them, two of each gender, fuzzy, charming, easy to find homes for. Migno has remained blissfully—to my way of thinking—unattractive to male dogs in these parts since.

But not tonight. The dark yard seems full of phantom dogs, appearing eerily out of the broom sedge in the garden plot or fading into the froth of the asparagus ferns near the clothesline. Since Ben left, no one tends the garden or the asparagus. Face pressed against a cold windowpane, I make out only the shadows of dogs. When I turn on the porch lights, the dogs disappear. Migno, barking, races as far as the muscadine vines, but she is not barking her usual fierce, this-is-my-territory-by-God-and-don't-you-forget-it bark, the one packs of coon dogs do not challenge.

She is not chasing these fellows away. She is eager to follow them, to find them, to know them.

When Migno's puppies were born, Monique was living here, after Steve's company closed and he had to go to Florida to work while she stayed here teaching. Monique fell in love with the puppies, put a special box for them under the back steps and kept it clean and dry. I was amused, watching her, especially since she swore she didn't want children. She got pregnant that spring, married Steve, and now has a baby girl she adores.

My heart starts to ache a little for Poco, Migno's daddy, the sass-ass-iest beagle dog God ever made. Surely it was only an hour ago That Little Girl Dog took up here to become Poco's love and the mother of Migno.

I do not forget how delighted Poco was in this fragrant female some-one dropped off near our mailbox one night. His rapt attention to her kept me from calling animal control. I never like calling animal control, but I refuse to let someone else choose my dogs for me.

Watching Poco become more and more possessive as the newcomer got to smelling better and better, I decided enlightenment might lurk in what was to come. I fed her but kept calling her That Little Girl Dog, hoping I wouldn't get attached to her. Poco was attached enough for both of us.

She wasn't pretty, had scraggly brown and blonde hair, stubby legs, bowed ribs, a skinny neck. Clearly no family background. Nor any imagination to speak of. She was content to trot along behind Poco, doing his thing. None of this mattered to Poco because she smelled right. He saw no advantage to choosing a girl like him, a sleek, tricolored beauty, sturdy, curious, intelligent, well-educated. Poco's nose was stirring his genitals, and he had no choice but to respond. His organs were ordering him to fuck.

I use this infamous four-letter word in an effort to be clear. I know no better word for this context. For *fucking* is my meaning, not *having sexual intercourse*, not *sleeping together*, not *making love*. The term *fuck* is the best in our language to convey that essentially mindless activity, that total surrender to implacable physical forces whose sole aim is to get the animals concerned to reproduce. Those other terms are less urgent or imply something beyond the demands of reproduction. Some might consider *mating* a more appropriate word, but I offer *fucking*, with its pushy, onomatopoetic quality expressive of sexual activity in primordial form.

Watching Poco's increasing delight with the way That Little Girl Dog made his body tingle, I supposed Poco believed it was she who made him want to fuck, instead of her smell and the *idea* of fucking, which Mother Nature places slightly below the surface of male consciousness, ready to surface and consume his consciousness. Mother Nature sees to it that the male dog gets the idea before the female, that he is primed for action. Poco enjoyed being primed.

Pretty soon That Little Girl Dog was agreeable to his desire for reproductive activity, and then nothing could stop them. They fucked in the yard, down at the barn, out in the pasture, on the front porch. Poco was ecstatic about having his consciousness consumed.

I could not help noticing, however, that fucking did not consume the consciousness of That Little Girl Dog. She never seemed as anxious or as eager about it as Poco did. She was happy to acquiesce, to submit, sometimes to tantalize him a bit, but her relative calm vis-à-vis Poco's excitement leads me to suggest it is not the nature of females to forget everything when mating. The stakes are higher for us, and perhaps even the most primitive females sense that if the thing goes well, we will go beyond the act of mating. Our bodies will produce young, and this is more important than fucking. Producing young is what fucking is *for*.

The reproductive act itself, however, is all the male is going to get. No wonder then that fucking can become the most important thing in the world to him.

What happened next in Poco's romance illustrates Nature's determination that every female dog in heat becomes impregnated. We live in such far country that we don't have many neighbor dogs, yet That Little Girl Dog attracted a number of courtiers. Word—or perhaps perfume—got around. Like these creatures tonight, dogs appeared out of the grass, grinning in their entire being. They looked, for the most part, like degenerate coyotes, though there was one good-looking blue tick hound mighty pleased to find something far better than coon hunting.

That Little Girl Dog was not averse to added attention. Poco knew it right away and didn't like it one bit. Too enamored to scold his love, he showed no irritation with her, though he was plenty worried about his numerous rivals. His solution to the problem: to cover her as much as he possibly could. I noticed the other dogs stayed back when he was mounting her.

After a while I felt right sorry for Poco. He was frantically fucking all the time. His eyes glassed over, and he didn't seem to be enjoying it as much as he had at first.

It reminded me a little of the way things were around here when Dwain Jackson was getting the wanderlust. He wanted to roam, but he wanted to keep his woman at home covered, too. At the time I didn't know exactly what was going on—still don't—but I know that in humans the sexual act bonds, even when we don't mean for it to, so like That Little Girl Dog, I acquiesced as much as possible. At least it felt like as much as possible. However, I was going through a pretty rough patch of identity crisis that muddled the scene further, and I finally had to give it up.

Humans have to deal not only with fucking but also with thinking about it. Consciousness complicates fucking.

As for Poco, he managed to hold out until That Little Girl Dog lost interest in him and all other males. As her perfume faded, so did her courtiers, and no one seemed unhappy about the shift. Not such a bad system.

Although it is highly probable that she linked up with that good-looking coon dog one evening, her puppies were Poco's. They looked almost like 100 percent beagle dogs, had none of their mother's shag, proof that Poco's furious fucking had stamped them good. They did have her stubby legs.

Although the male of most species generally does not know or care much about his offspring, Poco's strategy turned out to be a good one in the important sense of ensuring his survival. He got hit by a car on the curve at Daddy's big barn a few weeks after he mated. He managed to drag his dear little body into the Matthews cemetery up there before he died. Grieving the loss of his sassy presence, I kept Migno out of the litter That Little Girl Dog produced. Migno is Poco's immortality, such as she is.

She's her mother's immortality, too, because That Little Girl Dog died of tick paralysis a few months after her pups were born.

I call to Migno, down among the muscadine vines, but she doesn't come. I try to reassure myself this isn't a sure sign of her coming into heat. She never has come much when I called. Beagles are as bad as cats for not coming when called.

I go to bed, trying not to worry. In the night I hear Migno howl a long, lonesome, high-pitched call, a keen yearning, an about-face change in her attitude toward these interlopers, an attitude that must puzzle her in body if not in mind.

She who usually keeps other dogs away simply by the ferocity of her bark is falling under a spell that makes her turn to strangers and howl for attention in a most undignified manner. Suddenly she needs her enemies. Soon she will not have to beg, will be the center of attention that she will lap up, forgetting her heritage of aloof dignity.

There's nothing to be done. She is powerless against this force, this need to breed. No matter the ignominy of the mate, she will accept him. What Joseph Campbell calls the Will in Nature is too strong for her. Shakespeare reminds us with a shrug: "It's a bawdy planet."

I climb alone into bed considering whether sex is best characterized as a cruel joke Nature plays on one or the other of the parties. Female spiders kill their mates. Female praying mantises devour theirs in the act of copulation. The canine female becomes an object of dispute and loses all dignity in this mating game. I've heard human males deride her for her willingness, a willingness that excites them, that they long for in their own kind. Abandoned soon after mating, a female dog raises her young alone and gets no credit for her accomplishment, only a coarse comment: "Look at that old bitch with the long dugs."

In humankind, the male wants to spread his seed afar. Almost as soon as he has made a deposit with one female, his eye is roving, looking for the next one. The female, however, as soon as she has bonded through sexual intercourse, wants to make a nest. Viewed coldly this way, our sexual makeup comes under Frost's designs of darkness to appall.

Migno's howls in the night magnify in my mind the force of reproduction ringing the globe. It may be the greatest force in the world. No bomb can rival it. No other natural physical force, not a river rushing, not Niagara Falls, not an earthquake, nothing else has that sustained, omnipresent power. It is going on around us all the time, this fucking, this manifestation of a Will that insists, "This is first: survive, survive, survive."

The weight of my sheet and of the quilt I bought for my celibate bed soothes my skin. My blood courses to the keening in the backyard. My body picks up on the force of reproduction, recalls its capacity for pleasure. I remember Ben's coarse beard and sensuous mouth, the scars on his hands.

A few days earlier a friend asked me, regarding my life alone, "What are you doing about your sex life?"

Her question startled me because I had not given it a thought. With two capable and eager partners and my general pleasure in the physical side of life, I had enjoyed sex. So why wasn't I missing it?

"I guess I'm riding horses," I said.

Tonight riding horses does not seem enough.

When I close my eyes I hear katydids singing, a throbbing music that invades the blood already infected with Migno's howling.

I visualize, behind closed eyelids, the bugs that were here a few days ago, mating all over the place. I don't know what they were: mayflies or yes-you-may-flies. Joined abdominally, two faces, four wings, they stuck together, fluttering around without a care in the world. Or maybe they were taking care of their only care. There were crowds of them in the grass, on the manure pile, in the barn aisle, in the hayloft, on the barn roof.

"You ought to have a little more pride," I said to them.

Lying in bed now, I wonder if I was prudish. But I think it isn't prudery that makes me frown on such goings-on. It's fear of this force.

Fear, not shame, gives me the feeling of surprise and disappointment I have when my calm, detached Dulcie squeals, squats, and pisses because there's a stallion nearby she hasn't even met. My mare Dalal, also a dignified female, will perform these same maneuvers over the geldings, doesn't wait for stallions, when she's in estrus.

I don't blame insects, horses, and dogs for being bawdy.

The life cycle of most insects is a few days long—at least in the stage of wings and abdomens. The sex act is their one big act. No wonder they don't worry about being seen. What else do they have to think about? Sex is their *raison d'être*.

After the mating period, female horses and dogs become absorbed with their offspring at birth and watch over them until the young are old enough to look after themselves. In the meantime, for both sexes in both species, life is a long meal interrupted by occasional flights from danger, a lazy eye here and there on the world at large, the swish of a tail at a fly. Nature is wise to ensure that most animals don't have to think about sex, that they simply switch onto autofuck.

Why then make humans capable of thinking about sex? Instead of being entirely swept away by it, we have a head that may restrain our glands, our appetites, short-circuit the autofuck switch.

"Listen," we can warn quickening pulse rates and glowing genitalia, "it is better not to mate with that particular specimen. He may ride a horse well, but he doesn't have a job and shows little prospect of getting one."

Because genitalia do not give up easily, we may have to go on, "Yes, his smile is devastating. I can name six devastated women out there to prove it.

"Steady, girl. Remember fucking is not all there is to life. You have reproduced, already obeyed the Will in Nature, and I might add, with excellent results. Don't forget there are many things in human lives, long and fruitful ones that we have, that are more important than fucking."

Can we settle on *as* important as fucking?

Give me a few more minutes. I'm sure I'll think of something.

SEASON OF WOODPILES
AND HAYLOFTS

THE TEMPERATURE dropped to twenty last night after a day of high wind blowing the cold in. I wore my red L. L. Bean river-driver shirt to bed under my sweatsuit and kept my socks on, running from the warm office to jump under the quilts and comforter after writing until midnight. At the foot of the bed I have the two fleecy Scottish sheepskins we bought on the Isle of Aran in 1985, Ben, the girls, and I. Aware of the icy air while sheltered, I'm more comfortable than I've been all winter. I feel like a hero in the *Iliad* with my sheepskins.

This morning I hung out clothes because there was sun. In spite of being mild, our winter has been rainy. The sun looked wonderful but felt thin. After four hours on the line, the clothes were not dry. I brought them in and draped them about in the dining room, where the wood heater hummed. Only slightly damp, they dried quickly. I felt comforted in this old method of readying clothes for another wearing.

The woodpile is sinking out of sight. I survey the wreckage each time I take in an armload. Some of the logs are soggy and dirty, having been on the bottom a long time. I try to pick enough dry ones to mix with the wet ones. Although Steve cut some little stuff last week when he was visiting Monique, we have already burned most of it. She is visiting him in Florida this frigid weekend. Good time to go.

Since Ben left, keeping wood enough to supply the wood heater has become something of a worry, a new one for me, having heretofore had on the place men who liked to cut wood. Dwain Jackson cut wood for recreation, loved everything about it from chainsawing the tree to splitting big chunks into burnable-sized logs. His attitude was pioneer, and he took great satisfaction in subduing the woods. He cut living trees, choosing oaks that had grown double, cutting only one of the pair.

I always felt a little sorry for those twins. Having cut green wood, we had to wait for it to season, but with Dwain's enthusiasm and abilities, we rarely ran out of seasoned wood.

Ben also enjoyed this work, which he approached peacefully. In summer Ben marked dead trees with blue ribbons. "That way," he said, "God decides which trees will be burned."

This approach was pleasing because I never like to cut a living tree. It also saves time in letting the green wood season. Trees that are already dead but standing are pretty well seasoned. They smell fresh and seasoned right away, lack the raw odor of logs from a living tree.

Ben kept a good supply of logs stacked under the carport. I liked helping load the logs onto the truck in the woods. Sometimes if we couldn't get the truck close to the felled tree, we'd make a short chain, Ben tossing me a log, I tossing it onto the truck. This was demanding work because the logs were unsplit and heavy, but I liked the rhythm we got into. The rhythm took out some of the fatigue. Ben was a good one for rhythm, for all his offbeat ways. It's the last of his wood I'm burning now.

I like to believe my woodpile has taught me the meaning of cold, and I view the modern trend in turning up the thermostat as a potentially fatal indulgence. I tell myself that having to produce with my own labor the stuff that keeps me warm makes me more humble about my place in the universe, more apt to notice the advantages of mutual existence, like my ancestors. We moderns who are willing to let Georgia Power be the Great Wood Stacker in the Wings are asking for a cold awakening.

On the other hand, perhaps I idealize my ancestors. Humankind has more often been wastrel of wood than respectful, denuding tree-rich land for ships, houses, cathedrals, burning entire forests to make charcoal for industrial use, with little thought of replenishing the harvest. It's modern humanity, rudely awakened, that has turned to reforesting.

Yet we continue to show little respect for these magnificent creatures whose growth process provides us with clean air. The powerful limbs of an oak tree lie at the side of our road where a power crew is working.

The crew has pruned the tree, amputating most of its limbs in deference to the god humming in the electric wires passing close to the tree. These limbs, so long in growing, will not be used. They will be ground up and cast to the winds. At best they may become pressed board, a weak imitation of wood.

At County Line School they are adding to the lunchroom because the school is growing by leaps and bounds—nothing in common with tree growth, which is slow and steady—as more and more people move into this part of Barrow County. To clear for the new building, they cut a row of oaks that someone had planted at least fifty years ago and that had had hard work of it to flourish so near the asphalt of the parking lot and the highway. They were big trees, with deep, far-reaching roots. Their trunks and branches have been cut off, their roots torn out of the soil, and all were stacked up and burned, as if their lives meant nothing. My Druid blood says this is a sacrilege we will pay for some day, gasping for air.

Wood-hunting, I went for a walk yesterday, the first since knee surgery. How good it is to appreciate walking. When I reached the rocky spot where several oaks regularly died in dry summers from not being deeply rooted, a spot where Ben often cut our wood, the intense physical labor of wood gathering rose up and confronted me. Weakened after surgery, I feared such work, bleakly admitting that it is labor I cannot do, even when in full strength. I was painfully aware of the limits of energy.

Looking at two oak trees of the telephone-pole size Ben preferred, their bark harboring the telltale scaly gray moss that means they are dead, I envisioned them cut and stacked in the woodshed, neat insurance against the frost. Yet unless I gave up all other work—writing, teaching, cooking, and housekeeping—I would not have the energy to cut that wood.

Nor would I have the strength and skill. I am happy for woodcutting to be men's work. I expect I will have to let out the news that Ben left me the log-splitter. There are several men I know who will no doubt be interested in me once they know I have a log-splitter and dead trees.

It doesn't matter that I don't have a chainsaw. They have their own chainsaws.

Cold is forecast all week, lows in the twenties and teens. In spite of worrying about wood, I love the cold. Thanks to the mild winter so far, I still have a barn full of hay. If my woodpile blues get too bad, I go to the barn and appreciate my stash of hay.

Going to the barn is pure pleasure in winter, for the horses relish their rations, come running when I ring the old farm bell that signals the equine meal is served. In summer they sort of saunter up or won't come at all, secure in their flourishing pasture. Now, with the fescue eaten to ground level and the air biting cold, they come cantering, a small herd of thunder, tails high, nostrils flared. Prancing, they circle each other in the little paddock behind the barn, vying for position.

When I lift the barred gate, Cumiche, Monique's gray Arab chief, tosses his head, enters without interference, then trots up the aisle and into his stall. I lock him in, go back, and lift the bar again for Bon Courage, whose strawberry roan coat shines through his winter fuzz. A saucy teenager, tall and rangy, he hesitates at Bandit's stall but moves on to his when I scold him. Took flattens his ears at Dalal and KJ, claiming the third spot. The two ladies come in after him. Devon and Bandit hang back together. They have never been much interested in politics. Pooky comes in wide-eyed, while sweet old Dulcie ambles in last. Soon all are crunching their grain, snorting and stamping. I treasure each note of this music.

Although I am sure the thermometer would not show it, the barn seems warmer for their presence.

Climbing the ladder into the loft, I feel an immediate change in temperature, thanks to the insulating quality of hay. When I cut the taut baling twine on a couple of bales, the coastal Bermuda hay lets go a fragrant sigh of summer. Thinking about having a talented hay maker in the family reminds me that I am a rich woman, and I call down to the horses that they ought to feel pretty well off, too.

My brother-in-law, Raymond Reynolds, is famous for a few things in Barrow County. One is gargantuan physique: He's nearly six feet, seven inches tall, and the word *herculean* hardly describes his physical strength. Fabled strength of character and integrity add to his renown. Raymond is a man you can count on. Raymond is also famous for making the best hay in the state of Georgia, maybe in the entire Southeast, and it is well known that he packs his bales full and prices them fairly. At his barn, fights have been known to break out among horse owners over hay. I tell him family loyalty means he has to give me first rights.

When he calls to say the hay is going to be baled and ready the next day (hay making is a short-notice labor), I do whatever I have to do to get out there to help load it. Raymond is generous with his flatbed trailer and his farm help at these times.

Loading hay is monumental labor, and I always hope they will let me drive the truck, which they usually do. Nevertheless, loading the bales on the trailer is easier than a fight with the horse owners lined up at Ray's barn.

I throw down the number of sections of hay I'll need, climb down the ladder, and drop them into each stall. In the barn I don't use hay nets or racks. Horses were meant to eat off the ground, and I keep their stalls clean. Horses make short work of grain, but eating hay takes longer. They munch with an intensity that I find thrilling in a way hard to explain. It's primal. First things first.

Enjoying the society of the horse meal, I climb back up to the hayloft and sit on a bale of hay with bales high beside me and behind me, drawing my legs up and clasping my knees. The sounds of the horses eating and their perfume drift up to me. It's a good time and place to be alone—I don't mean lonely—good for contemplation, for meditation. I feel peaceful in the hayloft.

A hayloft may be a hint of heaven, a first step from earth to celestial realms, where labor is rewarded with safety and nourishment.

The floor of my loft is satin smooth, its pine boards polished from years of pushing bales along the floor both in stacking the hay in summer and in using it in winter. Ben tore down an old house for the lumber to build this barn. I helped him load the material onto Raymond's flatbed trailer and bring it home one Thanksgiving weekend. Ben saved the best tongue-and-groove wallboards for the hay-loft floor and laid them well. There's a lot of love and work in this floor.

The trick of warming in the hayloft I learned burrowing into the hay-loft at Grandmother Russell's as a child. On Saturdays my beloved friend Lynn Smith would come out from town, and we would set off across the fields, bundled in wool jackets and caps. Our thick corduroy pants, lined in red plaid flannel, were proof against most Georgia cold. Playing in the woods behind Uncle Bill's barn, we pretended to be characters from King Arthur's knights of the Round Table, Robin Hood and his merry men, or Tom Corbet, space cadet. If we felt deeply chilled, or when the wind howled to irritation, we climbed into the hayloft, burrowed in and told stories, close and companionable. Because Uncle Bill did not bale his hay, just tossed it into the loft from the mule wagons, we could drape it over the rafters and make a cave, a hideout.

To this day, nearly forty years later, I have no better friend than Lynn. We have often sat in this hayloft and told stories, confiding our troubles and our dreams, in the past ten years. Her daughter, Jennifer, and my Nan played with each other in this place through their childhood and puberty, becoming as close in friendship as Lynn and I are. We recognize and are grateful for that kind of dimension in relationships.

Harry O., Lynn's father, was a storybook grandfather, sharing his own considerable horse lore and love. I claimed him as an almost-father, and my girls called him Granddaddy, the same as Jennifer. He kept horses with us for several years and came almost daily. I cannot recall a time I was not glad to see his jaunty, rotund figure. He gave us the farm bell, which Ben decided should be hung in the hayloft, and the two of them hung it there one afternoon.

I can still see Harry O. and Ben going about the farm, mending fences, putting up a new gate, repairing stall doors. Ben became like the son Harry O. never had, and Harry O. became a gentle but strong father figure for Ben. Their friendship was a joy to watch.

The day Harry O. died, I came home from work and found Ben in the hayloft with a six-pack of beer.

"What's wrong?" I asked. There was usually something wrong when Ben retired to the barn with a six-pack.

"Jennifer called," he said.

I waited. Jennifer called our house all the time, but I knew this was different.

Ben didn't speak for a long time, and from his silence I learned that the news would be serious. I became aware of my breathing, Ben's breathing. I waited for the words, my throat tight.

Finally he said, "Harry O. is gone."

"Gone? Gone where?"

My blood and bones despaired, knew "gone" meant the Great Journey, but my brain, my speech denied everything. Yesterday he'd been well, hearty.

Ben could not bring himself to say Harry O. was dead.

"Just gone," he said, "gone."

DEATH SCENES FROM
THE TAPESTRY

A HAWK quarries a mouse down on Rocky Creek, where the broom
sedge grows patchy on the bank bordering the arrowhead field. I am
kneeling in the grass, looking for arrowheads, imagining the Indians
working stone for arrowheads in this tranquil spot by the creek two or
three hundred years ago. I have, through the years, found perhaps two
dozen flecks of white quartz that are plainly hopeful arrowheads
broken at some stage of their manufacture.

The hawk drops out of the sky as if from nowhere, close. I am used to
hawks speck-high in the blue. His wingspan and his proximity make him
look large, his colors more vibrant. The flash of the red tail, if such is
possible, is more thrilling than when I catch its glow against the sky.

The mouse, sleek, gray, plump from abundant summer seeds, is
heading from one clump of sedge to another, but he does not make it.
In the hawk's claws he falls limp, turns from scampering, living mouse
to bloody food in an instant.

The hawk rises with his meal. I kneel as if at an altar of revelation,
stunned, terrified, and comforted by the knowledge of how casually this
transformation occurs.

Another late afternoon, driving in from school, I surprise a hawk rising
out of the brier patches in the pasture, a rabbit in his talons. Startled by
the car, the hunter drops his prey, but the rabbit is dead, its soft brown
and white coat splattered with its own bright blood. It falls against the
backdrop of gray sky, a wasted rag bag. As soon as I park the car, though
I would like to inspect that rabbit, I go in the house. The rabbit is the
hawk's dinner, and it would be impolite—and irreverent—to interrupt
more than I already have.

A fledgling swallow falls out of the nest beside the front door, the nest tucked into the gingerbread carving supporting the balcony floor overhead. Perhaps he was pushed. Five siblings in one red-mud cup is a crowd. It is a damp evening, but no rain is falling now after an afternoon storm. The baby huddles on the porch floor, shivering.

Adult swallows swoop and soar over the little one, chirping urgently to him about flying. This rescue operation is a community effort. There are two other swallows' nests on the porch, at the tops of tall columns, and the adults from these homes get into the act along with the baby's parents. The porch swirls with swallows.

The little one tries to stretch his wings, and when he does he looks more feathery than fluffy. A papa bird lights in front of him, excited, stretching his own strong blue wings. That's right, that's right! For the most part the youngster does not respond to this encouragement. He remains a pitiful fluff ball. He is not ready for flight.

At dark the parents go to bed, and the baby huddles against the wall of the house. I think about the wild orange cat that sometimes comes onto the porch in the night. But I am ill-suited to put the creature back into the nest. My touch would contaminate him so that he would surely be rejected/ejected.

Nor am I willing to take the responsibility of feeding him. I earnestly doubt my ability to teach him to fly. Priority claims on my time and energy line up large.

This is the second covey that these adults have hatched this year. One covey is thriving in the nest at the top of the corner column, and another is hatching in the nest on the column by the steps. We are not hurting for swallows. If one falls, is that cause for grief?

Jesus said his eye is on the sparrow. Okay, but the fact that the sparrow falls does not mean that God is not watching. Death is part of life, a deeply important part. It is too often we who are not watching, who avert our eyes.

The next morning the baby is still there, and the parents again have started flying lessons. Good parents do not give up easily. Life exerts itself to the last.

In the evening when I return from night classes, no youngster on the porch. I think I count only four babies in the nest. I get the flashlight and shine it on them to be sure. Only four.

A beautiful spring morning—Earth Day, in fact—and I go out on Bon Courage. On the way home through the rocky woods above a patch of swamp near the river, I hear dogs yelping wildly. Fearing they have a calf down, I try to ride near enough to see, but my young horse is too nervous. Does he smell blood?

I ride home and unsaddle quickly, turn him into the riding ring to cool. Grabbing a shovel, I head back toward the disturbance, trotting through the woods. The trot is a ground-covering, energy-saving gait, horse or human.

I cross the clear, graceful stream that skips down the stony slope before puddling in the swamp, then muck my way across the swamp, thanks to rubber riding boots. Through the trees I see four dogs howling over something. Nearing them, I smack the shovel hard on the ground and shout, "Get out of here! Go on, NOW!"

Startled, the dogs oblige, skittering off toward the riverbank, leaving the cause of their frenzy. A beagle, tan, black, and white, heavy with pups, sits hunched, panting, wet, an ugly flap of raw, bloody skin showing on her back.

Quietly standing a little way off, I see she has been shot. There is a vicious, dark bullet hole beside her spine. She turns puzzled, hurt, patient eyes on me. It is useless to say I'm sorry, that I wish it were not so, but my blood grieves.

I head home, wondering what to do. I have no gun, no means to put her out of her misery.

Back at the barn, Gus has arrived for his Sunday ride. He has a revolver in his car. We walk back silent through the woods. The frenzied dogs have returned but veer away again when they see us.

She watches us approach patiently. Her coloring, like fallen branches, dry leaves, and pale grass, makes her hard to see.

I say a prayer to the Great Spirit. Forgive us this violence that makes the world spin. Take back this spirit.

Gus fires twice, and still her body is able to drag itself a few feet, lies twitching perhaps five minutes as her eyes glaze. Fat, blue-green flies swarm over her, darken her shape.

"Let's leave her for the possums," Gus says.

I agree that burial in these deep woods seems unnecessary. She is already melding.

At Harry O. Smith's funeral all of Old Winder is there—and it's OLD, arrives with canes, wheelchairs, walkers, hearing aids. Harry O. was eighty-one.

The funeral home plaque indicating his room says "Mr. Harry O." No other appellation is needed for this longtime newspaper editor and community servant. The reception rooms are thronged. It's unnatural not to see him walking among these dear friends, laughing and joking, bourbon glass in hand. How he loved a get-together! In his coffin he lies easy, dignified. No disease has ravaged him. As he took life, he took death, in stride, and made it look easy. Home from a pleasant dinner with his friend Miss Evelyn, to bed, to sleep forever.

In the church I watch the old people file in, find seats. These are the people who built Winder, have lived here for forty, fifty, sixty years. They are old growth that made this little town a true community. And they are dying. The new growth, celebrated for its numbers here at the edge of metropolitan Atlanta, does not have Old Winder's feel of steady purpose, of commitment. The new feels raw, unrooted.

Jessica has come with me, and we sit holding hands, remembering this good man whom we loved, who loved us. Dwain and Harriet come in and sit two rows in front of us. To take the row between us come old Cotton Cavett and his wife, a remote relative of Grandmother Russell's. Cotton, who is as old as my father, likes to remind me every time I see him that we are kin. Because I find him pompous, I have to resist the urge to remind him that he and I are actually no kin at all. Today he does not notice me.

Cotton speaks to Dwain, and Cotton's wife asks him who Dwain is. Then Cotton starts explaining our family history to her: "It's that Jackson boy from Statham, the one who married Sally Russell. They're divorced, though, and she lives out on that farm with this bearded fellow, looks like a hippie. I saw him when I took the grandchildren out there last summer to ride ..."

Jessica and I start to laugh. We try to hold back, but the bench trembles with our laughing. Fortunately, tears rolling down my face could easily be crying. I am bubbling inside, delighted at the irony and delighted that my daughter appreciates it as I do. I am sure Harry O., our "large, sweet soul that is gone," must be laughing, too.

It is Easter Sunday afternoon, and I am walking in the woods down at Wingo's, celebrating the joy of walking, of being, of the assurance spring is that the world runs on resurrection. I sit for a moment on the high bank on the west side of the pond. I have never sat for five minutes at Wingo's without seeing something special move on the water.

Today I see something special standing at the water's edge, not moving.

Before I notice it, I see two saucy Canadas sailing among the greening lily pads, stopping to nip a bite under water, then sailing, sailing, sure of themselves, of their abilities, of survival. Oh, for the confidence of a Canada goose.

Then, as if it has spoken to me above the goose show, I become aware of a dead tree at the water's edge, a hickory. It is dead, most of its bark fallen away, exposing a pale, smooth underside. The bark that is left is rotted, pocked. Yet there is vitality in the tree, for it is nourishing insects with its decay, and birds come to feed on the insects. At its base there is an inviting hollow before which the ground is packed, as if the home hearth has been swept.

I let my gaze climb the tree to a woodpecker hole at its broken top. I can hardly believe what I see there. The tree is alive! It has put out several new limbs that have grown to about the roundness of my arm, and frothy green leaves flourish on them. I shake my head, refocus my eyes, not sure of what I've seen.

I climb across the steep bank for a closer look. From the water side, the tree looks almost normal, has healthy bark and greening limbs. It is, in fact, exactly half dead and half alive.

How many years ago did lightning strike the fiery wound? Yet something in the tree refused to give in to the fire, and it survives. Even its half-dead side teems with life and gives life.

In the midst of life we are in death. And vice versa.

Circle Heart Dandy has a horrible sore from what was a minor cut on his right front fetlock joint. It festers with pus, and antibiotic ointment makes no headway against the infection. Black flies feast at the spot, gorge themselves on gore, no matter how often he stamps.

After more than a week, I begin to despair that the wound will heal. Infection has spread nearly to the bone, and proud flesh has enlarged the wound from nickel size to silver-dollar diameter. As I am applying ointment one evening, the sore writhes under my fingers. It is crawling with worms.

Stories of western mountain men report maggots eating at trappers' wounds and the men surviving to tell about it. Studying Heart's wound, I see the worms of death gnawing, as they do in the grave, yet his body is renewing itself in partnership with the worms' work.

I keep watch with Heart, and day by day the worms consume only his rotted flesh until they and the angry sore disappear. His soft gray hair grows over the scar until I can hardly find it. Horses, they say, have a greater ability than any other animal to heal without scarring. This is a great gift, the ability to heal without scarring.

I dream that something is wrong with my face. In the mirror I see only a huge bruise, painful, throbbing under my fingers. Thanks to the clever camera work of dreams, nothing is visible except the bruise, but I feel it is covering my entire right cheek. The cheekbone aches.

Then the camera pulls back, and I see my entire face. What I thought was a bruise is an intricately stitched tapestry. My face is a tapestry of dark red and blue flowers with dark green leaves. The threads are orderly, the stitches expert. Although my skin stretches tight across my cheekbones, there is no longer any pain.

A new camera shot reveals my face made of living flowers, the velvet, dusky violets that flourish beneath the fig tree in spring. Ben planted the fig bush at the eastern end of the back porch from a cutting of his Aunt Plumma's hundred-year-old tree. The soil is rich at that spot, and the tree is heavy with fruit in season. Through the years violets have thrived there, flash flooding the side lawn in spring, starting from a single shoot Jessica brought home from kindergarten in a white Styrofoam cup. Laughter bubbles within me at this vision of my face alive with these flowers.

The last shot of the dream shows, from a bird's-eye view, a field of flowers, violets and impatiens, daffodils and Queen Anne's Lace, daisies. I am in the field, but I do not know where, and it does not matter where I am. What matters is that I *am* a field of flowers, a bird sailing over the field, a woman aware of herself as bird, field, and flowers.

I wake up laughing, peaceful.

ANOTHER SIDE OF THE
BAWDY PLANET

FEW WOULD ARGUE against the statement that humans are the sexiest animals on the planet. Because we do not have sexual seasons and do not mate for life, we stand accused of licentiousness. Reliable evidence to support the accusation is not lacking. The French novelist Colette, in a cynical mood, wrote, "L'amour c'est une des grandes banalités de l'existence." I think she meant that what we try to elevate by calling it *love* is in fact banal fucking and ought to be recognized as such. Well into middle age, Colette was suffering over a man, and she wanted a simple if harsh explanation for the complex and difficult nature of human sexuality.

I earlier raised the question of what humans might find more important than fucking, and I failed to answer it directly. Nevertheless, the answer is direct enough: making love is more important than fucking. Conscious of their complex sexual natures, humans have long known that what goes beyond fucking—that is, making love—is highly desirable.

A harder question to answer is how, before the in-your-face and in-your-wherever-else attitude of brash, noisy, insistent, neon, glossy, overpublicized fucking, do we *remember* that making love is more important?

Making love does not employ the attention-getting tactics of fucking. It is quieter, takes thought, takes time. But it lasts longer and is more essential to our humanity. Human beings in whom consciousness has any sway at all will admit we often fuck without making love. On the other hand, more among us than might be suspected experience the delicious intimacy of making love without fucking. I submit that human sexuality at its best achieves a seamless union between making love and fucking with a consistent partner over a long run. That may not be 100 percent true, but in my experience it comes pretty near the truth. I'll leave it on the page.

Thinking about this question of human sexuality, with all its glories and its heartaches, I am watching a flock of about fifteen geese on Wingo's, a chilly evening in late December. The geese are making casual circles in the middle of the pond, chatting idly, waiting for a few others to arrive home before starting supper. Pretty soon, a trio appears over the tree line along the river, and the pond geese take up honking and awnking, flap their wings, stretch their necks, make faster and tighter circles. When the returning geese glide onto the water, it seems to me that three others there are especially glad to see them. They pair off with homecoming joy. One pair eases away into the reeds for a few moments of privacy.

I can't help recalling Ben's homecomings after he first went to Herd Island to build a coastal haven for us. He flew home sometimes in his blue and silver Cessna 150. He'd buzz the house, and I'd run out to the yard to watch him land adeptly in the front pasture, on that makeshift landing strip he built, a strip my highly qualified pilot brothers dared not land on. Nor could I resist running down the hill for that first hug. Ben's hugs are the best in the world.

Geese make long-term bonds in mating, and I am sure the birds on the pond this December evening are mates welcoming each other. Yet it isn't the breeding season, so they aren't thinking sex. It occurs to me, and the thought is somehow shocking, that they are making love, letting each other know they are glad to be home safely, glad to be together again.

Suffering over a man, I have envied other animals their established sexual rhythms, which seem to me more freeing than the human state of being constantly sexually active. I didn't think animals made love.

After the geese move to the dining room on the far side of the pond, where their watery table is laid with marsh grasses and other water-loving plants, a pair of beavers pop out of their lodge near the bank where I am sitting. Their wet, dark heads shine with their rich oils as they swim gracefully out toward the deeper water. A beaver is a clumsy-looking creature on land, but in water it illustrates the powerful grace that comes with knowing your element.

In the center of the pond, the beavers nip at each other among the faded lily pads, splashing, and, I swear, though I cannot *hear* it, laughing. Their attitude says they are laughing, delighted in each other's company. Because it isn't their mating season, I conclude that they are, like the geese, making love, expressing affection and joy in the mate's presence, regardless of sexual activity.

It is nearly dark now, and my eyes lose the beavers somewhere out on the darkening water. I am growing chilled, but I want to wait for the first star to appear in the water. I always hope to catch it at the moment it plops onto the glassy surface, but I never can fix my attention to that degree. In the blink of an eye, there is a star or two or twenty in the pond.

On my way home across the pasture, I stop to pet the horses. They nuzzle me for carrots, which I do not have, and soon wander back to snatching grass. I have eight in the herd at the moment, two mares. Dulcie has always been a standoffish person, selecting her own society, though when it comes to breeding, she exhibits remarkable graciousness and magnanimity.

Tonight it is, as usual, beneath her dignity to sniff for carrots. She remains a quiet ghost down near the oak trees at the edge of the lily pond. Closer by, another gray ghost, Cumiche, the Arab chief of this little tribe, is shadowed by Dalal, a bay half-Arab mare. Dalal is not in estrus. Horses never are at the dark of the year if kept out of artificial light. Yet she is content to be close to Cumiche. Their preference for each other's company is obvious. They are making a little love. The other geldings, Took, Bandit, Devon, Bon Courage, and Pooky, respect the relationship, keep their distance.

A gelding is a much-neglected example of what can be accomplished by harnessing sexual energy for something besides sex. Geldings are strong, talented, affectionate, hardworking, generous, willing, cooperative. They are congenial. This little herd gets along well. You couldn't keep a herd of six stallions and two mares without most of them getting seriously hurt. You couldn't have one stallion in such a herd without guaranteeing serious pain.

No wonder human sexual liaisons are complicated and often painful.

I have a friend who says she's looking for a man with all gelding qualities except one. Maybe that's what we all hope for in civilizing mankind. I am sure it was women who began to civilize mankind, and we are still trying, with uneven success. For who can deny that a civilized man, one who harnesses his sexual energy for the good of himself and of others, is a much-neglected example?

Under the night-blue sky brilliant with stars, I head up the hillside, aware of the reassuring presence of horses on the landscape behind me.

I remember an encounter with a civilized man.

When Lindy Clack sold the last of my cows, he came by the house to pay me. I walked up from the barn as he stopped his dually in the back yard, got out, stood waiting for me, as deadly good-looking as ever.

"Got seven hundred apiece for your two cows," he said, leaning against the left front fender of his truck. "You want cash or a check? Fella paid me in cash."

When I started out, people still believed actual money in hand meant something. I like the feel of a good wad of it. I said I'd take the cash.

"I sold 'em for seeder cows," Lindy went on as he counted my money and handed it to me. "We had 'em all checked for pregnancy—you know I had some of your dad's cows, too—and nine of 'em weren't pregnant. One of yours wasn't pregnant."

He shook his head, pushed his Stetson back a little. "You know when we went up to Cornell University back in the early fifties, spent three days up there, they told us this artificial insemination and egg-carrier cows business was coming. I laughed. But I'm not laughing now."

I was struck, thrilled actually, by how perfectly straightforward yet genteel he was while talking that sexy talk.

I thanked him for coming to get the cows so promptly.

"That's nothing to thank me for, just my job," Lindy said. "I used to go get Preacher Roy Etheridge's cows. He was Bob Etheridge's great-uncle, you know, lived up in Nacoochee Valley. He'd write me a penny postcard saying, 'Mr. Clack, I'll expect you Tuesday morning between six and seven to get the cows.' No phone call, but plenty of notice.

"So I'd get up there about daybreak and we'd eat breakfast, then load the cows. Well, he had about the prettiest creek bottom. He'd lined the sides with flat rock to keep them from washin'. Carried the rock in a pick-sack on his back down there. When I said, 'Preacher, this is the prettiest creek bottom I ever saw,' he said, 'Well, I'm just the caretaker here. I'm trying to keep it in good condition. I know I've got a deed, but we're all just caretakers.'"

Lindy's blue eyes got a slightly faraway look in them, as if they were seeing that well-tended mountain creek bottom again. I could almost see it myself.

"I've never forgot that," he said.

As he got back in his truck, I said, "Well, Lindy, if I can't thank you for getting the cows, I can thank you for that story."

He smiled. "It's a good 'un. I hope we're still making some people like Preacher Etheridge."

As he drove away, I was hoping we are still making men like Lindy Clack, men who can with infallible courtesy connect sex and reproduction to being caretakers of the planet.

Treasuring that experience as one in which humans show a flair for going beyond the immediate, I let myself in the back door. The house is dark but cozy from log fires burning in the wood heater in the dining room and in the living room fireplace. I do not turn on lights, take my coat and hat off, hang them on their hooks in the pantry.

In the living room, papers litter the floor and the seats of the sofa and all chairs because Lynn and I spent the afternoon by the fire working on a book of my poems that Nan and Jessica asked me to put together for them. I did not finish it for Christmas as planned but hope now to have it to the printer soon after the new year. Lynn and I have had fun for weeks, selecting the poems and a few essays from my *Winder News* columns. This has been a healing project, one that helped me focus on my own worth at a time when rejection made me feel, against all logic, worthless.

I switch on lamps, sit on the floor among the piles of poems and essays, start to sift through them again, feeling for their proper order.

After a few minutes, I lose concentration, think about making a cup of tea. But it isn't tea I want. I feel my house empty around me. A treasure is missing. For the first time in many months, I admit to myself that I miss masculine intimacy in my life. I don't mean sex—fucking, if you will. I mean sharing daily intimacy of thought, word, and touch with a beloved partner.

For nearly a year I have been sure that I did not want or need this kind of intimacy any longer. Misanthropy did not bring about this decision. Common sense did. I like men, have always liked them. But I figured I'd given two partners the best I had to give and if that wasn't enough, I'd stick to my children, my family, my friends, a rich group of personalities, full of love and friendship. That, with the horses and the farm, would be enough. I was happy with the decision. I felt numb to physical desire.

Men at my workplace and in the endurance-riding community surprised me by trying to change my mind. Although I am sure I am not sending out any come-hither signals, they come hither. They offer to change my single status, at least temporarily.

I say no, thank you, politely but firmly. I am not too flattered by their attentions. Several have been scraggly sorts, and at least one was married, supposedly happily. Others, however, have been fair prospects—if you are looking for prospects.

Lynn, while not denigrating my charms, warns me that these men might be after the farm. I admit the thought has crossed my mind.

I remind myself that it's hard for a good woman to stay single. I've seen too many good women take up with unworthy men. I think this happens because as part of their survival systems, most men carry deep recognition of good women, while women, deeply programmed for others' survival, don't pay enough attention to what they themselves need and want. What I wanted, I thought, was solitude.

Tonight I am no longer sure of that. I leave my papers on the floor, switch off the lamps, poke up the living room fire so the last of the logs will burn, stoke the stove in the dining room for the night, then start upstairs, thinking the last thing I want to do right now is climb into bed alone. So I stop at the landing, where I sometimes sit to think, while looking through the window lights over the front door across my pasture to the hickory ridge on the other side of Rocky Creek. The echoes of Somechoes Farm like to bounce off that ridge, bringing our voices back to us. I know by the tree line where the ancient arrowhead factory was, where I sometimes gather the fragmented echoes of another group of humans who lived and worked here. There is perspective in the view from the landing.

Geese, says my bird-watchers' handbook, form long-term bonds. The book is careful not to say that geese mate for life. I think this mating pattern is true of humans. We need long-term bonds, but we do not necessarily mate for life.

Alone on the landing, I consider that I am good at long-term bonding. I stayed graciously married to Dwain Jackson for nearly eighteen years, gave him two children and a preference for marriage. He is happily married to a good woman now. Dwain Jackson knows how to pick out a good woman.

When the great wanderer Ben Blessing showed up at my door asking for farm work, I never expected him to stay, nor did I ask him to stay, though I told him he was welcome. Early on I made a unilateral decision to take Ben as partner. Unilateral partner choices are risky, yet the fellowship, friendship, and love we shared went on for nine years, a long-term bond by human time measurement.

My back to the wall on the stair landing, I remind myself that I am forty-eight years old and have had two good partnerships, which should be enough for one woman. But in my heart I am unconvinced, I feel a thaw setting in.

My Grandmother Eaton would have said that what's wrong with me is that I'm going through The Change. I remember how mysterious that phrase seemed to me at age nine, the first time I heard her use it, and I still think it thrilling: Going Through The Change. It was a thing of wonder and terror that happened to women in their forties, a metamorphosis involving, as metamorphoses do, a loss and a gain. Bleeding and hot flashes were necessary. From my grandmother's tone when she applied the term to various women, I knew that in her harsh judgment some handled The Change better than others.

Perhaps humans do have sexual seasons after all, at least women do. Following childbirth, many of us have little interest in sex for a time. We adapt to our partners, but truthfully, as one new mother I know said, "You don't want them near you like that." During a woman's childbearing years there are times each month, too, when sex is unwelcome.

In the natural swing of a woman's life, The Change might be fairly considered nature's way of equalizing males and females. Without the responsibility of reproduction, we women are free to enjoy our partners sexually in a way not previously possible. Because men's sexual desires decline somewhat during the same time—it is no longer their responsibility to insist that new humans get started—a balance of love and desire might be achieved at this time of life.

I know about modern birth-control methods, but I am thinking of our deep biological selves in this case. We should not lose sight of our deep biological selves.

In the dark at the top of the stairs I shiver at the thought of hot flashes, of metamorphosis, of loving partnership. I think of caterpillars curled into cocoons, dissolving to liquid heartbeats that give birth to butterflies.

Almost without thinking, I go back downstairs and out onto the back porch deck. I stand under the huge and thoughtful night and feel the stars and the infinite space between them.

Perhaps I am hoping that under the wide and starry sky fame and love will sink to nothingness, but that is not what happens.

Surprising myself, I address the Universe with assurance, with audacity.

"Okay, Universe," I say out loud, "I like the rascals. I don't like living without one as well as I like living with one. But if I'm going to consort with another man, this is how it's got to be: he's got to be loving, kindhearted, even-tempered, loyal, and economically sound; have a good sense of humor; respect the dangers of alcohol; be satisfied with his work and good at it; like horses and love France or vice versa; appreciate women as people; be my intellectual equal and proud of it; know how to court and be willing to court."

The Universe does not comment on this audacious list.

Climbing into bed, I puzzle over my list. It is not an order or an ad in the Universal Personals. I have no intention of man hunting. What is it, then? Perhaps it is a talisman, a protective charm evoked by a changing woman, aware of vulnerability as she summons courage to cast off a deadening fear of loving.

Part Four

STOCK EXCHANGE

STOCK. n. a source of something; assets; a store; an endowment for a son (or daughter); livestock

EXCHANGE. v. relinquish something and receive something else in return

CHICKEN POTPOURRI

THIS MORNING I went down to the barn to let the chickens out of the coop Ben has made for them. He usually does the letting out on his way to work, but this morning he asked me to do it. We have had the chickens three weeks, and there have been no eggs so far.

The first chickens, gift of Jim Kline, another amateur chicken raiser, turned out to be five roosters and one poor, pitiful, rooster-pecked—or, we could say, rooster-peckered—hen. There were no eggs and no wonder. The hen had no peace in which to lay an egg. But we added six hens and subtracted all but two roosters, and barnyard society is much improved.

The way we added hens and subtracted roosters is this: I heard Kenton Hayes over near Braselton had barnyard chickens for sale and would trade. Kenton, a big man wearing overalls and a prodigious black beard, had his chickens and roosters set up in the back of an abandoned chicken house on Highway 53. It looked sort of like Kenton might be set up with them.

Kenton said he'd take three roosters and give me six hens if I'd give him six dollars. That sounded okay to me, but I had only three dollars on me. Kenton took my three dollars and said I could pay him the other three next time I came by. I didn't do that until about two weeks later, and when I did, I apologized for taking so long. "Shoot," Kenton said, "that doan bother me none. I'm not settin' 'round here worryin' 'bout no chicken."

This morning there was an egg in one of the dozen nests Ben has carefully prepared. It's a good-sized egg, too. I watched the seven hens scratching in the barnyard after I let them out of the pen and wondered which one had laid this surprise. Did she notice? Is it a virgin egg or the first of the new season or of the new home?

Who was the first human to discover that eggs are edible and nourishing? What a day, to learn the bird could be eaten over and over this way. You can have your chicken and eat it, too, if you're sensible.

Counting the cost of the pen and coop, as well as the price of the new hens, I figure the first egg cost me one hundred dollars.

Soon we get four other eggs and are down to twenty dollars each. No, that's not right, because we spent ten on corn and laying mash.

I am not going to count the cost of having the chickens in dollars and cents or even sense. There is this reward: the satisfied feeling I have when the covey comes running as I approach the barn, following as I call "Chick-chick-chick! Chick-chick-chick-chick!" I talk to them freely, discussing their abilities and duties. They are providing an outlet for something I don't yet quite understand. Maybe I never will. I experience the joy of provision with the chickens, of usefulness. I know a feeling of honest pride, an I'm-the-one-guarding-the-flock feeling.

That one little red hen is starting to look much better now that she isn't the only hen among five roosters. Do females usually do better when they don't have to meet the demands (of whatever kind) of too many males?

Having the females outnumber the males is not such a bad arrangement for any species. Some females get male attention, while the others are left in peace to be creative.

I mean that little red hen is looking *a lot* better. Her feathers are coming back smooth, pretty, and shiny, and she is getting fatter. She prances around confidently, and well she ought. Anybody who survives five roosters can be rightfully proud.

Roosters have horribly coarse, clawed, and yellow feet—vicious feet. I used to think human feet were ugly, but I was wrong. Human feet are supple and soft, a good thing to have at the end of a leg. Rooster feet define ugly. Actually, "ugly ain't no word" for those feet, as Rabun Treadwell used to say. Roosters in general are not admirable, for all their combs and feathers. They admire themselves too much. I find their strutting unpleasant. Strutting is—? Comical? Undignified? Uncalled for? Nauseating? All of the above.

A girlfriend once told me she couldn't stand for a man to strut after he'd made love to her. Reminded her too much of roosters. "But some of them do it," she said. I really cannot confirm that observation.

Our roosters are what the country folk call Domineckers. I delight in that corruption of the French *Dominique*. There's an aroma of indomitable Saxons sassing Normans in it. Domineckers are good-looking as roosters go. They are black-and-white speckled, sort of a gingham bird, with that flash of red comb on top. Ours have smooth, slick feathers. If you forget their feet, they are elegant.

We are supposed to get twenty-five new chickens next week. We are sharing an order of one hundred from Sears with Jim Kline and Dale Crandall. Will thirty-four chickens be too many? We will have to kill and cook some if they thrive and multiply. I wonder if I can kill a chicken.

They may indeed multiply if the hen that is setting her nest is successful. She has about a dozen eggs to keep warm. It's exciting on the farm when you're hoping for birth.

The new chickens add to the cost of this venture, but I said I would not keep accounts. The experience of chickens is going to be worth several hundred dollars at least. I like the way they scratch around in the barn aisle and go in the stalls and eat the windfall grain that the horses splash out of their troughs. The chickens eat the grain in the horse droppings, too. Flies and grasshoppers do not last long with chickens around, a real bonus in the barnyard.

Finding the eggs is a treasure hunt every day. Some hens lay in the straw boxes provided in the coop, but others leave their treasure in the bare horse troughs or in a sandy corner of a stall. If I forget to check the troughs before letting the horses in, I may lose an egg. April has gone in more than once and reappeared over the stall door with egg on her face. The laugh is part of the treasure.

I like eating these eggs. They have strong yolks, deep yellow, almost orange, and thick, greenish whites. Their taste is robust, reflecting the variety of a barn chicken's diet. We feed a little grain each day, but most of their feed is foraged.

I like going down each evening to get the flock back into the pen, even when some are dumb—a daily occurrence—and cannot find the gate. I have to be patient as they squawk up and down the fence outside the pen, missing the opening. When I think I will not have time to be patient in the evening, I simply leave them in the pen all day. That will not be an option when we get the new ones, unless we build a bigger pen.

The new chickens arrive in a box that Jim Kline brings to his office at school. I am glad I work where I can find a box of baby chicks in an office, an entirely appropriate find in Gainesville, the (self-declared) chicken capital of the world.

The chicks are yellow, with tiny brown feathers showing in the wing area. They are fluffy and adorable. Jessica and I oooh and aaah over them when I get them home. Nature makes babies cute so we will put up with the mess, which is considerable with all babies. Eating starter feed and drinking and splashing water, these chicks keep the bags in the bottom of the box soggy, requiring constant changing.

The first night—a warm early September one—we keep them on the screen porch in a big box, but three smother before morning as they crowd together trying to feel warm and safe. Let that be a lesson to us all.

The next night I bring them inside in the box they came in and put them in the dining room. Next morning everyone is fine. Ben turns the old quail-rabbit-dog pen into a cozy home inside the chicken coop because of Jim's warning not to turn chicks out with big chickens. Jim says the adults will peck the chicks' eyes out.

Something is stealing the eggs from under the setting hen. One morning I count the eggs and find only nine instead of twelve. Another morning there are only six. Then only three. I do not know what to do besides pray they will hatch soon. I feel for the poor mother, setting so long, all her faith and patience for nothing.

One evening at twilight I am at the barn to check the flock and turn out a couple of horses. As I am closing the chicken pen gate, I see a snake lying near it. A big snake, about four feet long and thicker-bodied than a garden hose. In its center it's as thick as my arm. It is gray, without decorative markings. It does not move or seem inclined to move. I know it is not poisonous, and I also know what has been getting my eggs.

I go for the shovel, but as I reach for it, I know in my blood I will not be able to strike true, so I run toward the house and call, loud, for Ben to come QUICK! I've found what is getting the eggs!

Jessica in her upstairs bedroom hears me and relays my message to Ben, watching the evening news. "I'll bet it's a snake," she adds.

Ben comes nonchalantly down the slope and spies the snake. Without a word he takes the shovel and strikes a hard blow at this marauder. He cuts it almost in two, but the snake manages to slither under the tack room. We stare at the place where it lay, incredulous at its disappearance.

Ben lies down in the dusty, chicken-litter strewn coop to peer after the snake. One of many good things you can say for Ben Blessing is that he has no fear of getting dirty. It is almost dark now, but he can make the snake out. It has its head up, is swaying back and forth. We feel sure it must be dying, but old superstitions about snakes' powers of regeneration make us uneasy. We try to prod at the snake with the shovel, to oust it from its shelter. It will not be dislocated.

Ben goes to the house to get his rifle. There is enough light left when he returns to allow him to shoot the snake in the head. This may be the first time I have seen Ben shoot. The snake drops, lies still.

We are both breathing hard.

"I guess we've got ourselves a chicken snake," I say.

"I don't think it's a chicken snake," Ben says.

But when he pulls it from under the tack room, it is unmistakably a chicken snake, brownish gray with a yellow, ugly belly.

Next day someone tells us that chicken snakes sometimes swallow four or five eggs one after the other and crush them by winding around a pole or a limb to help digestion.

Our chicken snake did not make it to the limb. He'd eaten the last of our poor hen's brood and was too sluggish to escape.

We throw his carcass into the pen, thinking it poetic justice to let the chickens eat it. Chickens usually will eat anything, but they refuse to have anything to do with that chicken snake.

Crows, however, are not so squeamish. When we throw the carcass into the big paddock, they make short work of it.

My sister Susan and her husband, Raymond, live three miles up Mulberry Road from us on another farm. They have three chicken houses, new ones, and are raising sixty thousand chickens every eight or ten weeks. That's what I call earnest chicken farming.

Georgia chicken farmers can turn out chickens better than God. In tiny Barrow County (in land area we are 152 out of 159) 250 farmers raise sixty-two million chickens a year, and we're running in fifth place behind Jackson, Hall, Habersham, and Madison Counties. And I did not count my three dozen chickens in that tally. But that is how when you go to the grocery store or stop at the finger-lickin' fast-food place, you have chicken till your stomach bulges.

I am sorry most of us no longer have the joy of yard chickens, and I think we ought to take time now and again to consider how birds have long been a friend to humankind in the good fight against starvation.

After Harrison Poultry came to get Susan and Raymond's first batch of chickens, Raymond brought me three that escaped the chicken catchers. He thought they would make up for the ones that smothered and maybe a little for the ones that the snake ate. I thanked him.

It is a relief to receive a grown chicken. Having failed to get any babies of my own this season, I watch the little ones from Sears anxiously. They are growing pretty well, have lost their baby feathers, and are now that shiny rust color that gives the Rhode Island Reds their name. They are sassy, too. No danger of having their eyes pecked out by the older hens now. Raymond's chickens are white leghorns, so we have a pleasing mix of brown and white hens with the two Dominecker roosters threading the flock with tweed.

I am happy to report that chickens will eat almost anything besides a chicken snake. In addition to their foraged horse grain, they eat old lettuce leaves, rotten celery, petrified bread crusts, moldy yogurt, unidentified mold-covered globs from the fridge, vintage jalapeños, burned biscuits, green beans with freezer burn, potato peelings, tea bags, and coffee grounds. When my fridge does not need cleaning out, they eat grasshoppers, crickets, butterflies, plain flies, flies' eggs, their own eggshells, and of course cracked corn and commercial chicken feed. After watching the chickens eat, I do not want to know what is in commercial chicken feed.

When my mother heard about my chickens, she began to save scraps for them, too, and they are in high cotton when a saver as talented as my mother looks out for them. She saves popcorn, bread crusts, bits of toast, orange rinds, apple cores, carrot peelings, baked potato skins, soggy cornflakes, and cucumber slices. The chickens eat it all.

Sometimes they eat the mint by the back steps and rosebuds off the bushes by the front steps. The thorn with the rose of chickens, I suppose.

Having chickens is better than having a compost heap. They ingest and digest and turn matter into fertilizer overnight. Sometimes the fertilizer gets spread onto places I don't think need fertilizing, like the back porch steps, but I don't do much to keep the chickens from roaming.

I feel good about recycling all my leftover food, and I stand amazed that from this checkered diet the chicken produces something as fine as an egg.

The young hens have not laid yet, and with winter coming on they are not likely to. Never mind. All the chickens provide a kind of poetry in the farmyard. I don't wonder that artists like to paint chickens. I enjoy their pecking and squawking and cackling. I have had enough eggs all summer to make pound cakes and breakfast omelettes at will and to give a dozen eggs away now and again. A good feeling.

As hard as I have been on my roosters about vanity, I must note that the cocks' crowing is a joy. Their morning clarion calls do not awaken me unless I want them to, and when I lie listening to that lilting music that often starts before dawn pales the dark eastern shore of my world, I forgive the cocks their strutting. With voices like that, they have reason to strut. Although I know they are not strutting about their voices, I agree with Thoreau that it might be worth keeping cockerels merely for their songs.

MR. PEABODY'S STORY

RUNNING a small summer horse camp and taking in horse boarders to help pay for our riding passion, we had a dozen horses at Somechoes Farm that year. At the end of the camp season, I had the vet come to do a Coggins check. A friend whose young sons were two of our favorite campers, he performed this yearly procedure cheerfully in spite of the terrible Mr. Peabody.

Mr. Peabody was an intelligent, talented, well-trained, and good-natured pony, but he had one fault: he hated vets. Too refined to take his hatred out viciously, he simply refused to be vetted. He would stomp, snort, toss his head, crash through the stall door, run away—in a word, refuse. I repeat that he was not vicious, but his evasive tactics could be dangerous to horse and doctor alike.

Peabody hated the veterinary procedures that I handled myself, such as paste worming and yearly immunization shots, but we had achieved an uneasy truce one afternoon when I had been trying to worm him for over an hour and dark was falling fast.

"Peabody," I said to him finally, "I am supposed to be smarter than you are. I intend to prove that I am by getting this wormer down you without either of us getting killed."

I spoke with confidence because I had had the brilliant idea of blind-folding him. It worked. Unable to see me approaching with the syringe and a little confused by the blindfold, he took the wormer. After that we went on with our lives in relative tranquillity about home vetting.

Not so with visits from Dr. Powers. The minute Jim's blue pickup hit the barnyard, Peabody would start stomping around in the stall. When Jim got out of the truck, pandemonium was liable to break loose and Peabody, too. It took all the help we could muster—me, Ben, Nan, Jessica, and the vet assistant—to get sedation medication into the horse so he could be tube-wormed or have a blood sample taken.

Jim Powers was a kind, good man and a capable veterinarian. There was no reason for Peabody to hate and fear him. All we could figure was that somewhere in Peabody's past lurked an unhappy vet experience that the pony could not forgive.

I was at the barn that afternoon in late August when we got the bad news from the Coggins. I heard a loud wail from the house direction, a wail that seemed to have started with the cry, "Mama!"

I came to the end of the barn and shaded my eyes with my hand to look up the hill toward the house. Nan, Jessica, and Jennifer Lowry, who boarded her pony, Hobbit, with us, were running across the yard toward me, tears streaming down their faces.

"What on earth?" I asked as they came up.

"Peabody has a positive Coggins!" Nan sobbed. "Jim's office just called."

"But that's not possible," I said, and I truly didn't believe it could be. We checked our horses yearly. All horse events we attended required riders to show proof of negative Coggins tests. Several campers had brought their own horses to camp, but we had required negative Coggins tests for them, which they willingly provided.

I went to the house and called Jim, trying not to show my concern in front of the little girls. But all of us had been to horse education seminars at the University of Georgia School of Veterinary Medicine. We knew that a positive Coggins indicated equine infectious anemia, EIA, dread blood disease of the horse world, one for which there is no inoculation and no cure. EIA, transmitted by blood-sucking insects, is highly contagious in the active stages, sometimes wiping out entire herds. It is no exaggeration to call it the AIDS of the horse world.

Jim was not optimistic. Our only hope, he said, was to pull another sample after twenty-one days to see if the results were the same. In the meantime we would have to isolate Peabody from all other horses, one hundred yards minimum distance. A state inspector would come to see if we were complying.

Temporary isolation was possible because there was space for Peabody in my father's cow barn, half a mile away. Bovines were not at risk for the equine disease. The nearest horses were those on the Beckemeyer farm, about three hundred yards away. I dreaded telling Del and Fran Beckemeyer about the crisis, but when I went to them, they offered support and sympathy in their usual good-hearted way. Del said not to worry, that a vet had told him the virus dies before a fly or mosquito covers a hundred yards. Knowing they had to be concerned for their horses, I found such civility and kindness almost overwhelming.

The girls had always been good barn help, taking their turns at the chores without a word of complaint, because to have Somechoes Farm we knew that every creature had to earn its own way, humans included. For the children I stipulated that earning their way meant doing a good job in school (no grades lower than B), and performing specific house and barn chores. At this time, however, I elected to take the sole responsibility for Peabody's care because if worse came to worst, I hoped a gradual separation would ease the pain for the girls. Peabody was Nan's first horse, her first love, but she had outgrown him that summer and had graduated to Circle Heart Dandy, a tall, bighearted Appaloosa. Now I was more than ever grateful for that new affection.

We had kept Peabody because he was such a good teaching pony. Well-trained, he had patience, but an inherent pride made him insist that the rider do it right. If the learner was too sloppy, Peabody would simply stop and plant his feet until the cue was correctly given. Then he would move out beautifully. He taught many children to ride well.

Mr. Peabody was no mistaken appellation, and his distinct ego made him a favorite. In addition to accepting without question his right to tell humans at what point he would go no further, whether with riders or vets, he was always running for office in the herd and usually winning. We enjoyed his campaigns as he jockeyed for head horse position when a new boarder or a temporary camp horse would come in. Watching new arrivals keenly from the moment a trailer pulled into the yard, he would canter to the fence and observe all activity of unloading and stabling, standing ears forward and head up or pacing the fence line, eager for the kickoff.

Not mean or hateful, he was firm and sure of himself. Other horses soon found it was the better part of valor to let Peabody run things. Not until Heart came did Peabody meet his match. A confident, unconcerned leader, Heart was willing to let Peabody be a strong second-in-command, but where the feed line and certain mares were concerned, Heart claimed first rights and no buts about it. Without holding grudges, Peabody was constant in his vigil for a chance to move up. The next election might be different.

I rode Peabody up to my father's cattle barn and installed him in his new quarters the day after we got word of the positive Coggins. In a bare paddock about fifty feet by fifty feet, the horse had access to an open shed on the side of the barn where there were a hay manger and water bucket. Thinking of how he was accustomed to eighty acres of sweet green pasture and woods, two ponds, and a dozen pals, I could hardly hold back tears.

We notified all the owners of horses that had been at the camp during the summer. Although I had no way of knowing how this had happened, and although my rational mind told me there was no way I could have prevented it, I felt acute shame as I called to reveal this dreadful development.

On my way to school in the mornings I stopped by the barn to throw Peabody some hay and check his water. In the afternoons I returned to lunge him and feed him his grain and more hay. Lunging him was torture because it accented how eager, talented, and well-trained he was. To relieve the boredom, I set up little jumps for him, and he would take them with finesse and pride that hurt my heart.

The state inspector came shortly after the bad news. A humane man, he sat with me on the back porch and quietly explained the options. We could keep Peabody as he was, but he would have to be branded, and there would be regular inspections. He could be put down. He could be sold for slaughter.

My barn was under quarantine for thirty days, and if at any time Peabody returned, the quarantine had to be reinstated.

I explained that we would like to wait until we had pulled a second

Coggins before taking any action other than isolation and quarantine. I was still hoping there was some mistake.

The inspector agreed. Dr. Powers could call him with the results of the second test.

As I visited Peabody every day, the inevitable happened. I came to love him more deeply because our bond became more important. I was his source of physical and emotional comfort. He watched for my arrival and whinnied a commanding "Hurry!" when I pulled up in the car. I knew he was affectionate, capable of giving as good as he got from the adoring little girls he'd worked with, but I never thought to steel myself against his nuzzling, his prancing, his low whickers. His obvious pleasure in my company was flattering. Returning his caresses seemed little enough under the circumstances.

So I brushed him and lunged him and told him about life back at the farm. Pitying him his paddock, I took him out for long rides three times a week. Although he was only 13.3 hands, he had a big-horse trot and a rocking-horse canter. By crossing the river onto LaMarche's land, where no other horses had permission to go, I could ride relaxed, covering ten or twelve miles, enjoying time with my horse while the autumn hills gained splendor day by day.

Peabody was lively and willing. I could not believe he was sick.

Word came in from every horse that had been at our barn that summer. All had passed their Coggins tests. This was much to be grateful for. After thirty days, I had new tests pulled on my horses. Getting Peabody's was an ordeal, of course, especially since at the cattle barn we did not have a good place to contain him until Jim could give him a tranquilizer.

The samples came back with no change. Everyone was negative except Peabody. We tried to be thankful for the considerable blessing this represented, but our hearts were breaking.

The state inspector came back, too. This time he said he would have to brand the pony. I could not watch. After the inspector had gone, leaving me with papers that made the disease more official than ever, I went into the paddock. Peabody walked to me and put his nose against my chest. I felt sick at my stomach when I reached up to stroke his neck and saw the damning marks.

I could not bring myself to a decision. The horse looked so healthy. We had wonderful rides. I bargained for more time. Since my only hope was that the test was a mistake, I decided to wait thirty days longer and try again.

The girls had stayed away for the most part, and I preferred it that way. On their rides they had to be sure to give Granddaddy's barn a wide berth, but they could hear Peabody's high, lonesome whinny when they crossed the big pasture below the barn. Sometimes they would tie their mounts down in the woods and come on foot to give the pony a carrot and a hug.

If October is more beautiful in any other part of the world than it is in North Georgia, I don't know where that might be. As Peabody and I trotted down roads scattered with autumn's fleeting treasures of gold, ruby, and amethyst, I was painfully aware of the passing of time. On Saturday mornings I would get up early and take him off across the river to see the sun rise over the wooded hills behind New Hope Church. The slant of light in the afternoons reminded me that dark was on the offensive. The days grew shorter and shorter.

Although it was only he and I, Peabody never lost his intense interest in what was going on in the social structure he inhabited. He was glad to see me when I arrived, but as I entered the paddock he would come up with his old attitude of investigating the possibilities of power. He was never threatening. It was simply a statement of his self-confidence, and it pleased me.

I knew, however, that he was lonely.

It was early November when Dr. Powers came for the third Coggins. Although I had tied him before Jim arrived, Peabody jerked back when the truck pulled in and broke the lead line. He spent nearly thirty minutes racing around the paddock before I finally caught him and we could sedate him.

The results of this test were also positive.

The day we received that news I walked the half-mile trail through the woods to the cattle barn. Peabody saw me and began his prancing and snorting. Usually he pranced around me as I crossed the paddock to get the halter. Once I put the halter on him he would quiet down for his grooming.

That day I could not begin to brush him. I buried my face in his mane, knowing the terrible brand near, a deadly snake. I wept bitterly. Here was a beautiful creature, full of life, with love and talent to give. Yet in his blood was something evil that could kill him and others, a lurking that might never strike, but if it did, it would be utterly lethal.

I knew that I would not ask Jim Powers to put Peabody down. I would never let any vet put this horse down. He had fought vets all his life, and it seemed to me a terrible, final indignity to let a vet kill him. For both parties.

That left only the slaughterhouse or keeping him and giving up all our outside horse activities. Although we had been too grieved and shamed to do any competitive trail rides that fall, the latter was not an option. We could not take in boarders or continue the horse camps if we kept Peabody.

They came for Peabody in a big stock trailer, and he walked right on with me. I fed him an extra ration of grain, standing with him in the depths of that dark trailer, stroking him as he buried his nose in the scarred red feed bucket.

Ben, who didn't like to fool with the horses, was with me, and although he didn't like to deal with money matters either, he handled the money that day. The traders gave us a hundred dollars. My father came, quiet moral support. He, Ben, and the two traders stood outside the trailer, talking. No one hurried me.

Finally, I ran my hand one last caress down the smooth, muscular neck, soft with winter coat. I kissed his cheek.

"Good-bye, Mr. Peabody. You're still earning your way, and you'll be with other horses right till the last. There'll be lots of politicking."

I came out of the trailer, and they slammed the gate shut. I handed over the official papers. In a moment the rig was gone.

I was forty years old, but I stood in the road crying like a child. Daddy stood beside me quietly, and in that special way he had, he shared my pain and thought of a way to help it a little.

He put his arm around my waist and said, "Once when one of my cows was killed on the road, an old countryman said to me, 'Y'know, Doc, them as ain't got cain't lose.'"

To love is to have in abundance. And to know, inevitably, the pain of great loss. But the greatest loss would be not to love.

COWS FOR PATIENCE
AND PROFIT

TODAY Lindy Clack came back to pick up my two steers and take them to the cattle sale. This was the second time he had been summoned for this task, and I still blush, thinking of what happened the first time he came. I was more than a little nervous about what might happen the second time, but I had been following Lindy's advice for two weeks and thought it would be possible to load the animals onto his trailer.

Lindy Clack has been raising cattle as well as buying and selling them for other people in Barrow County for about forty years. I had heard a lot about Lindy from my mother and from my sister Susan and her husband, Raymond Reynolds, but I did not know Lindy. My mother thought he was one of the best-looking men in the county. When she was a young woman, going down to the American Legion on a Saturday night with my daddy, she would sometimes mention that Lindy and his wife were there. "That Lindy is better looking than Gregory Peck," she'd say, "and a genuinely nice fellow, too." Susan says he's "deadly good-looking."

I knew my brother-in-law respected Lindy's judgment about cattle. It was he who told me to call Lindy to come get the cows. "He'll do you some good at the sale," Raymond said, "and doesn't charge but six dollars a head."

"Do me some good?" I asked.

"Get you a good price."

That first day Lindy came, I could see why my mother thought him good-looking. Tall, slim, tanned, he wore khaki pants, a plaid shirt, and a Stetson that Susan says he hangs on the gun rack in his truck before he goes into church. He wore also that easy grace of men who are expert at work they love. He was quick with his smile, genuine good humor evident in his handsome face. I figured he had to be in his fifties.

Any hope I had of impressing Lindy with my cattlewoman skills was soon smashed. I had lured the two steers into the small paddock behind the barn only that morning. When I tried to get them to come near the cattle trailer, they knew in their T-bones and sir-loins that it was a monster out to get them. They were not inclined to trust me, who had been neglecting them, albeit kindly, for over a year. Consequently, the two steers behaved like nursery rhyme cows, which is to say they jumped over the moon, or tried to. Although they didn't succeed in jumping over the moon, they did crash through two barn doors, bash in the side of Lindy's truck, bend the bars on the gate of his cattle trailer—all before they tore down the fence in the back paddock. The last we saw of them they were hightailin' it toward the river bottom.

Lindy's rig was already pretty bashed up, so I didn't feel too bad about the new dents, which hardly showed through the crust of manure coating most of the apparatus. What I did feel bad about was I knew he could tell in a second that I was trying to raise cows like my daddy raises them— that is, with as little attention as possible. Lindy is too polite, too much of a gentleman, to point that out.

All he said was, "You got to tame your cows, Sally. Shut 'em up in that big paddock and feed 'em every day, hay and grain. You'll never tame 'em as long as they stay out there in the wide open pasture with all the grass they want, especially now summer's coming. Make 'em depend on you. Look after 'em. When you've got 'em so you can rub their noses, call me again. Prices are good right now, but you don't want to wait too long. Things go dry and people'll be selling."

My face scarlet, I asked, "What do I owe you for your trouble?"

"You don't pay me till I sell your beeves," he said.

The truth be known, I entered the cattle-raising business in hopes of making a little easy money, always a precarious state of mind. I did not know anything about raising cattle. I had heard from a horse dealer that you could buy cows fairly cheap when they are young and sell them for about twice the price or more when they got fatter and bigger, without putting too much time or money into them in the meantime, given the fact that I had plenty of land and grass.

I did not want to look after cows. I had enough to do with looking after ten horses. Unfortunately, horses cannot be considered a cash crop, which is what the horse dealer was trying to impress me with when she told me about cows. Each of the three foals I raised cost me more in breeding fees, feed, vet bills, and training than it would have cost to buy two trained young horses. I manage to make money on horses only by boarding them, by running horse camps for children, or by teaching weekly lessons, activities that require a lot of time and energy. Cattle, I figured, would be different. All cattle do is stand around eating. You don't have to groom them or ride them. Or teach other people to groom them and ride them. There was even the possibility of doubling my money.

So, figuring I could invest about a thousand dollars, I approached my daddy about buying some cows. He agreed to sell me two castrated males six months old and two cows in calf for a total of twelve hundred dollars. I planned to fatten the steers and raise the calves, then breed the cows again, if all went well.

The cows were Black Angus, likely bred to Daddy's big Hereford bull. One of them had a six-month-old calf by her side. Daddy thought she would have another one in about eight months and said he'd come get the current calf "before long." Three months later the calf was still with its mother, growing into a fair-sized heifer. One summer evening, standing on the front porch, I looked out there in the front pasture and thought I could see a tiny calf by the cow's side, along with the big one. Both were trying to nurse.

It was twilight, and I thought my eyes might be deceiving me. I went down to the pasture. No mistake. Our lady had a new baby.

Excited and pleased, I was nevertheless worried about this mama trying to feed two offspring, one of which was practically a grown girl. I thought I could feel the calcium going out of the mama cow's bones. I ran back to the house, called Raymond, and asked him what to do.

"You mean you've got a nine-month-old calf, and now the same cow's got a new calf?" he asked, incredulous.

"That's right," I said, "and I don't know how to separate them. What should I do?"

"I don't know if I can help you with separating them, but I can tell you one thing to be sure to do," Raymond said.

"What's that?"

"Keep that cow!"

Ben came in about then and said not to worry. He would lasso the big calf and get her into the paddock. Ben roped her easy enough—he has good eye-hand coordination—but when she took off with a moon shot in her eye, he made the mistake of trying to hold on. He went airborne about halfway down the hill, rope in hand, but soon let go. When the calf felt his weight go, she hauled buggy over the fence into the back pasture.

I ran right past where Ben landed, not knowing if he was dead or alive but knowing that if I could close the gate into the back pasture, we would have separation accomplished. I made it to the gate before the frantic calf did and voilà! separation achieved, although I suppose strictly speaking serendipity isn't an achievement. Other than minor rope burns, Ben had reentered the atmosphere unharmed.

The poor replaced calf bawled all night long, and we didn't get much sleep. The mama cow was not disturbed by cries of her old baby. She was more interested in the new one. My daddy came and got the big calf the next day, and we were out of those woods.

That's all the trouble the cows caused me. In fact, both of them eventually leapt my fences to get back into Daddy's pasture. He had the bull. Some of his stock were always wandering into my territory, so I figured we were about even on grazing, and he did, too.

The steers have been another story. Part Hereford and part generic, they were earmarked for hamburger. I named them College Fund and Hamburger Steak to remind the girls that they were not to get attached to these animals. Which shows how much I knew about cows. Fat chance that anyone can get attached to creatures as perverse as cows.

I used to think that one of the advantages of having horses was the fact that because of the horse's nature, I was bound to learn patience. My brother John thinks patience may be the greatest virtue, and whether it is the greatest or not, it is surely a great virtue, one that helps us live more calmly with ourselves and more kindly with others. After several years with horses, I thought I had learned how to wait, how to be unperturbed by unexpected outbursts, how to be satisfied with small successes in training, how to relax, tune in to this imposing creature whose thought processes are so different from mine.

Having cows taught me that as professors in patience, horses are rank undergraduates. Cows are the faculty.

Cows are superior to horses in teaching patience because horses at least have memories. They recall that yesterday you gave them feed and were kind. They are willing, after a few days, to bet that you will continue in this behavior. Soon, though they retain their unpredictable base, they can be reasonably predicted. They will go into the stalls you have assigned to them. They respond to rubbed noses, apples, grooming. You can attach a halter to their sweet faces and lead them. You will be reasonably satisfied that patience has paid.

Cows, on the other hand, do not remember anything. If yesterday you fed them and talked sweetly to them, they have a faint recollection, but they're never *sure*. So they hang back. And they freak out if one little thing is different from yesterday, which they can't recall anyway.

You don't know the definition of "freak out" until you have seen a cow perform the maneuver. It's "Katy, bar the door," and that won't do any good. They will crash through barn doors, gates, fences, trucks, tractors, and Stone Mountain because no dim light in their brain tells them they cannot.

So I tried to remember to approach my steers with patience cocked, but the truth is, they got along fine most of the year in the pasture without my having much to say to them. They seemed as happy with that arrangement as I was. I approached them infrequently.

During the winter I fed them, taking hay out most days while the horses were eating in the barn. (I don't put hay out for horses and cows together because the horses won't let the cows eat.) The horses remember about feed time and are usually up at the barn gate, waiting to be let in. The cows, however, have to be called and called. And called.

I remember many a January evening when the wind was howling down the draw and my patience, as well as my fingers, toes, and nose, was dangerously close to being frozen, that I called till my throat ached: "Come on! Come on! Come on!"

When the cows finally heard me and remembered that I might be about food, on the coldest days they galloped up. But on warmer days, they might come part of the way, then stop to stare at me and snort ferociously, as if they had spotted a refugee from a *Star Trek* episode. They could take a long time to recall that I am simply the woman who throws out hay to them. Such behavior does not inspire affection. It makes it easy to call them Hamburger Steak and T-Bone. It fosters the urge to kill.

Sometimes I saw myself standing out there in the cold wind, yelling my throat raw, a woman with two college degrees and a variety of other professional certifications, gainfully employed, and I had to ask myself what I was doing in a barren pasture on a winter evening, calling cows. Occasionally, if the wind was right, I could hear my daddy, up at Horseshoe Bend Farm barn, calling his cows at the same time. His case was more ludicrous than mine, maybe, for he was a prosperous doctor and well past retirement age.

That's when I had to conclude that we aren't too different from our cows. Something in our blood makes us have to get out here and take hold of the food chain, step into a place in it, though the circumstances of our lives do not require us to do that. We distrust the too-easy life, think we'd better be ready for a return to the primitive. Maybe we don't think about this. It's knowledge in our blood, not our brains.

Watching my cows jump back when they could relax and chomp into a bite of Raymond's fine coastal Bermuda hay, I realized that they tune into their survival instincts at every opportunity, assuring themselves that they can get away if they have to.

Their behavior is close kin to what I am doing, raising a few beeves when there is plenty of meat down at the Big Star supermarket and the Golden Corral steak house.

After my cows embarrassed me so much in front of Lindy Clack, I did what he said. It took a while, but I coaxed them back into the big paddock, which is large enough to keep them from feeling hemmed in or trapped, and I visited them morning and night to give them hay, feed, and water. Within three days I had them following me into the little paddock behind the barn. In another three days I had them following me into Dulcie's stall, which Ben had doubled by taking out the partition between it and the next one.

I had to admit, then, of course, that my laziness had caused all the trouble in the first place. I was learning not only patience but humility.

Although the cattle did not show the kind of affection horses are capable of and generous with, I got to liking the two steers, which sentiment I had hoped to avoid, but I reminded myself sternly that they were born for this. A dry spell was bringing the price of beef down. As Lindy had predicted, people were getting rid of cattle they were afraid they would have to feed through a summer drought.

Finally the day came when I could get the steers up almost any time of the day, so I called Lindy. When he pulled up, he stopped at the back door, not wanting to go all the way to the barn if it wasn't necessary, and asked, "Did you get 'em up, Sally?"

"Sure did. They're pretty quiet today."

Lindy had brought a young man to help him. I guessed Lindy didn't have too much confidence in my following his instructions about taming the cows. But at the barn, when he saw how docile the steers were, how they let me come right in their stall with them and rub their faces, he said, "Looks like you've done a good job with your steers."

I flushed with pride at such praise from an expert.

Lindy leaned against the tack room door while his helper backed the trailer into the barn aisle and set the portable barriers to block the spaces between the trailer sides and the barn walls. Lindy directed him to put one of these panels against the gate into the paddock, too.

The steers hesitated a little when I got them into the aisle and shut the stall doors. But they went on trusting me. I urged them gently to go toward the trailer. They went.

They stopped at the threshold, puzzled by having to step up. Then they jitterbugged a little, and cow dung flew. Well, it's not cow dung. Nor is it bull shit. Steer shit? Whatever you call it, some of it hit Lindy. I remembered that Susan said she'd never seen Lindy dirty, not even dusty. Uh-oh.

He said, not as a curse, but matter-of-factly, politely, "I'm not going to put up with that shit."

And he didn't. He closed in the back panel, took a pitchfork off its hook on the wall, and gently prodded the two animals. They got on the trailer, and his helper slammed the gate.

I don't know if you can prod gently with a pitchfork.

Anyway, the steers were loaded, and Lindy was pleased. He was so pleased that he told me a story.

"This just goes to show you that what the old mule trader said was right. You know, I used to go down to the mule-trading barn in Atlanta regular, and most of the old traders were gypsies. Of course, they're all gone now, but these gypsies, they knew stock. And they all wore suits to the sale. They were good con men. Whenever one would come up to you, he'd always put his arm around you and say, 'How's your daddy?'— trying to get to be your friend, you know. Well, there was this one fellow, he was Irish, with big puffy lips, always smoking a cigar, and he had a red face. Well, he'd always say, 'Feed your stock, son, and they'll know ye. Feed your stock, son.'"

I loved that story. It made me want to go to a cattle sale, and I said so.

"You just let me know when you want to go, and we'll go," Lindy said, and I knew he meant it.

Lindy got in the truck and cranked it up before he said again, "You've done a good job with your steers, Sally, a good job." He paused, reflected, probably decided he'd better not give a woman too much cow praise, and finished: "Of course you had good steers to begin with."

Raymond called me every day after that to find out what I got for the steers. It took about a week for the check to come—$1,255. We paid the sale barn $17 and Lindy his $6 per head to take them there, fees that were subtracted before we were paid. I was more than satisfied. I had made back my investment and still had two cows and two calves.

About a year later, Daddy's health got to a point where he felt he ought to get out of the cattle business, and I sold my cows when he sold his herd. I felt it only fair that Daddy have the calves, but I made almost $1,400 on the cows, so in the end, I did double my money. Not without a few crashes here and there, but my patience and humility quotients went up, and I got to know Lindy Clack. I figure I made more than a respectable return on my stock investment.

SOMEONE ELSE'S COWS

ALTHOUGH I have raised only six cows on Somechoes Farm, I have enjoyed the numerous cows of serious farmers near me—that is, of neighbor Del Beckemeyer; my father, A. B. Russell; and my brother-in-law, Raymond Reynolds.

Wait a minute: I have to admit that none of those men are serious about raising cows. I think you are serious about raising cows only when they are your chief source of income. Del, A.B., and Ray all have other incomes, generally comfortable, but I guess we could say they raise cows in serious numbers.

The reason I enjoy their cows more than I do my own is that I have no responsibility toward their vast herds (up to 250 cattle), other than that of a helpful neighbor. I ride my horses among them, appreciating the mama cows' serenity and pride regarding their babies, admiring the gleaming fluffy coats of new calves and sleekly shining coats of fattened older calves, breathing the good cow grass-milk-meat perfume, without a twinge of worry about the price of grain, where I'll get the money to fertilize the pastures, or what beef is bringing at the sale.

Sometimes stock escapes to my pasture or, more frequently, to the roadside grass that is, in the opinion of cattle, going to waste. I am glad the cattle like the roadside grass because I, as the person nearest their fenced pastures, have the pleasure of herding them back to their home ground. I early discovered that this task conducted on horseback provides the most pleasure, but I don't mind doing it on foot if I don't already have a horse under me. The cattle are used to being chased back home, and if you sort of suggest to them that it's time to get going in that direction, they will eventually head off amiably. All you have to do is get peaceful inside yourself and be willing to allow them the time to figure out what you want. This may appear a good little stretch of time in the age of copier machines at a zillion copies a minute, but it's not the swish of a tail at a fly when viewed in the time frame of the evolution of cattle. Most cows will get it figured out quickly by their time stick, say five to fifteen minutes. For the ones who don't, who go crashing off in the opposite direction, you have to be philosophical, keep walking with the others toward home. The strays wind up with the herd because cattle, like horses, are herd animals.

When you have a horse to help you, there are hardly ever any strays. Or more accurately, when you are there to help the horse, there are hardly ever any strays. A good cow horse will do the job almost without a rider. The rider is there only to get the horse's attention focused on the job. A horse on his own will not pay much attention to cows, but with a rider to give him a hint, he may well find them entertaining to boss around.

The best cow horse I ever had was Easter, a chestnut-colored Morgan/quarter horse gelding that came to us as a three-year-old. He had had excellent initial handling and training, which, combined with a good nature and comfortable gaits, made him a pleasure to ride. He had a tendency to shy, but I could often predict what he would choose to find spooky, and if I actively ignored tree-stump timber wolves and other death-trap alarms such as whitened bones of cattle, he would go along okay. When he did stop dead in the trail, his mind trembling at the bolt switch, I would try to talk him out of his grizzly bear or chide him for cowardice. He was reasonable enough to make this approach successful.

When Easter first came to the farm, I rode him on our land, which at that time did not harbor any cattle, for the first few rides. His shying improved with each ride, but it remained obvious enough to make me wonder what he might do when he saw his first cows. I headed out for Daddy's cow-rich pastures one morning with some trepidation.

No sooner had I passed the Johnsons' house than I saw about a dozen cows out on the road because a gate was down. Easter had his ears forward and his head up, watching those cows, but he did not seem nervous about them. I am nervous about cows on the road, so I decided to ask him to help me get them back through the gate.

It didn't take Easter long to understand what we were trying to do, and he was able, to my surprise, to focus on more cows at once than I could. If one tried to slip past us, he'd pivot to head her back to the herd, then pivot again to catch another one trying to get away. I just sat there, and the cows gave up rather quickly before his agile presence. Within a few minutes we had them safely back in the pasture, the gate closed. As we resumed our ride, Easter pranced across the pasture as if he knew he'd done a good job. After that, whenever there was serious cow herding to be done, I took Easter.

My favorite thing to do with somebody else's cows, however, is to spy their new calves, in spring preferably, but any time will do. Most calves are born in the spring, and although I am pretty good at finding pleasureful events, I have not discovered many more delightful than riding a good horse across the pasture counting new calves on a cool morning when pale lavender flowers hardly bigger than grains of sand are blooming thick on winter cow droppings and dew lies like starshine on grass, flowers, and dung.

Whether the calves are curled asleep in the sun, which they often are, or whether they are nuzzling their mothers' milk bags with insistence, which they often are, their vitality and beauty is so powerful I almost feel the world turning. Remembering Wordsworth, I feel the newborns "trailing clouds of glory." The peace from which the calves emerge into the noisy, bright world remains in their relaxed attitudes, their languid eyes, their soft, clean coats. Curiosity will take the place of peace, and fear must arrive if they are to survive, but the first morning of a calf's life is a glimpse into that dimension of beauty and safety we call glory.

The look of pride and puzzlement on the cow's face is another reason to enjoy new calves. I am willing to bet the cow is the embodiment of what most of us feel about motherhood: "Look at this wonderful (literally: full of wonder) creature. I did it, though I'm not exactly sure how and I'm a little worried about taking care of it. Nevertheless, I am, and it is full of wonder."

The new mother naturally is wary of anyone getting too close to her baby, but from horseback I have a good view of the pair without getting too close. I am careful not to frighten them or, rather, not to make the mother nervous. The calf is not afraid of anything at this point, which makes his mother nervous enough. She knows danger is out there.

As the calves grow, the beauty of their untarnished coats disappears. The first rains after a calf is born initiate her into the marred beauty of earth. But as their curiosity and their friendships with each other grow, young calves continue to be a joy to watch. Their playfulness brings laughter, comfort, a kind of peace.

My favorite thing NOT to do with other people's cattle is to confront their bulls. Spending as much time as I do in the pastures, however, it is inevitable that I meet bulls from time to time.

Del Beckemeyer and Raymond Reynolds are careful farmers, paying attention to the right time for particular farm chores. This is not the case with A.B., who tends to wait for circumstances to remind him that a thing needs to be done. For example, when all his cows are out in the road, he knows the fence needs mending.

Del and Raymond castrate the male calves early in their lives, perhaps the first week or two. Waiting to castrate a calf makes the job more difficult, and the longer you wait the more difficult it becomes, until it becomes impossible for you to do without a veterinarian. Nevertheless, A.B. will neglect this chore until his fellows are several months old. Consequently, he usually has a few young bulls in his herd, fellows too tough to be castrated. His Big Daddy bull does not take any insubordination from the bullish youngsters, but now and again, one gets uppity enough about his testosterone supply to make the pasture dangerous.

In general the papa bull's testosterone supply does not spell danger, except in cases of particularly vicious bulls. Fortunately, you will never mistake a papa bull for anything less lethal. He's the burliest, biggest thing in the pasture, his ponderous supply bags are evident, and his entire demeanor says, "Don't mess with me." Give him a wide berth, and he won't pay much attention to you. He's more interested in when he's going to next use some of that testosterone.

With uppity youngsters, such is not the case. The papa bull keeps them away from the fertile cows, and they soon tire of messing around with each other. Frustrated, they may learn that it's fun to charge at things, including each other. It's my personal opinion that this charging gives them a rush of adrenaline that offsets their testosterone attention-getting mechanism. They can look like steers or heifers from a distance. You might get uncomfortably close to one before you know it.

You would think A.B. would have learned to castrate his calves from what happened to him and a young Black Angus bull.

He was alone at the big barn at Horseshoe Bend late one evening, checking on a couple of young bulls he had up for Lindy Clack to take to the cattle sale. They had grown too big to castrate without the vet and likely big enough to impregnate cows. A.B. never did like to pay a vet if he didn't have to. The young bulls would have to go.

He had been feeding them for several days, and they were pretty tame. That evening he got careless about watching where they were in the lot and what they were doing while he was in there. He liked to have a drink of vodka when he was at the barn. Maybe he'd emptied the vodka bottle a little too far down. Anyway, he wasn't paying attention to the bulls when he opened the gate and went in the lot with them.

In his mid-seventies, A.B. had a fibrillation, an irregular heartbeat. As a doctor he was too inclined to treat himself, which meant his choice was to go along with his offbeat heart. I reminded him of the French proverb that says the doctor who treats himself has a fool for a patient, but he didn't pay any attention to me. He said he knew about pacemakers and shock treatments for his condition, but the thing didn't bother him that much. He took a nitroglycerin tablet now and again.

The evening I'm telling about, he checked the water supply for his young bulls and saw they needed some. He had to leave the lot to get the hose, thread it through the slats in the barn side, turn the faucet on, then come back around to put the hose in the trough. When he'd done all that, he started back through the gate, a long, metal five-bar one, and somehow it slipped out of his hand and swung all the way back. He walked over to pull it closed. He had closed it about two-thirds of the way when he realized one of the bulls was charging. He knew without thinking that he could not step aside in time. But A.B. is a survivor. Whirling, he gave a loud shout and threw up his arms, startling the bull into swerving. A.B. felt the animal's hot breath on his bare arm as the bull swept past.

He did not remember how he got out of the lot, but he remembered leaning against the walnut tree next to the corn bin, breathing hard, waiting for his body to stop trembling. When it did, he noticed something peculiar: his heart was beating regularly. No fibrillation. Just his old, steady beat.

Knowing that it is almost impossible for a person to take his own pulse accurately, A.B. drove to the hospital in town and asked to have an EKG. It revealed that his heartbeat was normal for a man his age.

He came by my house the next day to tell me about this phenomenon, laughing about his method of treatment but glad it worked.

"Sounds to me like the French proverb was proved right again," I said, "but I'm glad you lived to tell the tale."

It was a year or so later that another one of those testy young bulls charged me and April, Dulcie's blue-roan daughter, when I was first training her. April was cheeky herself, a little spoiled, the truth be known, because we petted her so much when she was little, forgetting that what might feel okay from a foal will knock you over from a horse. Yet April never offered to buck or rebel in any other way when we started riding her. She was as willing and cooperative as her mother.

Nevertheless, a young horse has a lot to learn, and I prefer that charging bulls not be on the syllabus too soon. I kept a sharp lookout for the older males that spring as April and I took little rides each afternoon. I had spotted one good-looking chestnut-colored fellow who had such broad shoulders and such a shapely body that I could see why he was full of himself. He eyed me, no matter whether I was riding, on foot, or in the truck. A time or two he pawed the ground and snorted. He was itching for trouble. I kept out of his way.

Then one day April and I came upon a little crowd of Daddy's cows that had gotten out of his pasture and into Del Beckemeyer's vineyard. In the herd was this uppity young bull. In Del's pasture next to the grapevines, his two horses were galloping up and down, excited by the cows and by April's approach. The wisest thing to do at that moment was to head for home and come back in the truck to herd cows.

But the cows were in the vineyard, it was spring, and they might decide to dine on the tender shoots of the vines. It was altogether possible they would trample and destroy the grapevines. I had spent too many blissful autumn mornings eating Del's scuppernongs to take that chance. I told April it was time for her to learn that she was ahead of cows in the pecking order, including cheeky young bulls. Pointing her toward the herd, I gave them their orders: "Get along now, doggies! Get along! There's plenty of grass in your pastures! Get along now!"

They headed agreeably toward the road for a few yards. Del's horses kept policing their fence line, one of them with a high, loud whinnying. April had a lot to distract her, but she zeroed in on the herding job and soon had the group tight and aimed toward A.B.'s gate. I was watching the young bull, trying not to let my nervousness communicate to April.

Suddenly, he slipped away from the others and whirled to face us, pawing the ground.

"Now get on along there, young fella. We're not afraid of you. Get on along!" I said, but my voice croaked. I was not at all sure this statement about not being afraid was true.

April was sure. She let out a saucy whinny and headed right for that bull at a high-steppin' trot, her neck arched, her entire self indicating that she was not one for funny business.

The bull dropped his aggressive stance and trotted back to the herd, head down. He looked the other way while I opened the pasture gate to let the group through and scampered away from us as soon as he could.

I was glad to have proved that a saucy young horse is saucier than a saucy young bull, but I recommended to Daddy that he make hamburger out of that fellow as soon as possible.

I enjoy messing with other people's cows, but messing with their bulls has served to make me sure of one thing: I never want to keep a bull.

I have never wanted to keep a stallion, either, and for the same reason: too much testosterone in too much unpredictable muscle, bone, and flesh.

Or maybe it's too much testosterone in too much *predictable* muscle, bone, and flesh.

WHY I KEEP STOCK

A DARK FEBRUARY NIGHT. The fog is so thick that coming back from Gainesville from my night class, I have to creep along after I turn onto Mulberry Road. Turning into my driveway, I jump a rabbit who zigzags up the track in front of my car.

Although he may be panicked in his individual rabbit brain, his age-old rabbit blood tells him that zigging and zagging might confuse his enemies and compensate for rabbits' lack of speed. This poor rabbit does not seem to be moving fast, certainly not compared to what this Honda can do. Yet his zigzag maneuver is one of the few defensive tricks he has in his evolutionary hat. It doesn't do him much good. The average rabbit lives about a year, if his luck holds.

I slow and let him figure out that he'd best head for the hills. He dives through the hog-wire fence, probably leaving a little of his fur, but thinking (can a rabbit think in any sense of the word?) he's a lucky so-and-so tonight.

The rabbit's real ace in the survival game, the only important game on the planet, is his ability to reproduce. Give him sufficient ground cover and some vegetation to gnaw, and he and she will make almost as many rabbits as you, the fox, the hawk, and the owl can eat.

Maybe having a life of mostly lovemaking makes the short life of a rabbit worth it. And other creatures benefit from rabbit love: fox, hawks, owls. Although humankind in this part of the world is currently ignorant of the delectable dishes rabbits can star in, this has not always been the case. Thankful that nature produced rabbits in abundance, we used to eat them in the South. But I haven't had a good rabbit stew since the autumn night about seven years ago I accidentally ran over a rabbit on Mulberry Road, again coming home from a night class.

I could tell that he had jumped square into my bumper and that the tires never touched him. So I stopped, got out to look, and found he was, indeed, dead of a blow to the head. Although I knew the crows would enjoy the rabbit for breakfast next morning, I decided to enjoy him myself. Dwain was at home then, and when I arrived with a rabbit, still warm, he was happy to clean it.

I reported this occurrence the next day at school at the lunch table in the faculty dining room, reveling in the fact that we would have rabbit stew for supper. A colleague shook her head and said, "Sally, you are the only person I know in the world who would do that."

While I'm pretty sure by "that" she meant "eat roadkill," I took her remark as a compliment.

As I park tonight in the backyard, I see the light on in the barn, which means that Sharon has left horses up and I will have to go down to let them out. I don't mind. I have to feed them all in the morning at 7:00, and so I'll leave their water buckets cleaned and filled tonight.

I'm tired, however, having been up and at work either writing or teaching since 5:00 A.M., and it's now nearly 10:00 P.M. Because I have two fifty-pound bags of feed in the back of the car (bad weather is in the forecast), I have the perfect excuse to drive to the barn, so I do, without going into the house to change clothes first.

Sure enough, Dulcie and Pookie are still up. They take longer to eat than the others. Sharon must have had to go to work before they finished. I don't mind having to let them out. It's a luxury to have a horse to hug on a cold and foggy night.

Not that Dulcie cares whether I hug her or not. Self-sufficient, she prefers her own society even in the pasture with other horses, though a more willing horse for working whatever job given her does not exist. Dulcie may be the definition of integrity. I rub her long old nose, warm my fingers in the thick gray coat beneath her mane. She gets the thickest coat of any of the horses, which is a good thing because she never has extra fat on her bones. I check to see that she has eaten all her supper. In her old age, she has had trouble with chewing, but tonight she has finished her grain and most of her hay. As I lead her out, I note again that arthritis is worsening in her hind legs. It takes her a minute to get them going.

When I let Pookie out, the young fella trots off to find the others, stepping high past Dulcie.

Then I clean the stalls. In my good shoes, I try not to step in anything too serious, which is a challenge because it has been raining, and Dulcie's stall has a leak at the back, where she courteously deposits her droppings in one spot.

Pookie is not courteous about his droppings. The other stalls are clean because the horses did not stay in them long. I have filled the wheelbarrow but decide not to empty it in the manure pile behind the barn in the dark and my good shoes. I park it out of the way.

I wash the eight buckets I will need in the morning. Next I have to lug the sacks of feed to the feed room. This is not easy because I am tired, the barn aisle is muddy, and the wheelbarrow is full and thus cannot be used to help negotiate weighty feed sacks down the little slope from the car to the barn.

I manage to grab the top sack out of the back seat with a good grip around the middle, as if picking up a fat child by the waist. Having opened the feed room door and the feed barrel in anticipation, when I reach the feed room, I find it fairly easy to heave the bag over the edge of the barrel, keeping it "head up," the right direction for easy opening.

Back to the car for the second bag. This time I do not get a good grip and have to put it down on the seat again, stand up, take a deep breath, grab again. Wondering as I lift whether I can hold steady enough to negotiate the distance to the feed room, I experience a moment of sharp clarity: I understand in my bones and blood why ancient tribes could not keep old people around after their strength was gone. I understand what it means "to be a burden" in the strictest sense of the phrase. I *know* that in lives that required physical strength from dawn to dusk, what a burden anyone would be who could not pull at least some weight. I understand, too, the vague fear of becoming a burden that runs in the veins of most of us today as we age, even in a society that has chosen to help the unfit survive, a society that takes on anyone from premature babies to drug addicts. We call it "social consciousness," pat ourselves on the back, feel virtuous, but are we perhaps being foolishly complacent?

I manage the second bag into the feed barrel while fearing becoming a burden and thinking that complacency means being comfortable when a bit of discomfort is in order. Unwise complacency may be an automatic product of too much comfort.

I close and latch the feed room door with stiff fingers, flick off the lights, see myself shivering in damp shoes in the muddy barn aisle, and laugh at the idea of being too comfortable. But let the truth be spoken: we are too comfortable today, too far from having to produce food to recognize how basic its production is. Or how tyrannical daily feeding, milking, cleaning can be.

As I get in the car, I admit that nurturing my stock causes me some inconvenience, but I do not depend on the few horses and cows we have for food, and so this inconvenience is of my own making, cannot be called tyranny. When the hawks and the foxes got the last of my hens, I abandoned that link of the food chain. I am free to choose food chains like A&P and Winn-Dixie. My life is ringed with safeguards.

I back the car up the hill to the house—glad Gus taught me that trick with a front-wheel-drive car. With the mud there is tonight, I might never get out frontward.

Bone tired, I crawl into bed, thinking about that ol' rabbit curled up in the brier patch down near the mailbox. I remember Julian Jackson's tales of depression-era rabbit hunts that gladdened the Jacksons' otherwise meatless table. I think about the cows and horses in the pasture and our shared history. I recognize self-sufficiency, strength, and wisdom earned from relationships with wild and domesticated creatures. I fall asleep secure in the deep-down toughness of the human animal.

A GIFT OF HORSES

WHEN MY CHILDREN WERE YOUNG, they asked for horses, and with no idea of the danger, the expense, or the rewards, I gave horses.

Eleven-year-old Nan began the passion with a bay Welsh/Thoroughbred pony called Mr. Peabody. In spite of falls and early personality clashes, with the help of a good riding instructor, she learned to ride safely, to care for her horse, and to respect his nature.

Inspired by Nan's tenacity and enthusiasm, her eight-year-old sister, Jessica, was riding within six months, and so was I.

Looking back, I don't know how I managed to buy three horses that year on a teacher's salary, but I did it, and from the beginning our horses returned a thousandfold our investments of dollars, time, energy, and love.

We knew the richness of their diverse personalities: bossy Mr. Peabody, sturdy Yo-yo, genteel Scout.

We began to appreciate the immense dimensions possible in horse-human friendships.

We learned the responsibility of dominance and the value of patience in any partnership.

Through recovery from accidents that included broken bones and a brain hemorrhage, we learned that when the need for courage and love is great, so is the capacity for them.

We learned the importance and the joy of equilibrium.

Priceless lessons.

We reveled in horse paraphernalia. Saddles, bridles, lead lines, blankets, buckets, curries, brushes, hoof picks—these never stayed stabled. They littered the car, the porch, the house. They adorned our lives.

Barn chores were our recreation. We loved the perfume of feeds and hay and the sound of the horses snorting over their rations. We hung an old farm bell in the hayloft, and the horses learned quickly to come when we rang it. The ponderous *clang-clang-clang,* accompanying the muted drumming of hooves as the horses cantered across the pasture at mealtime, was music in the air.

Bordered on all sides by three thousand acres of wilderness and farm trails, we enjoyed an unequaled riding environment. On horseback we knew the deer, turkeys, foxes, raccoons, owls, and hawks of this world as we could not have known them otherwise.

The children named the trails: Tortoise Shell Trail, because it was littered with tortoise shells bleached by time and weather; the Unicorn Trail, because there was a tree magically shaped like a horse's face but with a "horn." We touched the unicorn's nose for good luck each time we rode by. There were Road Trot Run and Hand Gallop Hill in the open pastures, places for speed. We prized the River Trail, winding two miles in the deep woods, keeping pace with the meandering Mulberry River. We thought nothing of riding ten miles on an afternoon.

When I try to describe the affection, the unity, and the joy we knew sharing the love of horses, I remember an evening in late summer about a year after horses came into our lives.

There had been a thunderstorm, but the sky was clearing. A lingering mass of clouds draped the western horizon with purple and coral. As the evening deepened and cooled, a mist enveloped the pastures and woods, a veil of peace.

Jessica and I were walking to the barn to turn the horses out.

"Let's ride, Mama," she said.

Slipping bridles on Yo-yo and Scout, both paints, we climbed aboard bareback. Nan, seeing us from the back porch, ran to join us. Mr. Peabody proudly took the lead.

Leaving the barnyard, we stepped into the mist in silence. Ahead of me, the little girls in shorts and halters and black English riding helmets, bareback on their ponies, created a unique and indefinable harmony, like the gentle music of wind chimes.

As we threaded the lush green pasture within its blue veil of mist and almost-night, Jessica began to sing, her young voice silver and true: "Sing Allelujah to the Lord! Sing Allelujah to the Lord!"

Nan and I joined in her song.

By taking in boarders and running a small horse camp for three years, we expanded our equine family. This work with a variety of horses taught us to be flexible and to be sensitive to the character of the individual, whether horse or human. Sometimes we had twenty horses on the place and a dozen campers. We came to appreciate the patience of horses, their willingness, their generosity.

Then the opportunity came to spend a year in France, and we took it. We found a young couple to live in the house and care for a few horses. When we came home, our equine friends were waiting.

But the little girls had disappeared. Instead there were two teenagers active at school, working part-time jobs, driving the car, going out on dates. Although delighted to be riding again, I missed my buddies. When I began endurance riding, the girls cheered, but they did not ride.

Not to grieve, I told myself. This is the way of the world.

It really is hard to keep 'em down on the farm after they've seen Paris. After only one semester in Winder, Nan went back to France to study and travel before beginning college at the University of Wyoming. Jessica finished high school in three years, then spent a summer traveling the western United States on a University of Georgia geology course. She fell in love with rocks, tectonic plates, deserts. Because she was so young, I decreed she had to start college at my school, Gainesville College, and she was happy with that decision. In the summer she went back out West and dug for dinosaur bones with Jack Horner, whom she had met on her UGA trip. After two years at Gainesville, she took off for Colorado College.

At Christmas of her senior year, Nan announced her engagement. In May she would be married in Nebraska, one week after graduation. I was happy for her. I liked her young man. This, too, was the way of the world.

I wanted to do something special, the three of us, before she embarked on this next life step, and I wanted this special event to involve horses. For auld lang syne.

Colorado . . . Wyoming . . . the heart of the West. Surely I could find a place for us to spend a couple of days riding.

When I heard about the McNamara Ranch in Florissant, Colorado, not far from Jessica's school, I knew I had found our place. Although her main livelihood is a small sheep-raising operation, Sheila McNamara will take guests, three or four at a time, on trail rides. Her brochure promised serenity, solitude, the dignity of mountains.

The last six miles to the ranch are on a dirt road. Mountains and nothing else on every side. Did we miss the turn? Where are we? See any war parties? No, but there's a wagon train. Whose idea was this, anyway?

Then we top a little rise, and beside a lake glinting green in the afternoon sun, a cozy, cabin-like house and a gray barn are reigning. About fifty sheep graze in a field beside the house.

Sheila McNamara, stocky and trim in a black sweatshirt, jeans, and cowboy boots and hat, is in the yard. "I see you found us!" She shakes hands all around and introduces her fifteen-year-old daughter, Mandy.

"Mandy's been helping me tack up," Sheila says. "Why don't you go right in and change, and we'll have plenty of time for a ride before supper."

The cabin is pleasant with high, light-funneling windows. The golden pine walls of our room and the beds adorned with sheepskins and traditional woolen blankets of Indian design are utterly appropriate.

At the barn, lambs and horses are at home with each other. The horses are Squaw, a 13.3 pony who is so speckled she ought to be in a Buffalo Bill show; Chris, a tall, hunter-type Appaloosa, a/k/a Sparky because, Sheila says, he will dance for about five steps when you first mount; Teddy, a half-Arab gray whose lean, long muscles and sturdy legs charm this endurance rider's heart; and Pridenjoy, Sheila's chestnut quarter horse, whose manner and appearance leave no doubt that he deserves his name.

Because Nan is shortest, she chooses Squaw. Jessica likes hunters, so she opts for Chris. I am set to condition Teddy for an endurance season.

We ride out through the grazing sheep. Chris does, indeed, dance for a few steps. I feel proud of Jessica's relaxed seat and quiet hands. Reassured, Chris settles. Nan's pony dances a bit, too, but the girl is not alarmed. She knows how to ride.

Starting at nine thousand feet altitude, we climb what Georgians call a mountain, but I suspect westerners classify it as a hill. Stopping at the top, we gaze across an undulating range, beyond which mountains rim the world. The nearer peaks are brown and bare. Distant ones are snowcapped.

Descending, we cross open country, while Sheila names the hills: Eagle Rock and Castle Rock, Saddle Mountain and Mount Pisgah, Pikes Peak and the Sangre de Cristo Mountains. Her words ring in the shining air.

Trotting, our horses are eager and cooperative. Sheila leads the first canter. I bring up the rear from an old habit of checking out the group.

Nan drops back to trot beside me, smiling. "Mama, this is wonderful. I didn't know it would be so intimate. What a beautiful present!"

It takes Teddy a bit longer to settle than the others, but Jess helps me pace the horse. We are soon cantering in cadence and glowing with the pleasure of marshaling the strength of horses.

A red-tailed hawk takes off from a pine beside the mountain trail, flashing his burnished feathers. Jack rabbits bound across the range. Near an elegant home built against a hillside, three chestnut Hanoverians thunder across their pasture to inspect us. We pause to say hello.

As the sun is setting and the night chill invades the air, we trot-canter for two miles, then dismount a half mile from home to walk in.

Our blood is singing with the exertion and thrill of riding such horses through such spectacular scenery.

Sheila promises the next day will be better. We don't think this is necessary or even possible.

In the barn, unsaddling and putting away tack, rationing hay and water, the girls croon to their horses as they always have. I smile at the murmurings: "Good girl! . . . What a nice pony! . . . Thanks for the ride, Sparky. . . . I love you."

When we open the front door, enticing odors engulf us. Neighbor Nancy has been at work. We are treated to a royal feast of roast lamb, onions, mashed potatoes, broccoli and cauliflower, crisp salad, fresh pineapple, and homemade banana bread. For dessert: Texas-sized slices of carrot cake right here in Colorado.

Afterward, we go back to the barn to say good night to the horses, but we think it prudent not to tell them how much supper we ate. We walk a little way down the quiet road, stopping to listen to a night bird's unfamiliar trill.

Deliciously chilled, we come back to the toasty house to crawl under our blankets and sheepskins.

Next morning we are up early to trailer fifteen miles to the Dome Rock Wildlife Refuge. There we are joined by Steve, a vintage cowboy: weathered face and Stetson, red flannel shirt, jeans, boots, prodigious silver belt buckle. He is riding a liver chestnut Morgan mare that could not be easier on the eyes. His ornate Western saddle with flashy stirrups and his green plaid blanket, red fringed to perfection, are happy reminders of the human talent for decoration.

After tacking up, we mount and climb to a breath-stopping view. Is this heaven? The world is all sky and stone, gigantic stones of dusky coral, stones heaped into mighty pyramids, the casual architecture of the gods. In the distance, peaks of snow and sapphire write the horizon.

We wind down into a gorge that is, geologically speaking, not far from becoming a valley. Trotting, cantering, we cross again and again the singing waters of Four-Mile Creek. Sometimes we travel a narrow trail along the hillside. Other times we flash through willow rushes beside the creek, where crowds of tiny yellow butterflies feast on willow bounty.

I watch the girls, confident and happy with Squaw and Chris. I know my own joy in Teddy's long, inexhaustible trot. In this vast land where majesty begins, nothing could be better than being horse and human together. I am the richest woman in the world.

We soon start another steep climb and slow to a walk. We are winding up the mountain, and there is not one inch of the trail that is not beautiful.

Pine and aspen line the creek banks. At this altitude, the aspen are frothy with first green. We come into a high meadow where a lake gleams and pines parade the hills. Crumbling ruins of a cabin's chimney stand solemn witness to the power of mountain weather.

When we reach a dirt road, we move out again. Although we are still climbing, the road circles the mountain, and the ground is excellent. Teddy feels so good she thinks about bucking. No one can blame her.

Jessica canters up beside me, her eyes shining. "Can I have this for my graduation next year?"

We reach an overlook where the view again stops us.

"I wonder how high we are," Sheila says.

"I'm *really* high," I say.

At lunch I am proud of the competent way the girls tether their mounts, making sure they are secure before taking refreshment. We delight in thick-sliced ham and turkey sandwiches, bananas, chocolate chip cookies, and ice water—heavenly fare.

Siesta time is natural after such a morning and such a lunch. Every spot is comfortable. Stretching out, we doze in the sunshine.

Although it appears possible this *is* heaven, we are not yet permanent residents. Earth is a place of promises, and we have made ours. Too soon we must start down.

By the time we reach the valley floor, Nan and Jess sense that their mounts are beginning to tire. Teddy (the endurance horse) is still eager. Leaving the others, we canter ahead.

When I stop and turn to look back, I see in the distance the Morgan, the two Appaloosas, and the quarter horse walking across a hill, craggy stones rising behind them against the blue sky. The riders wave. The landscape radiates the history of the horse in this country, its history in our family.

GODSPEED, DULCINEA

To THOSE who love horses, there is nothing as heart-wrenching as a horse down.

To find that flowing grace, that strength in lightness, that four-footed, tail-flying defiance of gravity stopped cold, earthbound in a fierce (they are always fierce) struggle against injury or illness is our ultimate nightmare.

Even when we expect such a situation, as at the time of birth, a horse on her side makes our adrenaline charge.

Finding a horse down as part of a natural death, a death we ought to expect, does not change our terror, for humanity is a species that persists in finding death unnatural.

So it was the afternoon I came home from school to the sickening sight of Dulcinea stretched out in the sun in high grass, halfway across the big front pasture. Other than the two times she birthed foals during her fifteen years on the farm, I had never seen her lie down.

My heart leapt into high gear so fast I could not think straight. I wanted to jump out of the car and race across the pasture in dress shoes, silk blouse, and skirt. Knowing that doing so would waste energy in short supply under Georgia's hot June sun, I mastered the impulse with difficulty and raced upstairs instead to change into jeans and T-shirt.

Dulcie, long the beloved and honored senior citizen of our farm, had grown thin of late in spite of high summer grass, and she had been coming slower and slower to the barn each evening for her grain. I could not say this turn of events was unexpected.

Dulcie was an unregistered saddlebred, so I was not sure how old she was. When she came to us out of a hunt stables near Atlanta, they said she was thirteen. Knowing how people selling horses of her ilk tend to make them younger than they are, I felt she was probably nearer fifteen. At any rate, she had to be approaching thirty now, a venerable age for any horse. Nevertheless, grabbing a halter and lead rope, I headed across the pasture, hoping for an injury. I wanted to see a gash, blood, a swollen leg, anything that would say, "This is reparable. Help her to the barn. Call the vet."

There was no sign of injury. Covered with black flies, Dulcie could not lift her head, though the matted, bruised grass gave testimony to her struggles to rise. Her breath came hard.

Foolishly I shooed the flies away and knelt beside her head as they settled again.

Her sweet eye cleared. It was for her sweet eyes we had named her Dulcinea.

"All right, sweetheart," I said, hoping my voice would not break, "we'll see this out together."

Jim Powers had stopped vetting horses. The nearest large-animal vet was thirty miles away. It would take probably two hours to get him. I did not think we had that long.

I went for a sponge, a bucket of water, and a sheet to help against the flies, sobbing all the way to the barn and halfway back down the hill. Respect for the dignified spirit now facing the Great Indignity dried my tears before I reached the mare. Dulcie was the soul of dignity, not the kind of horse to merit blubbering.

After spreading the sheet over her body, I knelt to sponge her face. Her eye had clouded in my short absence, but it cleared a little as I sponged, and I fancied she knew me. The water ran off her cheek and puddled at my knees.

"It's all right, girl, it's all right. You'll be running soon. You'll leave this old shell behind, and you'll challenge Pegasus. I know it's been three years since you've run anywhere, but it's like riding a bicycle. You don't forget how. You'll gallop ahead of the horses of Apollo. That magnificent tail of yours will make them jealous. But be careful. It's best not to make the gods jealous."

When the bucket was empty, I sat down next to her, trying to position myself so that my shadow would shade her face. It was all I could do.

I put my head on my damp knees and grew still. When we can do nothing to change a situation, it is good to be still.

In stillness I became softly aware that my horse was not a bony lump of tired hide, wasted flesh, and shallow, rattling breath. Instead, she was, above all, a spirit rare and fine that had enriched my life and would continue to enrich it.

The great Greek horseman Xenophon wrote that the horse is the noblest creature man has conquered. An extravagant statement, but I do not dispute it. The inherent nobility of horses commands our love and respect. This nobility is manifested in their cheerful willingness to contribute their rich birthrights of affection, patience, loyalty, generosity, and strength to our service. It is close to what the French call noblesse oblige, but with horses there is no need for the sense of obligation. What they do, they do naturally. I return to the word *inherent*.

Dulcie was a horse of this kind of goodness. On this farm, she did whatever job we asked of her and did it with skill, industry, goodwill, magnanimity.

Although she came as a candidate for a camp horse, she was too hyper at first for the youngsters. I, however, fell in love with her eager spirit and claimed her for my trail horse. A conservative estimate would put the miles we covered together at three thousand, most pure pleasure trail, though a few were competitive trail miles. Never did she sulk, wring her tail, or balk on our daily rides of five, ten, or more miles. She shied once. That was the day we crossed the river and cantered out of the trees into Thad Perkins's pasture and saw five lightning-struck cows lying dead on the hillside. A legitimate shy.

She crossed creeks, swam rivers, and negotiated any other tight trail corner with confidence. The first time I showed her the Atlantic Ocean and asked her to go in, she hesitated long enough for me to say, "It's okay, girl. We don't have to swim this one." Then she splashed in among the waves with quiet dignity that balanced my glee. On the beach she of the long walk paced herself beside me while I searched crusty patches of shells for those delicate beauties called angels' wings. When we cantered the white strand, I felt as if I had found wings.

She taught many, many children to ride at our camp. They were proud when they had graduated to Dulcie, for this meant they knew how to walk, trot, and canter with confidence. To ride Dulcie, their instructions were these: Think the gait change. She will give it to you. They were accurate instructions. Eager to do her job well, she was in tune with her rider.

She produced two fine foals, a filly and a colt, grown now into strong, willing horses serving other families well.

When she could no longer take long trail rides or work in the arena for any length of time, I used her to check fence lines and clear short stretches of trails. Her brisk walk, in spite of advancing arthritis, remained a joy. Straight through the last winter, she was a pleasure for the children to groom and pet, though I would no longer set even the lightest on her back.

I do not know how long I sat beside my dying horse, remembering the luminous beauty of her life of service, but it was long enough for her to render me a last service. For as those memories of our shared time rose, there came, too, a renewed awareness of what a privilege it is to be a rider, to spend one's life with horses and with other humans who love them.

That these noble creatures trust us with their gifts means our supreme obligation is to be worthy partners. For the partnership to be honorable, we must bring to it complementary virtues of patience, loyalty, affection, generosity, and strength. We must not be petty, unforgiving, selfish, stupid. Although humans lack the horse's natural nobility, in our relationships with them we may achieve a higher plane of being.

In the end I could not stand the rattling breath. I wanted to do something to help. I went to the house and called Jim Powers. I said I knew he didn't treat horses anymore, but he knew Dulcie. Would he come?

He came within fifteen minutes, but Dulcie slipped away before he arrived.

Kneeling beside the mare, I saw that her earthly breath had gone. Through the deep wash of grief that swept through me, I experienced a sharp, bright sensation, an acute pleasure, but not of the body. I believe it right to call it fulfillment, a sense of completeness arising from this certainty that it is good to spend one's life in the company of horses. The feeling of satisfaction was almost tangible, a precious, unexpected, and undeserved gift, Dulcie's last offering, through the witness of her life and character, before she cantered off into the heavens.

In fantasy I see her yet, arriving at the gate of her paradise, scattering stardust off her hooves, snorting and tossing her head, transformed into that prancing wonder she was when first she came to us.

It is a rickety old wooden gate she comes to, gray and weathered, for what good is a gate in this place of freedom? It serves only as the spot for riders to line up, waiting for horses like Dulcinea.

I am sure there will be riders in that place because the pairing of willing horse and responsible rider is a holy thing. I am sure, too, that we will have to line up and be humble because in Horse Heaven, the horse will choose the rider. Only those of the gentle hands, the subtle seat, the quiet mind, and the kind heart shall ride.

Part Five

BOUNTY

BOUNTY. from the French *bonté*, meaning goodness in general; an act of generosity, a gift

IN DEFENSE OF
PERSIMMON TREES

AFTER IT STARTED TO RAIN so hard and Clarence Chastain dropped my house in the ditch along the road the day he was moving it up here, we had to wait a week for the grass to dry enough to bring the house on up the hill. There was no driveway yet, and Clarence was planning to run along the grassy terraces, where rashes of scrawny persimmon trees straggled, leafless in early April. They were a thin gray line, poetic enough, suitable in this pasture beside the site of Confederate Captain Williams's house. I remarked that none was large enough to get in the way.

Clarence set me straight quick about the value of a persimmon tree: "I'm goan use one or two of those trees to winch the house out of the ditch," he said. "You'll see how strong those little trees are."

He was right. Attaching his winch to a persimmon tree about fifteen feet tall and eight or ten inches in diameter, with the aid of a small truck operating the winch, he pulled the big truck and house out of the ditch and soon had our parade headed up the hill.

After it was all over and my house was safely on the chosen spot, I went down and looked more closely at that little persimmon tree. I rubbed its gray, checkered bark—it reminded me of gingham—and marveled. Like most other southerners, I suspect, I had taken persimmon trees for granted, considered them a sort of weed, not much good for anything. Yet there I was, falling in love with persimmon trees.

It was a good thing I fell in love with them because right away I had to start defending their presence at Somechoes Farm. When we started the restoration of the house, workers wanted to cut down a twenty-foot persimmon near the front porch to make their job of reinstating the columns easier. I stood up for the tree, claiming it would shade the porch as it grew. I also stayed execution of its brother in the backyard. The workers wanted it out of the way to stack materials.

Later that summer, when men came to work on pastures and fences, I again defended persimmon trees. Where they were well established, I thought it cruel to uproot or cut them down, and I gave instructions not to do so. I heard the men grumbling, "What does she want with that dad-burned plaguey weed?"

Although I was sure the trees were a blessing, I did not know anything about them. I asked a friend what you make from persimmons.

"Faces," he said.

I laughed then, but after twenty years with persimmon trees, I know this noble plant has much more to recommend it than its power to pucker. We moderns vastly underrate it. Wild creatures never do, and our ancestors made so much use of the mature trees that only the scraggly variety exists today.

When white settlers came to North America, magnificent persimmon trees thrived in primeval forests. Oak, ash, hickory, poplar, maple, birch, black walnut, and sweet-gum competition forced the persimmon to maximum growth of one hundred feet or more. Early Virginians knew the plant's Oriental kin, *Diospyros kaki,* and christened the new variety *Diospyros virginiana*—fruit of the gods, Virginia style.

The common name comes from the Algonquian *pessemmin,* and Indians taught colonists to appreciate the ambrosial qualities of persimmon fruit. Indian tribes from Arkansas to Connecticut used it as a staple in breads and pemmican. Captain John Smith at Jamestown wrote about the persimmon, "If it be not ripe, it will draw a man's mouth awrie with much torment." While this sounds like the distinguished captain was the butt of an Indian joke, settlers soon valued the persimmon so much they called anything a "persimmon" if they wanted to emphasize that it was a highly desirable type.

The reason persimmon trees today are scraggly is that early settlers discovered the value of the tree's wood as well as of its fruit. Of the ebony family, persimmon wood is hard and durable, particularly the black heartwood. First spinning wheels were fashioned from it, and later the giant trees were sacrificed wholesale to make shuttles for textile looms in the nineteenth century. Because the wood does not crack under sudden impact, persimmon heartwood was also used in heads of golf clubs and still is where purists refuse to settle for synthetic woods.

Bewitched by false and ubiquitous pearls of junk food and fearful of our own inability to choose a ripe persimmon, current humankind ignores the lush and nutritious fruit. The rest of the animal kingdom is not so dumb. Birds, squirrels, foxes, raccoons, skunks, white-tailed deer, and that maverick marsupial, the opossum, depend on persimmon tree bounty for fall feasts before the lean winter months.

Red foxes munch under my pasture persimmons, and whitetails come to graze there alongside the horses. On a gray November morning, I spy two does nuzzling for fruit in the fescue under a tree, while Took, a bay Arab gelding, rubs his neck against the trunk to make the fruit fall. I wondered why his mane was so tattered. What's a long flowing mane when persimmons are to be had?

One morning on my way to the barn, I discovered a raccoon curled tight in the topmost branches of a tree at the back pasture fence. Stuffed to the no-moving point, the little bandit snoozed all day long, rocking in the spindly gray branches resplendent with plump orange fruit. At twilight he nibbled a few persimmons before he climbed down.

The most comic creatures to grace our persimmon trees are possums. Rivaling the raccoons, these gourmands invade the yard trees to gorge on rich fruit. Absorbed in persimmon picking, they ignore barking dogs and passing people. They are so often found among the tree's branches that the tree is sometimes called possum wood. Audubon's painting of opossums shows them high among persimmon branches, dining on orange orbs. Numerous songs and stories from the Old South swear that most possum hunts end at the foot of the persimmon tree.

A folk song known from Virginia to Alabama verifies the long coon-possum-persimmon association. One version says, "Possum up a 'simmon tree, raccoon on the ground; raccoon say, 'You rascul you, shake some 'simmons down.' " In another version, the raccoon is topside and the possum is giving the shake orders.

In spite of enjoying watching all these creatures eating persimmons, I did not have the courage to try them until I saw Gus Baird picking the fruit and popping it into his mouth like candy. He taught me to choose the fruit that is deep orange, going purple.

"You have to eat it when it looks the most unappetizing," he said, "and smells like heaven."

That's it. The pulp of a ripe persimmon is a mushy mess, its skin shriveled. Although the skin never fully loses its tannic taste, I am not patient enough to peel persimmons. When they look almost rotten and smell ethereally of spice and orange, I chow down in delight. I substitute persimmons for bananas, zucchini, or sweet potatoes in my basic recipe for fruit- or vegetable-based bread. The results: ambrosial.

One fall afternoon a flock of about fifty bluebirds settled into the backyard tree, the one I had saved from the workmen. Only a few of its leaves remained, but fruit abundantly starred the gray limbs. The bluebirds found this shelter charming. Three or four birds would occasionally swing off into the nearby woods like leaves letting go. Then they would return, like leaves flitting back. At each grace-filled flight, each miraculous return, the perching birds fluttered, and the tree shimmered, a moving picture of iridescent blue and glowing russet. The birds lingered until the afternoon went as blue as their wings and the sunset deepened to the burnished orange of their breasts.

The following spring at the foot of that tree, sparkling gold and white in the grass, a thick crop of daisies bobbed up. Gathering the flowers for my breakfast table, for my desk at school, for my shut-in mother, I remembered the bluebirds and the blue October evening. Once again I put my hand on the gray-checked bark of the tree, to know its coarse warmth under my palm and to make, however simple, a gesture of gratitude for our connection and for the tree's generous proof that life is openhanded with its fairest treasures.

NOVEMBER

TODAY I RODE WITH GUS. It was cold, with high winds, and I had not planned to ride. Staying by the fire seemed like the better part of valor. When I went to the barn to give the horses hay, Gus was there and talked me into going with him. It didn't take much talking.

I chose Dalal, the mare Aunt Ina gave me four years ago, when Aunt Ina was ninety-one years old. Bay with a small star and three discreet white socks, Dalal is a great lady. Like Aunt Ina, she has presence. The people from whom I bought the mare said her name means "the Wind" in Arabic. Okay, though she is fit and has been known to buck, I'll take her out on this windy day. With good ol' Bandit for company, she'll be all right. With Gus for company, if I come off, I'll be all right. Gus tells endurance riders to wear bright pink or hunter's orange in the woods. "If you come off," he says, "you don't want to be hard to see."

Gus does not wear bright orange, however. He likes army fatigue pants and a long-sleeved white T-shirt. With this wind, he has put on a well-worn green jacket. He wears a white cyclist's helmet to protect his bald head. Nothing presumptuous about Gus.

Gus is happy for Dalal to lead because Bandit tends to be a pokey leader. Controlling the pace makes me feel more secure, so we are all happy. I guess. Gus is uncommunicative about feelings. I am not sure he would say so if he wanted to lead. He did tell me when he first brought his horses to board at Somechoes that he's outspoken but basically passive. I have found that an accurate description of his character.

The woods have their faces toward winter now, no October looking back with summer longing. The leaves are thick on the ground and make a noisy carpet, not having been softened and subdued by rain and cold. The openness of the woods in November reveals the supple, strong, supporting skeleton of the world. I notice the strength of trees more when they are devoid of the decoration of leaves. Trees are a reassurance as winter looms, life in death, an immortal part.

Dalal wants to go but listens to my requests to stay in her long trot, a comfortable gait. Responding to her powerful, graceful movement, my blood gets up, and I am keenly aware of my body's pleasure warm in a down jacket, snug riding pants, and riding boots. The brisk air against my skin extends this fine feeling of oneness, an awareness of our ability to expand in air. The sky may not be the limit.

Gus and I do not speak for a couple of miles as we trot along. Then he calls out that we ought to stop and pick persimmons from the tree at the back of the crab-apple orchard. He says the persimmons are flavorful from that tree. Gus is a highly intelligent human being, and one of his geniuses is garnering. We stop.

We pick the fruit from the limbs, the horses giving us enough height to do this easily. The orange orbs have a delicate pecan flavor, are indeed delicious. I give Dalal a couple, which she smacks with appreciation. Being a man, Gus does not waste good persimmons on Bandit, so I offer the steady ol' Appaloosa a persimmon, which he takes with surprise, then delight.

"I'm going to give him some Saint John's bread when we get to the locust tree," Gus says. "That's what he loves."

"We may never get there," I say. "These persimmons might keep us here all day."

We eat a few more, and I cannot decide which is best: their heady, spicy aroma filling my nostrils or the delicate, sweet pecan flavor of persimmon meat on my tongue. Persimmons leave a tannic taste, a faint hint of the powerful pucker they give when green, but as the tannic taste fades, my mouth tastes better than ever. I remind myself to consider savoring more seriously.

We canter up the pasture terraces toward the woods trail, then switch back to the trot. Soon we hit the old logging road through the woods along the river, and the horses know this is a good cantering place. They like jumping the low hickory tree that fell across the trail in an ice storm years back. This trail makes me want to shout "Wha-hoo!" and

I usually do, even when riding with someone as quiet as Gus. Today I let Dalal run all the way to the old bridge. Gus and Bandit come along with gusto.

Then we walk a good way along the narrowest part of the river trail. The river is high but not muddy. The water runs coppery green, throws off sparks of light, whispers to the banks. I am glad Gus is a quiet riding companion. Words would be wasted here.

When we turn up toward the pasture behind Daddy's big barn, we let the horses have another good run. Bandit decides ambition might not be such a bad thing, but Dalal lays her ears back when he gets too close, and he is easily discouraged. When we pull up near the barn, both horses are high. They prance through the barnyard and turn toward home.

The locust tree is near the road, not far from the barn, and as we approach, we see a buck, portly in his sleek gray-and-white coat, his head raised regally in the way of stags. He watches us with curiosity and caution. The poetry he adds to this exhilarating ride gladdens my heart, but my brain disapproves, thinking that if we were hunters, he'd be a dead buck. Especially since he is so beautiful and fat, too. Hunters count points of antlers. I never do, but I enjoy the sight of a good spread, which this fellow gives us.

Because we are on horseback and downwind, he stands and stares long at us, reluctant to give up his feast. Gus says the deer is trying to figure out why these huge deer coming have such terrible tumors on their backs.

I say I prefer not to think of riding as being a tumor. The buck angles away into the pines, turns to study us again, then melds into the brush.

We dismount to inspect the locust pods on the ground, our Saint John's bread. The horses love these pods as much as the deer do and chow down with excited little snorts. Gus and I gather a few of the juiciest pods for ourselves. Most of these are too dry to tempt humans, but some hide meaty fiber along one seam, fiber that surprises and delights with tangy, citrus flavor.

When we remount to leave the locust tree to the deer, we have to urge the horses away from the goodies. Gus, who is in the lead now, asks Bandit to trot. The Appaloosa knows he's headed home and takes off briskly. Dalal does not like being left behind. I am well occupied reminding her that I am the one giving orders when I see a hawk sail low off to my left, across the steep, terraced pasture. Although I know the danger of taking my attention from the horse, I have to watch the hawk, and I do. Her russet tail sparks the blue-gold air. She dips and rises, flying her red-cream-tan colors. As we pass through the wooden gate, I see another hawk far across the open field, dipping over the pasture next to my house.

The horses swing into the canter, the cold, golden afternoon invades my lungs, and the sailing hawks enter my veins as well as my view. Green fescue flashes beneath Dalal's feet, gray-brown dog fennel sways on each side, scraggly persimmon trees scrawl their way across the pasture. I sense the thick mass of oak trunk on the fence line, the fine old tree Daddy calls the whiskey tree. It is where, he says, the man who used to own Horseshoe Bend Farm would stop to have a last drink of whiskey because his wife refused to allow whiskey in the house. I laugh, remembering that tale, glad I don't need whiskey, with days like this for intoxication.

RABBIT STEW

IT'S AN ORDINARY JANUARY EVENING in North Georgia, with a hard freeze in the forecast, and I am at the barn, feeding horses. The dark, rich odor of molasses rises from the grain barrels as I dip sweet feed into buckets. Summer sun lingers in the perfume of hay bales when I pull off sections of hay, drop the required amount in each stall. I stuff and hang a net for Dulcie, who seems to prefer nets to eating off the ground. In spite of the cold, this is good work, a time for the body to reestablish rhythms after a day given to the mind.

Waiting at the gate, eight horses snort and shuffle: Cumiche, the gray Arab chief, lays his ears back often enough to keep the others in line and his right to be first inside the barn undisputed.

I have shut the stall door on the last horse when I hear someone holler up by the big gate at the house.

"All your horses up?" he says.

Looking west through the bright sheen of winter evening, I see it is Alex in his brown canvas hunting jacket and pants. I wave and nod, and my heart lightens at the sight of him, a tall, straight man of fifty with the reserved confidence, the muted southern arrogance of William Faulkner in his prime. In spite of having spent twenty-five years in the wilds of Alaska, Alex has retained his southern-gentleman air in mythical proportions—Faulknerian proportions, you could say.

"I'm gonna run some cows through here," he calls, and I wave again okay.

Since our father raises cows by a method that can best be described as benign neglect, his fences tend toward symbolism. When it gets this cold, his cows stay out more than in, grazing the road shoulders.

When I have filled the last water bucket and the cows are not coming through the gate, I know the Alaska contingent, unaccustomed to cattle that aren't caribou, is having problems. Grabbing a couple of sections of hay, I head for the house.

The front yard is excited with cows. Eight or ten are milling around, proof that total confusion can be illustrated. Alex has spooked three others over the fence into my pasture.

"They jumped that fence as good as two deer I saw up at the horse-shoe bend in the river this afternoon," he says, his voice reflecting a kind of dawning amazement.

"Well, they're kin," I say. "I'll try to lure these with the hay. You walk up behind 'em easy. Give 'em time to figure out what we want."

It takes twenty minutes to move the infuriating beasts two hundred yards into their proper pasture, straight lines and logic being foreign to cows in general and especially to cows kept in/out by symbolic fences.

By this time it is nearly dark, but when we walk back to where Alex has parked Daddy's battered blue pickup, I see the rabbit in the truck bed. Alex is a hunter, which is one reason he moved to Alaska, and even on vacation in Georgia (transplanted Georgians in Alaska often take their vacations in January), he finds pleasure in wandering our brown winter hills, taking a good shot when Providence provides.

"Where'd you get the rabbit?"

"Aw, I shot it in the brier patch down at the bottom of the big terraced pasture. You want it?"

"Does cleaning come with that offer? If it does, I'll make a stew for the family get-together tomorrow night at Mother's."

In the last minutes before dark, when the January sky is royal blue and airy gold radiates the western horizon, my brother squats by the faucet on the west side of the house and skins the rabbit. His hands are respectful as he takes out the entrails and cuts off the head. I throw these over the fence, where the crows will celebrate them in the morning.

Alex shows me a patch of blood in the hindquarter. "Soak this in a little salt water," he says, letting cold water from the faucet run over the slick, pink morsel.

Then he stands, and I take the rabbit on a paper bag. He wipes his hands on his pants.

"Guess I won't come in. I've got to get on back to Mama's."

I take the rabbit to the kitchen and lay it in the sink as the truck lights disappear down the drive. I let warm water trickle into a pan and put the rabbit in it. I lightly salt the section where Alex removed the shot.

The night and the light in the room make a dark mirror of the window over the sink. A figure there emanates light, startles me. It is a slim woman in her forties with silver and gold hair, a strong, handsome face. She is wearing an off-white wool sweater and faded blue jeans. I am startled by her because memory has brought up a dark-haired, serious little girl, an icy December nearly forty years earlier, and another rabbit.

That day my brother suggested we walk over to Brunnel Smith's farm to see if the rock quarry pond was frozen. He was eleven, and I, four years younger, was unaccustomed to having him recognize my existence. I went. We walked a mile through fields of tawny broom sedge in the thin, year-end sunshine. Pale cornstalks crackled in the last field we crossed to reach the old quarry pond, which, sure enough, was frozen over with a sheet of white ice.

Knowing the pond, half frozen or not, was off-limits, we could not resist the ice. Alex, more canny than I, stepped gingerly along the edge. I ventured out too far and—crack!—down I went. The pond was shallow. Drowning was not a threat, but soaked shoes, socks, and pants legs would spell spanking if Mother found out.

A spanking for me, that is. For Alex, they would spell the loss of his new .410 shotgun, which he was not supposed to have with him.

Feet muddy and soaked, teeth chattering, I walked out of the pond.

"Don't worry," Alex said, "we'll build a fire and dry you out. It may take a while. I'll see if I can get us a rabbit for lunch."

Proud of his woodsman skills, he cleared a spot for the fire and formed a ring of stones while I gathered sticks and pine straw. With his pocket-knife he cut two forked branches and made a spit to hang my socks from. He soon had the fire blazing, and I huddled barefoot before it. We placed my brown oxfords on the stones, as close as we dared to the fire.

Alex set off with his shotgun, and I was not the least surprised when he returned shortly with a rabbit. He cleaned it in the pond, and meat on the spit soon was sizzling over the flames.

The roasting rabbit blackened, but it smelled like a Homerian feast. My socks steamed on the forked sticks with the rabbit impaled between them. When Alex finally pronounced the meat cooked, we had to gnaw it with all our might, and we did, but it was so tough we couldn't make much headway.

We ate rabbit a lot when we were growing up. I don't think we had to. When Mother made rabbit stew, she billed it as a delicacy. She respected rabbit boxes and beagle dogs and young boys learning provision.

I am careful not to get rabbit blood on my sweater. My hands washing the rabbit in the warm water are the hands of generations of southern women accepting the gifts of their men, to give them back as nourishment, life for life.

I think about the tomatoes I canned last summer and have been saving for such a stew. There's frozen corn, too, from my brother-in-law's cornfield, corn I put by when the field overflowed and we saved what we could. I've got a fat onion, a couple of celery stalks, and a can of limas. There's plenty of oregano.

I smell the steamy, rich stew before I start to boil the rabbit. I imagine the pleased and surprised looks on the faces of my other brothers and my sisters at the family party tomorrow night when they hear I've brought a rabbit stew.

Sitting around the big dining table, we will probably tell the tale of the day Alex and I went to play on the ice at Brunnel's pond. Mother will exclaim again that she is glad she didn't know all the mischief we were up to.

I came down with a raging sore throat from that adventure and missed the Christmas pageant at the church. I was supposed to be an angel.

GIFTS

SUNDAY was my forty-ninth birthday. I have never minded birthdays, except, the truth be told, my thirty-fifth, when "in the midst of my life I came to myself in a dark wood" and tumbled straight into an identity crisis. Although I had read Dante, I did not know that my crisis, like his, was classic. I read *Passages* later, after I'd had all the symptoms. But they didn't last long, and the next year thirty-six sounded young to me. It still does.

At the moment, however, I am feeling a little down, fearing age-limited activity. Having always reveled in my physical being, I see decrepitude looming an amorphous monster in the wings, about to come on my stage. That's probably because right now I *am* decrepit, thanks to knee surgery a couple of months ago and a twenty-five-mile horseback ride on Saturday that left my muscles aching with the poison of too much lactic acid.

Sunday morning I creaked around like an old door hinge, but by afternoon I got up the energy to go by the Russell home place and pick two generous bunches of daffodils, one for Mother and one for Daddy. I like to take my parents flowers on my birthday. It seems appropriate to thank them. I hope they had a good time when they were getting/begetting me. From the pleasure I find in life, I suspect they did have fun. I may have felt right away the gift that life is.

I told Daddy I had come to give him a chance to wish me a happy birthday. He laughed. Then I thanked him for my birthday, and we had a quiet visit sitting on the sunporch.

Mother was irritated because I had not come earlier. Nursing-home life is a hard adjustment for her. According to ritual, I ask her about my first birthday, and she tells me there were three inches of snow on the ground the day I was born. My father was in North Carolina serving with a mobile army hospital unit. American involvement in

World War II was revving up. He wrote to my mother that he was relieved everything went okay, and although he hadn't wanted a girl, maybe someday I'd make him glad I wasn't a boy.

I found that letter near my forty-fifth birthday and saved it till the day when I showed it to Daddy and asked him if I ever had done anything to make him glad I wasn't a boy.

"Lots of times," he said.

That may be the worst and the best of my father in one story.

After delivering my bouquets, I went to Lynn's for supper with her, Martha, and Susan, my dearest friends, women I have known and loved nearly all my life. Lynn served broccoli chicken divine—well named—and a scrumptious spinach, shrimp, and mandarin orange salad. For dessert we had my favorite, cherry pie. Lynn made me blow out the table candles in lieu of cake candles. She brings an original touch to everything.

I came home about ten to find that Sharon, who is living at Somechoes for a while, had left an eloquent bouquet of spring flowers on my bedside table, new-spring gifts, gathered from fields and old house sites near us.

The daffodils, quince, and forsythia are living remnants of the lives of other women who made their homes here when this country road was long miles, often muddy and impassable, from town, when their days were filled with arduous labor and loneliness. Yet they found time and energy to plant flowers. The flowers have outlasted all their joys and troubles, outlasted the house, look set to outlast the barn.

The wild plum blossoms are gifts of bird flight, wind capers, rain song.

Sharon has an artistic eye and hand and has created a splendid bouquet. The plum blossoms are tall, white, frothy. The daffodils are of different types: a rich golden yellow with long trumpet, a pale yellow with shorter trumpet, another with ivory petals and orange trumpet. The long-armed forsythia weaves among the plum branches, its yellow silken shine offsetting the plum's froth. The quince's red gleams.

The flowers are in a quart mason jar, one I found many winters ago at one of the house sites where the flowers grow. I suspect one of my country women used to put up tomatoes or beans in that jar. The cows walked it up one winter out of the mud to the west of the crumbling chimneys. The chimneys are all that is left of a fine, antebellum house built of heart pine. Raymond Reynolds found a still in the house by accident one afternoon in the late 1960s. He hoped no one saw him find it because he intended to forget finding it before he got back to his truck, but the whiskey manufacturers must have seen him: that night the house burned to the ground, leaving not a trace of the still.

The flowers in the lamplight on the table beside my bed, with unbleached muslin curtains at the window behind them, look like a seventeenth-century Dutch painting. Besides spreading a feast for the eye, they waft over my bed a fragrance so light and sweet it might be the odor of peace. Sometimes I am a little sensitive to plum blossom perfume, but tonight my nose delights in it. My entire body seems attuned to the flowers, to the joy they represent.

Sharon is embarking on an entirely new phase in her life, and putting off her old one has left her close to penniless. She is working at Domino's, delivering pizzas. Yet she has given a gift of inestimable value. There are gifts to offer in abundance.

As I am turning back my comforter and fluffing up pillows, rejoicing in forty-nine years with daffodils, Jessica comes in. Home from college on spring break, she is breaking up with her boyfriend.

We crawl under the covers together and lie there getting cozy, talking. My girl's profile, delicate and shapely, lies between me and the mason jar of flowers. Her blond hair shines in the lamplight. Her dark lashes fill with tears over the inexplicable pain of love, a pain I know. We turn to each other and embrace without words.

In the luxury of the bed we are soon comforted, grow peaceful. We find something to laugh about, turn on our backs, talk idly until words become unnecessary. Jessica is a good one to know when words are unnecessary. After a little while, she gives me a good-night kiss, tucks me in, and goes to her own bed.

I am bone tired from Saturday's ride and dealing with poisoned muscles today. I groan a little, turning, settling in. But in my nest of quilt, comforter, and sheepskin rug, I feel rich and secure in spite of poison.

Sleep flows into my veins. I slip away. In the night I drift back toward consciousness and sense the flowers beside me, like an angel watching. I do not know how else to say it. They are a blessed presence, an embodiment of divine grace. Their form and fragrance make me smile in sleep.

When I wake at 4:30 A.M., my usual writing time, a spring storm is rising, so I avoid the word processor. With pen and notebook I crawl back into bed. The rain drums on the roof, sings in the gutters. Thunder grumbles, lightning flashes high and far away.

Under cover, surrounded by pillows, I am aware again of the vase of flowers glowing in the lamplight. Outside is dark, wet, danger, but inside there is my own warmth given back to me by my quilts, and there is this splendid bouquet.

The plum blossoms are clustered so thick on the black twigs that I forget the plain black sticks. In winter the black, scrawling arms of the plum bushes belie their ability to burst forth with such a bride. Soon this white froth, fragrant and lacy, will give way to green leaves. If sun, rain, and frost cooperate, the branches and leaves will bear fruit. For a short season, we will have bright red plums, a treat to eye and palate. They don't last long, the plums. Too many of us love them: rabbits, quail, deer, humans, horses. I suspect foxes eat plums when fox hunts for plum-fattened quail or rabbit are unsuccessful.

I recognize without grief that the flowers that are perfect today beside my bed, adorning my room, making glad my heart, are dead. These plum bridal boughs, these quince twigs covered with rubies, will make no fruit. These daffodils, planted for the joy of their being, bear their fruit only in the moment someone takes pleasure in their being.

One of the daffodils attracts my eye. It is all of the same color but is barely color. It is cream, perhaps ivory. I am wrong. It is not all the same color. Its cup is faintly brighter than the petals. And it is not cream or ivory. It is the translucent color of sunlight falling through clouds on a winter morning.

On this day after my birthday, I am comfortable with the idea that all things are not meant to bear fruit and with the thought that the moment is its own fruit.

Although seasons are brief, they are faithful, returning again and again in the circle of time to bring their particular miracles.

BLACKBERRIES

A HAND-PAINTED SIGN tacked to a mailbox on Highway 53 last week shocked me because it said, "Blackberries $6/gal."

I have always thought blackberries are free.

I remember as children how my sister and I gathered blackberries for tea parties in our playhouse under the mimosa tree. Everything else on the menu was imaginary, but real blackberries gleamed on the tiny plates. Sometimes we couldn't wait for the tea party and stood at the bushes cramming in the sweet, dark fruit, lost in the blissful moment of blackberries.

When our mother sent us to pick blackberries with a lard bucket, we skipped to the work. This was the season of vegetables, and from our garden or the neighbors' we would sit down to suppers of fried squash; green beans cooked all day to a deep, caramelly country flavor; heaped platters of corn on the cob slathered with butter from our own cow; plates garlanded with tomato and onion slices larger than the palm of Mother's hand; cornbread browned to perfection in the big iron skillet, cut into pie-piece wedges.

The pièce de résistance (our father, recently returned from France and World War II, taught us French phrases) was the blackberry cobbler. Baked in a long, shallow pan, it sat on the stove until dessert time and then arrived at the table with the bowls for serving it. The bottom layer of dough had soaked purple with the juice of berries, butter, and sugar. The top layer was purple against the berries but white and fluffy in the middle, biscuit brown on top. Scattered grains of sugar crowned the whole, tiny white stars.

With four children at the table and like as not a visiting cousin or three, there was never any leftover cobbler.

Today, on Somechoes Farm, I pick blackberries for jelly. Along old fence lines where cattle used to browse, the blackberry bushes thrive. It takes me about an hour to pick a gallon because I have to stop to eat now and again or to watch a small white spider study the mayfly struggling in the spider's web among the brambles.

I am careful to respect other creatures that make their living off blackberries. Ants and wasps like them. There's a gray, spindly-legged, antennae-proud creature, the personification of BUG, that buzzes off loudly when I get too close to his sipping grounds, but he is not aggressive. I maintain munching blackberries makes most of us peaceful.

Snakes, they say, are a danger in blackberry bushes, but I have been picking blackberries for nearly forty-five years and have never met a snake in a berry bush. I figure snakes frequent blackberry bushes in hopes of catching a bird. Snakes are smart enough to know I'm not a bird. I don't worry about snakes.

The horses and the deer, however, are serious competition. In the horse pasture, you can forget blackberries. Horses will pull every one off the briery bushes as soon as they ripen. Among the bramble thickets in the gone-wild cow pasture, deer spend July nights in blackberry delight.

Even in daylight, I spy a fat, sleek doe browsing the bushes at the bottom of the terraced pasture. Before bounding away, she snorts at me, irate to be disturbed at her banquet. I call after her, "Don't get so huffy! I'll leave you plenty."

As I pick in jeans, long-sleeved white T-shirt, straw hat, and once-white, elbow-length dress gloves (they make picking less painful), I do addition in my head: labor, six dollars an hour, four hours total process; sugar $1.79 for five pounds; plus a dollar or two for electricity and jar lids (I use the same jars year after year). I conclude my jelly costs about five dollars a pint. I can buy top brands in the store for less money.

And less trouble. Considering the broiling sun, inevitable scratches, maddening chigger bites, and possible wasp attacks, I wonder if there's wisdom in making my own jelly.

Yet when the berries are shimmering more purple than the velvet robes of fairy tales, I cannot think of passing by such jewels. Picking blackberries has taught me lessons I carry into other areas of my life and sometimes gives rise to profound thoughts, or, rather, encourages me to note

how profound is the obvious. For example, nothing that is sweet, allur-
ing, and beautiful will be garnered without competition.

I think only from blackberries among thorns could I have learned that
black is *bright*.

I have learned that coming at the bushes from more than one direction is an advantage. A change of perspective reveals more blackberries
than I originally thought. I try to remember this lesson.

I treasure the satisfaction of starting out with an empty pail and
coming back with the weight of a gallon comforting my soul, proof that
provision is in the plan. I feel sorry for those who know bounty only
through specials at the grocery store. "Buy one, get one free" doesn't get
to the marrow of provender. Blackberry picking does.

I cannot recall emptying a blackberry bush. They are the personification of Plenty. It isn't hard to leave some for the deer and other
animals. What amazes me, however, is how few people pick these
treasures, how many are left hanging. Birds and wasps don't get to all of
them before the sun shrivels them to ashy brown.

Back home with my pail full, I admit that squeezing the juice is messy,
but I know of nothing creative that isn't messy at some juncture. Mess
is part of the process, may be what urges us to order.

I like to gather and squeeze one day and cook the next, working
in the early morning, when breezes bless my kitchen window. In my
120-year-old house, while I work I keep company with all the women
who have made jelly on this farm, more than a century of us, generations of Maynards, Wages, and Kennedys before me.

As my purple-stained hands measure the white sugar and stir syrupy
nectar in the pot, I consider the work of these earlier women. In a world
of omnipresent doughnuts and candy bars, I am pleased to recall what
their long-ago jelly meant, the singular contribution it was to the
decoration of a day, how it brightened biscuits, brought a sweet accent
of color and taste to plain fare.

I like the feeling that I can participate in the gift of sweetness with
these ghosts of summers gone. I know then in my soul that time is
not linear, leaves no one behind. It is, rather, circular, like the seasons.

With tongs, I lift sterile jars from boiling water and line them on a green-and-white checkered dish towel, ready for the moment of pouring.

I know this moment by its perfume. When a steady heat brings the juice to a boil that cannot be stirred down for at least twenty minutes, I sniff in earnest for a rich fragrance, a sweet, dark odor that tingles in the nostrils, makes breath excitement.

When this perfume rises, the juice will soon coat a metal spoon as it cools, and then I pour the nectar boiling into the hot pint jars, seal the lids fast and tight, and set my prize to shine on the window sill.

I listen for the tinny pop of each jar lid as it seals, a reminder of the mystery of vacuum and a reaffirmation of universal order.

Sometimes as I work, my mind springs forward to Christmas morning, when my two daughters are home from college, when my parents come for breakfast, when the jelly outshines its crystal dish. I see the dish going enchanted from hand to hand, as all spread the silken sweet on soft, white, butter-smeared halves of succulent biscuits. The revelers murmur in delight. They exclaim. My heart warms with honest pride in valued work.

I will find no such wonders in a jar from the grocery-store shelf. In my own jelly I make a bargain. I am rich with the poignancy of memory, the sweetness of now, the joy of anticipation.

WILD STRAWBERRIES

HOME after a hectic, people-filled weekend in Colorado Springs, Colorado, I am happy to be walking my own woods and fields. This solitude is my solace and the root of my best being. I am not made for apartments and streets thronged with people, dangerous with cars, or for restaurants, however deluxe. My restoring comes from home and home fare at my own table.

Although a time of celebration, the weekend was tense and stressful. Jessica has graduated from college. Rites of passage are telling, at least the graduation variety are. So much hoopla, ceremony, booze. Too much. And the added stress of being—how shall I say? *exposed*—to Jessica's father all weekend, a time to wonder if we did the right thing, no matter how useless I know such questions to be. A time for remembering the way we were, the way we didn't/couldn't manage to remain.

I need the fields and trees, the river running quiet, a glimpse of the fox.

I walk down to the river and stand there, aware of my own breathing. Fame and love sink to nothingness, and even a thing as clamorous as my last child's leaving the nest falls silent. I sit a while in the sand on the riverbank, watching the river flow, her coppery green waters aglow with the last sunlight of the day. I let the sand drift through my fingers, remembering the way Jessica's hair used to stand up all over her baby head, her early ability to make us laugh, which she has retained, her love of a pun, her sensitivity to my breakup with Ben, the way it's easy to be quiet with her whether we're on horseback, in the car, at home, walking in the woods. I grow peaceful, thinking of this girl-child–young woman.

When I take the trail that leads up from the river into the back pasture, as I reach the border of woods and field, I notice with a flush of excitement that the grass is jewel-strewn. I stop to look.

Wild strawberries! They are red as only strawberries are red among the green spring growth of sedge and fescue and poison ivy. I hesitate, squatting to view closer the ruby delights, though no ruby ever achieved anything like the glorious color of wild strawberries. I get a tantalizing whiff of their perfume. But I can't describe them. I'd sooner try to describe the Grand Canyon than a Georgia wild strawberry in the back pasture on a late afternoon in May.

The poison ivy doesn't deter me. I am not highly allergic to this noxious plant, have to get in juice-producing contact with it to suffer. So I pick the strawberries carefully among the ivy leaves without fear that this is a rash gesture. I gather four gems, hold them in my hand, close to my nose so that their delicate fragrance makes my mouth water. I pop one into my mouth. The taste of wild strawberry bursting on my tongue and against the roof of my mouth brings back a poignant memory.

I am sitting at the dinner table on a May Sunday at the Jackson household, a fairly regular occurrence while Dwain Jackson and I were steadies in high school. The main dish is pork roast with Little Daddy's barbecue sauce. Little Daddy is what I call Julian Jackson, Dwain's father, a slight, wiry man. He is a good cook, enjoys cooking. The roast is indeed tasty, ladled generously with the sharp vinegar, butter, and pepper sauce that is his specialty. I compliment this dish with sincerity, ask for more. Little Daddy is pleased.

"I wish I could make you a strawberry cobbler like Mama used to make," he says.

The way he says this, his voice seasoned with pride in and longing for his mother, the way it is whenever he speaks of her, makes me want to hear more. "How do you make it?" I ask.

"It ain't hard to make the cobbler," he says. "You do that pretty much like you do any other cobbler—some butter, sugar, and crust on top. The hard part is findin' the strawberries. I used to know where you could find 'em in the spring, on our farm and other places. Mama would be so proud when I brought home a bucket of wild strawberries. I can taste them thangs right now and the cobbler she made for supper. Bought strawberries ain't the same to wild strawberries for flavor."

"I love wild strawberries," I say, "but it's hard to imagine finding enough to make a cobbler."

"In them days you could," Julian says.

The next Sunday he makes a strawberry cobbler from bought strawberries, and I say it tastes good, all right, which is the truth. Well, it ain't the same, he reckons, as a wild strawberry cobbler, but we can be grateful for any kind of strawberries.

Thinking about Julian makes me smile as I scout around in the grass for more strawberries. There are a few but not enough for a cobbler. There are hardly enough to save for breakfast cereal, so I eat as I pick, savoring each bite. Kneeling in the grass, I have a good feeling. I imagine how it was to discover a thriving patch of wild strawberries, enough for Mama to make a cobbler, how it felt to be the rich son, bringing home a pail full of jewels.

BISCUIT LOVE

I HAVE BEEN THINKING about why no matter how busy I am with school, children, horses, writing, responsibilities toward my aging and ailing mother, I find time to make biscuits almost every day, and all are almost always eaten. The dogs may get a biscuit or two simply because I did not make biscuit toast in the morning and there is a pan of fresh biscuits for supper in the oven. When I throw biscuits out the back door, the dogs grab up this gift, wolf/dog them down, look up wistfully for more.

Although I rarely buy food at fast-food places, I admit their biscuits are respectable, light, tasty, and pleasing to the eye, golden brown and white in correct proportions. Biscuits have always been fast food. Women had to make them up quick for their large families and in large quantities. Biscuits were staples, serving to sustain the hungry when nothing else was on hand. Thus, it was fairly simple for the fast-food industry to adapt recipes that had been used for centuries to make quick bread. Nevertheless, you will never buy a real biscuit at a fast-food place because the nourishment you get from a biscuit is not all in flour, shortening, and milk.

Which is why I keep making biscuits. I am fulfilling my duty and showing love to my children, other family, and friends, by baking bread for them. Making bread equals love and duty was an irrefutable equation I absorbed in child- and girlhood.

Mama Eaton, my maternal grandmother, gave me my first lesson in making biscuits. She was not a gentle woman, Pauline Letson Eaton, but rather ill-natured, hot-tempered, imperious. Mother of five children, she did not take joy in her tasks of homemaking, but she fulfilled them faithfully for the most part. She made a memorable biscuit, high, light, crusty on the outside, soft, fragrant, and flavorful on the inside. We were happy when Mama Eaton was making supper biscuits.

I asked her to show me how, and she did, with her usual lack of grace, complaining that she had enough to do without Sally pestering her about biscuits. She showed me how much flour to sift into the bowl and how many spoons of shortening to cut in, but when we had cut it into the dry flour a little, she said, "Use your fingers to mix the shortening and flour. You can't make biscuits if you're afraid to get flour on your hands."

"Pour in enough milk to make a sticky, shiny dough," she said then, and she let me handle the sticky dough at first, telling me about working in a little flour at a time, but she soon snatched the dough away to her expert hands.

"You don't handle biscuit dough too much," she said, as if any idiot debutante would know that.

Perhaps to soften this experience, my mother told at the supper table that night, as we were buttering our biscuits, about how when she was a little girl she had been lucky to get a paper route because paper routes usually went to the boys in their Atlanta neighborhood. The Eatons were poor. Although Papa Eaton was a foreman with Georgia Power Company, he was also a union man who was often out of work on strike. The little our mother earned delivering papers helped buy groceries. In winter she was out late, past supper time, and her mother, our Mama Eaton, used to save a chicken leg and a biscuit for her in the warming oven of the wood stove.

"I remember how I looked forward to finding that chicken leg and that beautiful biscuit when I came in," our mother said, "and they were always there and always tasted so good." We could almost taste those long-ago love-and-duty biscuits.

My own mother could make biscuits to rank with anyone else's, and it is thanks to her further patient teaching that I went on to become a cheerful bread baker. The thing I remember about Mother's biscuits is that she seemed to be in a hurry to get them on the table, to see if they would meet approval, her need for approval being great, and how my father hardly noticed the light, delicious brown circles. We children noticed. We bragged, buttered, and syruped them and begged for more. This was not the approval she yearned for.

I never ate a biscuit that my paternal grandmother baked, but I know she baked them. Competent head of a household of thirteen children and dealing with a constant stream of visiting relatives, friends, and live-in teachers, she had plenty of experience in bread making. By the time I knew Grandmother Russell, she was too frail to cook, but the person who baked her bread was a biscuit queen. Modine Thomas was a fierce black woman whose biscuits you would not have criticized if they'd been rock hard and inedible, but there was no need for anything but praise. It was a treat to be invited to lunch at Grandmother Russell's for many reasons, but one was surely the chance to have Modine's biscuits with South Georgia cane syrup, sent up from Ailey by our aunt Pat. Modine did not care whether you praised her bread. If you dared say, "Modine, those biscuits were really good," the most she would say was, "Humpf!" accompanied by a scowl.

Modine never wasted a biscuit. Those that weren't eaten at lunch or supper were served as toast the next morning. I've seen fights break out over the last piece of Modine's crusty, buttery biscuit toast.

Later, when Dwain Jackson and I were courting through our high school years, I often spent time with his mother, Montine, helping prepare meals. She made her bread in a magnificent pine dough tray, so that no flour was ever wasted. The tray had been her mother-in-law's and became hers by the fact that Julian Jackson, the youngest in his family of tenant farmers, had cared for his ailing mother when she was stricken with what he called "female trouble." When his mother became too weak to do any work, he, a lad of eleven, made the biscuits, shouldering the responsibility of caretaking because his elder sisters were too far away with too many others to care for to do it.

Julian's devotion to his mother meant that when she finally died of a uterine hemorrhage that soaked the mattress so that it had to be thrown away, the other household goods came to him. No daughter dared ask for the treasured dough tray.

I remember Montine's telling again and again how the first time she made biscuits—she was seventeen—it was her husband of one night who showed her how to flour the sticky dough from her fingers and roll it into a soft ball from which the biscuits could then be squeezed, soft lumps to round lightly in the hand and pat into place on the blackened pan. I can see them now, the young couple, pleased with each other, baking biscuits their first morning as husband and wife.

Montine made good biscuits, but they were a little too lardy for my taste. She and Modine and Mama Eaton used animal fat, which had no evil status in a time when people burned more fat each day than they ate. It was a blessing to have lard, best from the pig you had raised yourself. My mother, trained as a nurse, had seen fat-clogged arteries and preferred high-quality vegetable shortening, even when we had raised a pig, and I grew accustomed to eating her kind of biscuit.

Hot, fresh biscuits are best, and biscuit toast never goes begging in our house. A cold biscuit is not to be scorned, however. I remember my brothers and boy cousins eagerly taking up pocket biscuits my mother had made for their Saturday hunts. These were the leftover breakfast biscuits with a slab of ham or cheese or butter and blackberry jelly, wrapped in wax paper to be tucked in a jacket pocket and pulled out on the cold duck flats or as the hunters walked windy brown fields in search of rabbits.

I pack a few pocket biscuits when the girls and I are going out for a long ride. Sometimes I made up a couple for Ben when he was going to be long away from the house cutting wood or bush-hogging. I ask brother John if he wants one if I see him on his way to his deer stand. He says yes.

I don't care how many good biscuits are made in fast-food or any other kind of restaurants, I am going to keep baking my own. I like being the one able to produce an instant picnic. I'd be a fool to give up the position of the one who produces nourishment that makes her circle a magnetic center, a place where love is visible, tangible, fragrant, and edible, in a pan.

THE BLUE OF THE
HERON'S WINGS

FOR YEARS I took the great blue herons for granted. They were a given at Somechoes, a staple of my time and place, like cornbread and turnip greens, red clay soil and hickory trees, valued but not at the forefront of consciousness.

Whether on foot or on horseback, wherever I went that there was still water, the lily ponds, the river swamp, Wingo's, Whiddon's, LaMarche's ponds, I would almost always stir up a heron. I once spotted three fishing at Wingo's. That day I was conscious of the herons. I had supposed that the heron I stirred up was the same bird dining in different restaurants from day to day. That day I realized there are more of these blue-gray, gawky creatures than I had imagined. It is good to know the world holds more herons than I imagine.

Because of their awkward and slow takeoffs, herons have keen hearing, and it is hard to catch them off guard. A heron hears footsteps far off and heads skyward, with a complaining awk-awk. I smile at the heron's awkward winging. He is clumsy looking, flying with his neck crouched between broad, slow-moving wings.

Many times I hear the heron rather than see him, and his inelegant squawk makes me smile too.

I rejoice over his keen ears and his keen eyes, too, keen to catch frogs and fish in the water among the reeds and lilies. A great blue heron once fished all the frogs out of the back lily pond before summer was over. I knew this had happened because the heron stopped coming, and it was mighty quiet down there, morning and night.

I wasn't worried about being done out of my frogs. Frogs can't help filling up a pond soon again if there's only a heron or two around. It takes more than herons to put frogs permanently out of business. For that it takes people with pesticides, oil spills. I knew the frogs would be back, and so would the heron. They were both common enough at Somechoes to take them for granted.

But the day I saw the blue of the heron's wings for the first time, all that taking for granted changed. I wasn't looking for a heron that day. I had gone looking for geese.

It's an early April afternoon with the air feeling like heaven has left open a window. Dogwoods star the daytime woods with white. Pink crab-apple blossoms give the window of heaven a helping hand with air beautification. Clouds are easing in. It will rain before morning.

Coming late from school I stop at the mailbox, and there are two letters, one from Jessica and one from Les. I sit on the front steps in the late sunshine to read them.

Jessica's letter contains a poem she has written in her creative-writing class at college. It is called "All the Men I Ever Loved Took the Bed When They Left."

Arresting title, I'll say that for her.

Then I read the subtitle: "A Praise Poem for My Mother."

I read the poem, and my hand holding the letter starts to shake. I want to read it again, but I can't because the paper is shaking. I hold it with both hands and read again. As an English and writing teacher, I know it is a true poem. As her mother, I know she has been paying close attention to who I am in a way I had not suspected. This knowledge makes my blood sing, like discovering the world holds more herons than I suspected. I sit on the front steps of the house, reading the letter and the poem, crying.

Next I read Les's letter, noting it only took four days to come from London. As usual it is a delight, overflowing with his delicious joie de vivre. I hear in his letter that he pays attention to and likes who I am. I remember his quiet, beautiful hands and how he makes me laugh. When a man has beautiful, capable hands and can make a woman laugh and wants to make her laugh, he is dangerous to her contentment with solitude. In fact, the truth be known, for some months now I have had to admit that Les fills all the requirements I gave to the Universe one night under the stars about what kind of man I would have if I had another one. It was an audacious list, but there was not a word on it about his being at least forty-five years old and a U.S. citizen. It seems the height of ingratitude to send him back now stamped Wrong Age/ Wrong Nationality.

I change clothes and head for the barn. Ringing the farm bell to call up the horses, I think the clear, deep clanging somehow expresses my triumphant feeling. The music of the horses' hooves as they canter up is another theme of happiness in my blood.

The horses soon are munching feed and hay, and I decide to shut Migno up in the tack room and head off toward Wingo's. There has been a flock of geese on the water for several days, but so far I have not had a glimpse of them, in spite of trying. Today, without a dog, I might be able to sneak up on them. I resist Migno's pitiful look. I like watching geese in their natural habitat. I like being able to spy on somebody's party and know that my skill at not disturbing gives me the right to watch.

I walk fast, filled with love and energy. Nearing the pond, I walk slower, sliding quiet feet in the leaves, stopping every few yards. In spite of my care, the wood ducks sitting in the back swamp on the west side know I am coming, and off they go, piercing the sky with their shrill cries. I feel sure they will alarm anything else on the water.

Sure enough, the heron gets up, awk-awking. I barely make out his gray-blue form loping over the pond.

I edge up the hill, heading for a spot high up the bank under the oaks and hickories, with a good view of the water below. Nothing moves out on the water. Nothing there, I think. The water glints pewterlike under a gray sky where clouds have erased the blue, bringing night nearer.

I have almost reached my spot when I see the Canadas, eight of them. In their gray suits and smart black-and-white waistcoats, they are standing saucy on the bank near the beaver house, near me. I stop, catch my breath, look away. Wild animals are more at ease if you do not look directly at them. The geese ease into the water with exaggerated casualness. I chuckle, thinking, "Okay, I know you aren't afraid. You just want to go swimming."

I sit on the bank while the geese swim toward the center and open water, keeping up their charade of unconcern. The farther away they go, the more the gray water and gray sky obscures them. No wonder I have not been able to see them in the late evenings.

Then the sky pours out a great racket as seven geese come flying in from upriver. They honk and anck, honk and anck, circling. Those below honk, call, flap, honk. When the new group lands, speeding smoothly onto the shining water, the others swim over, flapping and cackling. Two greet each other with extra joy. They swim into the swamp grass away from the others, it being springtime.

The beavers decide to join the party. A pair pop out of their stick house near the bank. They swim around, playing hide-and-seek in the new lily pads. One might be chasing the other, but since the chasee stops every now and then to look back at her companion and nuzzle him, chasing seems a misnomer for their activity. Spring is in the air and water.

Another pair of geese appears along the shoreline, low, off toward the river, singing a goose song. The wind whistles strong in their wide wings as they fly over me. My heart pounds faster at this uplifting sound. I hear, too, a buzzing sound in their throats, almost a motor sound, a goose purr. The others shout to them to land, and they skim onto the water with thrilling speed and grace. Everyone swims over to greet them with pleased carriage.

It starts to rain, a soft, pattering rain. The geese waltz the water into slow, widening circles. The rain sprinkles grace-note circles.

Another goose, a loner, is coming over the trees in the east. By this time it is so nearly dark that I lose him against the tree line and do not see him again until he lands. The others are excited, circling, calling. When he settles with them, they quieten immediately. Everybody's home safe.

The geese disappear in the gray light. I can see almost nothing out on the water now. Perhaps a few lily pads, perhaps not.

Out of the last light lingering along the shore, the great blue heron flies toward me. Because I am high on the bank and he is loping unafraid below, I see the flash of blue bands on the upper side of his wings, a stunning blue I have never seen.

Wings pulsing steadily and slowly, he crosses the air below me, and the color in his blue wings invades and captures my eye, a winged, powerful blue, now royal, now twilight-sky-in-the-mountain-lake, now night-sky-when-the-moon-is-full, now star sapphire, now royal . . .

He rises in his easy rhythm, taking his wings from my view. Although my gaze yearns after him, into the dark, his secret blue flies still in my inner eye, and I am happy. A flush sweeps my skin, a tangible joy. My blood is singing. Its cadence celebrates my wealth, this richness of blue and bird, shaken, pressed down, and running over, accorded to me at twilight, high on the bank of Wingo's pond.

BIBLIOGRAPHICAL NOTE

THE MATERIAL in this book is based on personal observation. I have, however, consulted a small store of nature books from time to time. Some of their information aided the development of the essays. Two of these sources were Audubon Society Nature Guides: *Eastern Forests,* by Ann Sutton and Myron Sutton, and *Field Guide to North American Birds, Eastern Region,* by John Bull and John Farrand Jr. Another highly useful volume was *The Birder's Handbook: A Field Guide to the Natural History of North American Birds,* by Paul R. Ehrlich, David S. Dobkin, and Darryl Wheye. I also found Donald Stokes's *Observing Insect Lives* helpful, especially concerning wasps.

For the myth of Orion, I relied on Thomas Bullfinch's account.

Dictionary definitions began with *The New Shorter Oxford English Dictionary* (1993) but may include author's additions or adjustments.

How much of the text owes a debt to Henry David Thoreau and Emily Dickinson it would be impossible to say. Worn copies of *Walden* and *The Complete Poems* on my library shelf, within easy reach, testify to their influence. These works, derived from lives of watching and writing, with little success as the world defines success, have given constant inspiration and joy.